ADOLESCENT STRUGGLE

for Selfhood and Identity

John J. Mitchell

Detselig Enterprises Ltd.

Canadian Cataloguing in Publication Data
    Mitchell, John J., 1941-
        Adolescent struggle for selfhood and identity

        Includes bibliographical references and index.
        ISBN 1-55059-050-2

        1. Self-perception in adolescence. 2. Identity
    (Psychology) in adolescence. 3. Adolescent
    psychology. 4. Narcissism. I. Title
    BF724.3.S35M58 1992   155.5'1825   C92-091579-5

DETSELIG ENTERPRISES LTD.
210, 1220 Kensington Rd. N.W.
Calgary, Alberta
T2N 3P5

Detselig Enterprises Ltd. appreciates the financial support for its 1992 publishing program from Alberta Foundation for the Arts.

Printed in Canada   SAN 115-0324   ISBN 1-55059-050-2

Dedication

This book is dedicated to the more than 400 teens and young adults who shared their thoughts, their frustrations, their ambitions and their secrets with me in order to help me better understand the adolescent struggle for selfhood and identity.

Table of Contents

Acknowledgments

This book was written while I was the recipient of the University of Alberta McCalla Professorship. This special research award provided me with an uninterrupted block of time, without which it would have been impossible for me to complete this book. I owe a very special debt of gratitude to Harvey Zingle, who has encouraged me at every juncture of my writing career, and who was extremely helpful in my being honored with the McCalla Professorship.

Special thanks are also due to the late Rev. Thomas Oddo, President of the University of Portland, who made available to me the facilities of the University of Portland in order to conduct some of the research required to write this book. A special "thank you" also goes to Rosemary Corah for her helpful assistance at the University of Portland.

Thanks are also due to Joan Schine of the Early Adolescent Helper Program in New York City. Her expertise and her willingness to share it with me, kept me in close contact with many frontline youth organizations throughout the United States and Canada.

Finally, I want to thank my father, Robert Vincent Mitchell, who edited this book with a critical, helpful eye. This is the eighth book I have written with his editorial direction, and each of them has been helped immensely by his encouragement and his penchant for precision of statement.

J.J. Mitchell
University of Alberta
Summer, 1992

Preface to Section One

The Struggle for Selfhood

Section One of this book deals with the adolescent self — especially with the need to protect this self and with the struggle most young people must experience in order to grow beyond their immature, childhood self. Our investigation of these topics is greatly influenced by two of the most important determinants of adolescent behavior: egocentrism and narcissism.

Egocentrism exerts its influence differently at different stages of human development; consistently, however, it interferes with the young person's ability to differentiate between the perceptions of an event and the event itself. The thinking of very young children, for example, is so controlled by egocentrism that they believe that their personal perceptions are identical to reality. It doesn't even occur to them that other people perceive the same event differently. Chapters Two and Three focus upon the ways in which egocentrism encourages self-centred viewpoints, perspectives and ideologies during adolescence.

Adolescents possess a rich and productive thought process known as formal thought. With its emphasis on objectivity, impartiality, and its ability to differentiate perceptions of an event from the event itself, formal thought operates by intellectual groundrules which oppose egocentrism. Consequently, formal thought and egocentrism compete for dominance within the adolescent's understanding of the world (both the physical world and the personal, private world). The outcome of this "competition" — outcomes which differ from person to person, from year to year, and from topic to topic — goes a long way toward determining the role of objective, reality-centred thought versus subjective, self-centred thought in the life of every adolescent.

Formal thought is premised on an objective, as-is, impartial understanding of reality. Egocentrism is premised on a subjective, as-if, self-enhancing understanding of reality. In these chapters we shall demonstrate how the struggle for adolescent selfhood is also a struggle with egocentrism. Chapters Four, Five, Six and Seven deal with narcissism and its impact on the adolescent experience.

As one might expect of a concept which fits so well with adolescence, narcissism is vague, imprecise and contrary. According to H.B. Lewis, "Narcissism is a positive experience of the self; it is the state of loving or admiring oneself." Most scholars are not as kindly. To Karen Horney narcissism means: "the person loves and admires himself for values for which there is no adequate foundation. Similarly, it means that he expects love and admiration from others for qualities that he does not possess, or does not possess to as large an extent as he supposes." Since narcissism has several meanings, the entirety of Chapter Four deals with this concept and the different meanings it holds to different scholars.

Chapter Five deals with narcissistic features which work their way into adolescent behavior. It also introduces the concept of the "minimal self" and its unique impact on adolescent selfhood, especially the ways in which it diminishes the adolescent's approach to life. Chapter Six focuses on how narcissism influences friendship patterns, interpersonal relationships and romantic involvements during adolescence. Chapter Seven discusses narcissism carried to unhealthy extremes.

Chapters Four through Seven investigate the prominent features of narcissism, especially:

1. excessive self-absorption;
2. grandiose inflation of the self;
3. radical fluctuations in self-esteem;
4. unrealistic expectations;
5. an exaggerated sense of entitlement; and,
6. the loss of concern for others.

These classic narcissistic features are discussed within the context of the adolescent experience. In these chapters we shall demonstrate how the struggle for adolescent selfhood is also a struggle with narcissism.

Chapter Eight describes some of the irrational beliefs and obsessive cravings which lead to self-deception, and, therefore, interfere with adolescent's capacity to honestly understand himself or herself.

chapter one

Some Introductory Comments

All rising to a great place is by a winding stair.

Francis Bacon

This book is about the forces which shape the self and direct the search for identity. Inevitably, this involves struggle, but experts do not agree as to how much of a struggle it really is. In this book, "struggle" means simply to make one's way with difficulty, or to labor with considerable exertion. No attempt is made to unduly glamorize the very real problems and difficulties of adolescence. Adolescent struggles, like those of their parents, are not necessarily heroic; they can be glorious and dignified but they can also be trivial and self-defeating.

In this book we shall investigate several critical struggles which greatly influence the lives of all young people in our culture. They are "part and parcel" of the adolescent package, and while some youth struggle with them far more than others, these struggles are among the most vital human realities of the adolescent years.

Stated briefly, these struggles include:

1. the attempt to overcome egocentrism and its distorting influence on the adolescent thought process; in essence, the struggle to think clearly;

2. the attempt to reconcile fundamental selfishness (basic narcissism) with the demands and responsibilities of group living;

3. the attempt to obtain authentic self-knowledge;

4. the attempt to construct a solid, worthy identity;

5. the attempt to negotiate the emotional and behavioral problems of identity crises and negative identity;

6. the attempt to handle the pressures of conformity and conformism.

However, before we begin our investigation of the adolescent experience in North American culture, a few "starting points" are in order.

Some starting points to help us better understand the adolescent experience

1. Adolescents are human beings and as such they share in the larger pains and joys of humanness. Like the rest of us, they must cope with fundamental day-to-day problems — they must learn how to live off their wits, how to get along with others, how to make do within bulky, indifferent institutions, and how to get what they need without offending the wrong people. As well, they must learn how to satisfy their basic physical, psychological, social and moral needs; how to make themselves feel worthwhile and human; how to receive sympathy, support and love from others; how to develop intimate relationships, to attain a decent sense of worth and value. In essence, they confront the same general life problems we all experience and they do so with urgency, apprehension and integrity.

However, these realities of "human-ness" are lived, negotiated and satisfied within the context of "adolescent-ness"! And in this regard, adolescents are profoundly different from the rest of us.

2. Adolescents are growing, changing, regressing, idling and improving all at once; they are "in-process," and, like children, they cannot be understood independently of the processes that define their developmental stage. Change, transition, modification and re-arrangement are the defining features of adolescence. In the midst of this developmental swirl they are simultaneously learning about themselves and the world in which they live; however, what they learn, and how they learn, is sometimes influenced as much by the swirl as by anything else. That is to say, the internal conditions of adolescence are as important to their behavior as the external environment in which they live.

The self grows throughout the course of the adolescent years; or, more precisely, it holds the potential to grow. The young person's capacity to know the self, and to live effectively with it, increase dramatically during the course of adolescence. The changing "me" is a fact of adolescence existence, and weaving the changing me into a coherent unity is the heart of genuine identity.

3. In very important ways (which are discussed at length in this book) adolescents are ineffective and inefficient learners. By this I do not mean that they are poor learners in the classroom — even though, quite obviously, many of them are. They are inefficient learners about matters which pertain to their own selves, to their own identities, and to their own inner workings. This "inefficiency" is based, in large measure, upon perceptual and emotional

limitations inherent to the period we call adolescence, and it contributes in very great measure to the trials and tribulations of youth.

4. None of us perceive reality with the impersonal neutrality of a camera. Every perception that our senses bring to awareness, and every thought our intellect brings to consciousness is reviewed, in one way or another, by our own mental apparatus. Without such a "review" we are at the mercy of an unchecked thought process, much as are children. Advanced thinkers, which adolescents are struggling to become, must be able to distinguish their thought from the objects of their thought, and be able to differentiate their perceptions of an event from the actual event. And, if this seems straightforward, it is not. Learning to separate the "as-is" from the "as-if" world is a giant first step in the adolescent's attempt to formulate a dignified interaction with family, school and community.

During the course of adolescence most individuals progress slowly toward a thinking pattern of objectivity and impartiality; a transformation which typically takes place during early- and middle-adolescence. During this transition period the thinking of young people is an enchanting, and often bewildering, mixture of concrete conventionality and radical rhetoric, stubborn narrowness and pliable intellectualism. From this intellectual-emotional potpourri, political ideologies, moral beliefs and personal identities are constructed, dismantled, abandoned and, finally, reconstructed.

The struggle to attain clarity of thought is, without question, one of the great challenges of adolescence.

5. The effort to become a clear thinker is complicated in the extreme by egocentrism, which exerts a powerful, and contaminating, influence on many important adolescent beliefs, including:

  a) the belief that other people are interested, even preoccupied with them, when they are not (the imaginary audience);

  b) the belief that they possess a singular specialness which makes them immune to unwanted consequences (the personal fable);

  c) the belief that they have discovered solutions to family, school and societal problems which, generally speaking, are not solutions at all (idealistic reform).

These beliefs create a cloud of misperceptions which profoundly distort the adolescent's perception of social realities.

6. The lived experience of adolescence — its sensation, electricity, vitality — is given much of its texture, flavor and energy from narcissism. Narcissism (described in great detail in chapters four through seven) contributes to the

adolescent's silent fascination with all things which nourish, stimulate or flatter the self.

Narcissism exists as a force within the youth community because so many of its traits overlap with adolescence: heightened self-awareness, preoccupation with appearance and beauty, the obsession with personal shortcomings, the craving for approval, the erotization of thought and fantasy, the concern with power and perfection — all of these are the traits of narcissism and of adolescence.

Even though narcissism is a normal and natural component within the adolescent personality, the emotional fabric of adolescence is "corrupted" by *excessive* narcissism. When such corruption occurs adolescents become consumed with their entitlements, they lose concern for the rights of others, and they abandon the behaviors which encourage what Alfred Adler called "social interest."

7. Adolescents both praise and condemn themselves, and from these judgments emerge episodes of self-doubt, inferiority and inadequacy. These feelings are not "neurotic," and they do not prevent youngsters from carrying out their duties or responsibilities. They do, however, result in a general condition of "emotional vigilance" which encourages interpersonal defensiveness and emotional hypersensitivity. This emotional vigilance, by which I simply mean the incessant attentiveness to threat, becomes an integral part of the adolescent psyche in early- and middle-adolescence. Frequently, but not always, this emotional vigilance subsides during late-adolescence and early-adulthood.

8. Adolescents reflexively strive to preserve their own centredness; as a consequence of this tendency, they are inherently attracted to events and people which validate, or are perceived as validating, this centredness.

Adolescents also defend themselves, and everything they identify with, against threat and attack; however, because of their tendency to mis-read motives, adolescents frequently perceive threats when they do not exist, and mobilize defensive behavior when it is not required. This willingness to tenaciously defend themselves and their loved ones produces some of the most noble, and, some of the most foolish, behavior in the adolescent arena.

9. Identity does not simply come into existence on its own. Adolescents require considerable guidance, leadership and coaching to attain a solid, wholesome identity. And even though many adolescents are remarkably resilient and demonstrate heroic determination in coping with day-to-day adversity, it is equally true that many young people, when left to follow their

own inclinations (especially early-adolescents) are prone toward self-destructive behavior which diminishes their self and derails their identity project.

10. Learning to share oneself with others, and learning to blend one's strengths with the strengths of others are *necessary skills* every young person must learn in order to grow beyond the immaturity of the adolescent self. Failure to acquire these skills, encourages a fearful, obsessive self-centredness which is emotionally and socially self-defeating. The failure to learn these skills has become, according to many youth-watchers, extremely widespread in North American society. Learning to share oneself comes easily to some youth, especially those who are popular, socially adept, and not burdened with excessive self-immersion. For others, extending themselves is a painful demand to which they respond with fear and apprehension. Whether it comes easily or not, learning to share oneself, and to participate openly with others, is a vital developmental task of the adolescent years.

11. One of the critical tasks of adolescence is to construct an identity sturdy enough to cope with the occupational and intimacy demands of the forthcoming adult world, and resourceful enough to satisfy personal needs, desires and ambitions within the immediate adolescent world.

Healthy identity is based upon the ability to assess one's strengths and weaknesses; upon a sense of community, and the ability to participate socially and emotionally within that community; upon a set of beliefs and values which guide *important* life decisions; and, upon the emotional resilience to cope with adversity and disappointment. Many youngsters never attain these "basics" of identity, but, quite obviously, many do.

12. Adolescents are simultaneously inclined toward self-knowledge and self-deception; they struggle immeasurably with the Socratic challenge to "Know thyself." As we shall observe throughout the course of this book, the quest for self-knowledge *is both facilitated* and impeded by the adolescent thought process.

Self-deception, one of the gravest impediments to self-knowledge, is fueled by two universal mechanisms during adolescence: rationalization — giving noble reasons to justify ignoble acts; and, blind spots — the failure to perceive painful or unwanted zones of reality.

These "starting points" in our investigation of adolescence are not intended to serve as *a priori* truths, or even as rigidly held maxims; they are, more than anything, hypotheses about the adolescent condition. They are, however, hypotheses which are well supported, I believe, by the existing data; and they are hypotheses which hold rich potential for generating new insights in our on-going attempt to understand this infinitely complex period of life.

In defense of adolescents as sophisticated thinkers and solid decision makers

One of the most difficult challenges facing an author who attempts to describe the "struggles" of young people is to do so without making them appear incompetent, juvenile, or governed by any number of traits which trivialize them. Equally challenging, one must not demean the society in which they live by unfairly blaming parents, schools, or governments for their problems and failures. Youth commentators, with a remarkable consistency, tend to commit one sin or the other in their analyses of adolescent existence.

Adolescents have their moments of brilliance and to suggest otherwise is slanting the news. They represent an immense talent pool which our society is unwilling, perhaps unable, to utilize in an efficient or dignified manner. (I have written extensively on both of these topics, see Mitchell 1975, 1980, 1985 for further elaboration). The irony, and all too often the tragedy, of adolescence is the way tremendous aptitude and advanced ability co-exists with ineptitude and incompetence, producing a collective of young people who represent both the very best and the very worst within our sometimes great and sometimes glorious culture.

Since so much of this book focuses on the shortcomings and the limitations of adolescents, perhaps it is advisable to point out, here in the beginning, that adolescents are capable of sophisticated and complex thought. The intent in this book is not to make adolescents out to be less than they are, but rather, to define and to demonstrate the components within their intellectual and emotional makeup which all too frequently overrule their intelligence, undermine their common sense, and contaminate their decision-making processes.

In their ability to think about themselves and the world in which they live children are, in the terminology of Jean Piaget, "concrete" thinkers — their thought is concerned with what "is." Concrete thought specializes in concrete reality. With adolescence, and the expanded intellectual capacities that come with it (collectively referred to as "formal thought") this narrowness is replaced by an expanded comprehensiveness of thought. As a result of these great mental advances adolescents acquire the ability:

- to think about the possible as well as the real;

- to think about implications as well as facts;

- to think about alternatives as well as givens;

• to think about hypotheses as well as descriptions;

• to think about "what if" as well as "what is."

All in all, the worlds of the probable, the possible, and the theoretical begin to rival material reality as the object of adolescent thought:

> In formal thought there is a reversal of the direction of thinking between reality and possibility . . . Possibility no longer appears merely as an extension of an empirical situation or of actions actually performed. Instead, it is reality that is now secondary to possibility (Inhelder, 1958, p. 251).

Adolescents also acquire the ability to inspect their own thoughts and to reason about them. This represents a breakthrough of remarkable significance since it allows investigation of the inner-self with far more elaborate methods than was possible at an earlier age. ("Far more elaborate" however, does not always mean "far more accurate" since self-investigation in adolescence is influenced by protectionist motives.)

Adolescents also become rather adept at propositional thinking. A proposition is any statement capable of being believed, doubted, or denied, hence propositions may venture beyond the confines of known reality. Propositional thinking allows the systematic probing of metaphysical ideas, and this, by definition, is the starting point of advanced intellectualism.

The importance of this thought modality in the intellectual development of adolescence is emphasized by Flavell:

> The important entities which the adolescent manipulates in his reasoning are no longer the raw reality data themselves, but assertions or statements— propositions—which "contain" these data. What is really achieved in the 7-11 year period is the organized cognition of concrete objects and events per se (i.e., putting them into classes, seriating them, setting them into correspondence, etc.). The adolescent performs these first order operations, too, but he does something else besides, a necessary something which is precisely what renders his thought formal rather than concrete. *He takes the results of these concrete operations, casts them in the form of propositions, and then proceeds to operate further upon them, i.e., make various logical connections between them* (1963, p. 205).

In this view, formal operations are really operations performed on the results of concrete operations. That is to say, higher order classifying and ordering which elevates the formal thinker beyond the constraints of concrete thought and the rigid solutions which derive from it. This is the "conquest of thought" as David Elkind is fond of saying.

Adolescents engage in all types of high-powered intellectual investigations. After all, their thought is characterized by abstraction, by comprehensiveness, by the ability to use propositions and logical postulates, by the capacity to anticipate consequences and envision outcomes in the future, by an increased power of memory (both short term and long term), by an enriched ability to focus and concentrate, and by advances in virtually all phases of language development. By every intellectual measure, adolescents demonstrate great improvement over the thinking abilities of children. Without question, adolescents are a powerhouse of intellectual potential.

This powerhouse, however, does not operate efficiently nor consistently. And, equally important, it is vulnerable to critical breakdowns — especially when the mind is required to objectively investigate itself, or when it must defend itself against criticism or attack. In the world of adolescence, this means all the time.

There is a certain lawfulness to the conditions under which the adolescent's high-powered intellect will malfunction, and under these conditions intellectual brightness dims into a conceptual fog where vague outlines replace clear images. It is the "fog" of adolescence, rather than its brightness, which creates so many miscalculations in day-to-day behavior. No claim is here made that adolescents live in perpetual fog; or that they do not exercise their vast range of intellectual brightness. Both of these are unacceptable diminutions of adolescent existence. The claim here is modest in its scope, yet profound in its implications; namely, that adolescents, *by merit of the principles which govern their thought process, are prone to mis-perceive and to mis-understand data which challenges, frustrates or contradicts their egocentric nature.*

With adolescents the issue is not abilities, but of exercising abilities; the issue is not capacities, but of utilizing those capacities; the issue is not potential, rather, the mobilization of potential.

chapter two

Egocentrism and the Adolescent Thought Process

Piaget has even further suggested that egocentricity of thought . . . has perhaps been the central problem in the history of human existence.
W.R. Looft

The traditional understanding of egocentrism

The theory of egocentrism advanced by Jean Piaget is primarily concerned with the ability to distinguish the inner workings of our own mental apparatus from the objects of that apparatus. That is, to know the difference between the perception of an event and the actual event itself.

In a most practical sense, egocentrism is "the inability to clearly differentiate the nature of the subject-object interaction, or, the subject-object relationship" (Muuss, 1982, p. 250). In sum, egocentrism refers to: (1) the incomplete differentiation of one's self from the outside world, and, (2) the tendency to understand and interpret the world in terms of the self. Both of these ideas attract our attention because many of the distortions, fictions and falsehoods so common to the adolescent experience owe their existence to the incomplete differentiation of self from the outside world, and to the propensity to interpret the world in terms flattering to the self — even when these interpretations are, by impartial standards, false.

The thought of very young children, for example, is so controlled by egocentrism that they believe that their personal point of view *is identical to objective reality*. Sometimes they do not even recognize that another point of view could possibly exist; and, at others times, upon recognizing another point of view, they will simply cancel, or "veto" it. This ability to cancel unwanted or unflattering information is egocentrism at its grandest. No other single feature of intellectual functioning so thoroughly typifies the child's orientation to reality.

Egocentrism is an embeddedness in one's own point of view. This embeddedness, this entrenchment within one's own mental processes, *exists without awareness,* and it causes the young child to automatically think that what she saw at the parade is the same as what everyone else saw, and to automatically infer that if a movie makes her sad it will have exactly the same affect on everyone else watching the movie. Egocentrism is an entire style of thinking, not merely a shortcoming within it.

As Piaget expresses it, the child reduces all experiences "to his point of view *and therefore distorts them without realizing it,* simply because he cannot yet distinguish his point of view from that of others through failure to coordinate or 'group' the points of view. Thus, both on the social and on the physical plane, *he is egocentric through ignorance of his own subjectivity"* (p. 75, Looft). Egocentrism always influences the child's thinking process to some degree. However, under specified conditions it literally takes over the thinking process, and it is to these "specified conditions" that we direct much of our energy in this book.

No matter how cautiously we approach the topic of adolescent egocentrism we cannot escape what is known in psychological theory as "the egocentric predicament." That is, the impossibility of knowing things or persons *as they are* as distinguished from the way we know and experience them through our own personality. For each of us is confined within a circle of our own ideas, the complete escape from which is impossible. This predicament hits at the heart of our attempts to investigate adolescent egocentrism because, by its very enterprise, the study of egocentrism is the study of how we misperceive, misunderstand, misjudge, or misinterpret reality — especially those realities which impassion the emotions. In our attempt to understand how adolescents misread reality we have no choice except to impose what we boastfully think of as our own "correct" reading of that reality. This is, indeed, quite a predicament!

Philosophical starting points

The theoretical starting points for Piaget's theory of egocentrism are similar to those of developmental psychology; the most noteworthy, at least for our immediate investigation, include the following:

1. mental growth naturally proceeds in a specific direction; that is, it moves from an egocentric orientation toward a sociocentric orientation to reality.
2. mental growth is characterized by an increasing differentiation between subject and object, between thought and reality.
3. increasing cognitive maturity is characterized by the ability to "decentre" that is, to not be centred solely within one's own

thought process; this process of "decentreing" is the heart of intellectual development.

4. children perceive *in gradually progressive steps* that they are not the centre of things and that other persons and objects have their own independent existence. (Muuss, 1982, p. 250).

Piaget believed that, in the course of normal development, thought moves from the egocentric to the sociocentric, from the idiosyncratic ideas of children to the validated and tested ideas held by older children and adults. Before anyone can become an advanced thinker he or she must grow beyond the constraining influence of egocentrism. Mature thought simply cannot occur until one can see perspectives other than one's own, and this is achieved only after the thinker is released from the narrowness *inherent to* egocentrism.

 Therefore, it is axiomatic throughout this book that mature thought *cannot exist until egocentrism is overcome.*

The significance of egocentrism

Without question egocentrism is one of the vital concepts in all of modern psychology. Its concern is with the very nature of the human thought process. And, crucial to our understanding of how adolescents develop, it assumes that every human, in the course of development, must transform from an inherently inept and faulty thinker (which all children are) to a mature and sophisticated thinker (which some adolescents are).

Looft, in his now classic overview of Piaget's understanding of egocentrism, went to special lengths to emphasize the great significance Piaget attributed to this concept: "Piaget has even further suggested that egocentricity of thought — the illusions caused by the immediate point of view — has perhaps been the central problem in the history of human existence" (p. 73). Piaget was so impressed with the significance of egocentrism that he concluded "a major portion of the developmental energies within the individual is invested into the process of overcoming his egocentric reference system" (p.73). And finally, "Piaget has placed the egocentrism concept in a central role in his theory of intellectual development" (p. 74).

Egocentric speech in childhood

In ordinary usage "egocentric" means to be concerned with oneself, preoccupied with one's own concerns and relatively insensitive to the concerns of others. The term carries a tone of *imperviousness* and *unawareness* rather than one of pure selfishness. Correspondingly, egocentric behavior is motivated by one's own needs rather than the needs of others. In its "pure" form it is seen in the characteristic self-centredness of children, but most assuredly such behavior also colors the conduct and speech of adults. (In projective testing, for example, an "egocentric response" is one that refers to "me" or to my personal affairs).

Egocentric speech provides us with solid instruction on the impact egocentrism exerts on children's behavior. Egocentric speech is comparatively insensitive to the feelings of others; it may carry no explicit communicative aim, sometimes there is no attempt even to make sure anyone is listening. The egocentric speech of children may make no clear social reference, or no social demand even though the speech is taking place in the presence of others. It is, very literally, talking to oneself.

In egocentric speech the child believes that *the listener will decode the precise meaning to a sentence without the benefit of precise language.* (Under conditions of anxiety or defensiveness adolescents and adults are inclined to this exact same behavior). Thus the child may blurt to mother "She dropped it on him," without explaining who "she" is, what "it" is, and who "him" is. Miraculously many mothers are able to decode such sentences, but, as a rule, teachers do not tolerate them.

Egocentric speech contrasts with "socialized speech" in which uttered sentences make sense, and the speaker expects the listener to pay attention to exactly what is said. With socialized speech the egocentric chains which bind speech to the self are broken, freeing thought to focus on the outside world "as it is," that is, allowing incoming data to be processed with a minimum of censorship or contamination.

The stages of egocentrism

Piaget recognized four stages of egocentrism, each of which builds upon the advances of the previous stage, each of which contains its own unique variations of reality analysis, and *each of which contains its own unique mode of reality distortion.*

Sensori-motor egocentrism (birth to age two): Infants are characterized by "radical" egocentrism, the inability to differentiate self from the larger world. The child cannot differentiate objects from the impressions they create. Egocentrism at this age is based upon the child's belief that the sensory impressions the child experiences are essential to the existence of the object. *Sensori-motor egocentrism begins to decline when the child recognizes that objects have their own existence independent of the child.* (Psychoanalytic theory holds that egocentrism is characterized by a state of undifferentiation and narcissism in the infant; a state of fusion between the self and the environment.)

Pre-operational egocentrism (two to six years): The egocentrism of this age makes it difficult for the child to differentiate between the symbol and its referent. "The child does not understand the relationship between the signifier and what is signified. Initially, the symbols are viewed as identical to their referents" (Muuss, p. 252). Children at this age believe that their own perspective (the outcome of their thought) is shared by others. To them, their particular understanding of things is the only possible understanding.

Concrete operational egocentrism (age seven to eleven years): The major cognitive task here is to master classes, relations and quantities. At this age the child can perform elementary syllogistic reasoning, and propose concrete hypotheses. These advancing abilities transport the child out of the more primitive limitations of the previous level of egocentrism, but, as well, introduce new thought deficiencies predicated on these very advances. For example, the child can advance hypotheses about reality but they do not understand that these hypotheses are their own "inventions" which need to be tested against objective reality to determine if they are true. At this level of egocentrism "children too readily accept their own hypotheses as something factually given and believe that the facts must adapt to fit their hypotheses" (Muuss, p. 252).

Here again, we see a deficiency: children cannot consistently differentiate between their own mental constructions (hypotheses) and objective reality (facts). Hence, when they cannot solve a problem because they started from a false premise they usually conclude that the problem is not solvable at all, or that the problem is really a trick being played on them. Their thought process inclines them to blame the situation rather than to examine their own incorrect hypotheses. At this stage the egocentric thinker *fails to recognize that many kinds of errors are to be found within the thought process itself.*

Adolescent egocentrism: formal operational thought (age 12-13 years to adulthood)

Since Piaget first introduced the concept of formal operations, the term "formal thought" has been used as a synonym for the thought process of adolescents. Formal thought does not come into being until the early adolescent period, and its arrival signals a dramatically new, and higher, plane of human intellectual functioning.

The ingredients of "higher" intellectual functioning, namely: (a) advanced reasoning, (b) philosophical thinking and (c) scientific thinking, all make heroic breakthroughs during this stage. Breakthroughs, which if they did not occur, would forever confine us to the concrete, narrow and rigid thinking patterns of children. Formal thought changes and advances the intellect in ways every bit as profound as puberty changes and advances in the physical body.

David Elkind believes that "the major task of early adolescence can be regarded as having to do with the conquest of thought" (1967). By this he means conquest of the limitations inherent to concrete thought. "Formal operations not only permit the young person to construct all the possibilities in a system and construct contrary-to-fact propositions, they also enable him to conceptualize his own thought, to take mental constructions as objects and reason about them." All of these intellectual advances culminate in a transformation of thought vital to our understanding of adolescent egocentrism. Namely: "Formal operational thought not only enables the adolescent to conceptualize his thought, *it also permits him to conceptualize the thought of other people*. It is this capacity to take account of other people's thought, however, which is the crux of adolescent egocentrism"(Elkind,1967, my italic).

We shall investigate this final point, the adolescent's capacity to think about other people's thought, at considerable length in the next chapter, and as we shall see, this new found capacity is a source of significant insight into the psychology of human subjectivity, and, as well, it is a source of considerable miscalculation, misapprehension, and in some instances, paranoia.

It is an ironic, yet unfailing, fact that all mental advances generate their own downside. In this instance, the adolescent's increasingly sophisticated capacity *to think about the thoughts of others* is susceptible to misinterpretation and error, most notably, the tendency to confuse the thoughts of others with one's own fears and anxieties.

Three themes run through Piaget's account of adolescent thought. The first is that the adolescent's system of mental operations has reached a high degree of equilibrium. This means that thought is flexible, as contrasted with the rigidity of the younger concrete thinker; it also is effective, which simply means less prone to error. In essence, the adolescent can deal efficiently with complex reasoning. The second theme is that the adolescent can imagine the many possibilities intrinsic to a complex problem. The third theme is that adolescents can compensate mentally for transformations in reality (Ginsberg, 1969, p. 181).

Piaget also discovered that adolescents usually are able to make reality secondary to possibility. For example, when confronted with a scientific problem the adolescent who employs formal thought:

begins not by observing the empirical results, but by thinking of the possibilities inherent in the situation. He imagines that many things might occur, that many interpretations of the data might be feasible, and that what has actually occurred is but one of a number of possible alternatives. Only after performing a hypothetical analysis of this sort does he proceed to obtain empirical data which serve to confirm or refute his hypothesis . . . he is not bound solely by the observed (Ginsberg, p. 203).

The struggle between egocentrism and formal thought

> *A great many people think they are thinking when*
> *they are rearranging their prejudices.*
>
> William James

One of the significant consequences of adolescent egocentrism occurs when the thinker fails to separate the problem from "me" the solver of the problem. Hence, for the sixteen-year-old contemplating dropping out of school the perceived issue is not the vast array of problems facing dropouts in general, not the problems of locating a job, not the problem of what one does all day with free time, the problem becomes how "I, myself, me" am going to survive as a school dropout. The entire objective scope of the problem is converted into a subjective "me" problem; a conversion in which matters of circumstance and larger social forces lose all significance. "Me" simply pre-empts the larger questions. This is but one reason why egocentric thinkers so consistently draw wrong conclusions: their obsession with "me" initiates their thinking with a false premise.

Perhaps this is why egocentric youngsters are so quick to exclaim: "This is MY problem" with a forcefulness which leaves no doubt as to the key word in the sentence. It is, perhaps, also why parents, teachers, older brothers and sisters find themselves saying with exasperation: "He just can't see the larger picture." "He just doesn't get it." "She can't see what she is getting into." As one sixteen-year-old, who was eight months pregnant at the time, put it:

> I think I'm beyond having my mother tell me what to do. Like, in the beginning it's not that I couldn't tell her, it's just that I didn't want to tell her about the baby. I figured it was none of her business. *I figured It's my problem* and I'll take care of it myself (McGuire, p. 149).

We observe that some teenage girls choose to keep their babies after an unwanted pregnancy, in no small measure, because they simply do not comprehend the scope of the problem, nor the implications of their decision. At sixteen, the question that her mind processes is not "Can a sixteen-year-old raise a child?" Rather, "Can I raise my child?" (Of course, both questions are perfectly legitimate, even necessary, and each must be asked). When the second question, however, is answered in the negative, it becomes, in essence, a negation of one's self — one's insecure and egocentrically invested self. "No" is an answer which cannot be given to this question because it represents a failure too great for the young teen mother to endure. *Highly egocentric youngsters deny or minimize reality rather than deny or minimize themselves.* This tendency to deny or distort reality rather than to confront the limitations of their immature self is one of the most profound deficiencies within the adolescent intellectual process. It is also one of the most widespread.

The contrast between the thinking of children and the thinking of adolescents

The thinking of children: concrete thought

The thought that characterizes the middle child is called *concrete thought.* This term, coined by Piaget, reflects the fact that children's thought is dominated by real objects, and is processed through a rather rigid structural apparatus. Concrete thought represents an advance over the previous stages of childhood thinking, and because of it children acquire certain mental "rules" which allow them to better understand the physical world. Most importantly they learn about (1) classes, (2) relations, (3) quantities and (4) mental representations.

With regard to *classes*, children learn to deal with the whole and parts of the whole at the same time. For example, if a child not yet at the stage of concrete thought is asked, "Are there more boys or more children in the theatre?" he may answer that there are more boys, more girls, or more children. His answer is unpredictable because he cannot think about a class and its subclasses (that is, the whole and the parts) at the same time. With the advent of concrete thinking, the child easily recognizes that children must outnumber boys because boys are only one of two subclasses (the other being girls) that compose the class known as "children."

With regard to *relations* the child comes to understand, for example, that brightness is a relative phenomenon. A 60-watt light bulb is bright in relation to a 40 watt bulb but not in relation to a 1000-watt bulb, and the same 60 watt bulb may be the brightest in a group of three bulbs. This recognition makes relative comparisons more effective, and absolutes less necessary. The concrete thinker becomes aware that the world is filled with phenomena related to one another "comparatively."

During the stage of concrete thought the child learns that quantity remains the same even though its shape is altered. For example, the nursery-school child usually believes that if the liquid in a short, wide jug is poured into a tall, thin jug, the latter actually contains more liquid. Because the liquid assumes a different shape, the child infers that the quantity has been changed. During mid-childhood the child learns that quantities remain the same regardless of the shape they assume.

Youngsters who grasp conservation of quantity respond to the humor in the following joke:

> Susy and her friend went into the restaurant and ordered a pizza. The waiter asked "Shall I slice it into four pieces or six pieces?" Susy replied: "Four pieces, please. We're not hungry enough to eat six pieces."

Children who have not reached the stage of concrete thought, and are thus not capable of such refinements of thought, think the joke is about pizza, or about Susy, failing altogether to recognize that the humor is found in the ridiculous deployment of impartial constants, in this case, fractions.

Children are capable of *mental representation* when they can represent physical reality symbolically. (Drawing a map of the route to the neighborhood store).

In summary, during the stage of concrete thought the emergence of four general abilities advances the child's capacity for thought:

1. the ability to think about a whole entity and parts of the entity simultaneously;
2. the ability to understand that some realities acquire their qualities only in relation to the qualities of another reality (that is, for a light to be "brighter," it must be brighter than another light);
3. the ability to understand that quantity does not change simply because its appearance has been changed; and,
4. the ability to formulate mental representations of physical facts.

The limitations of concrete thought

Concrete thought focuses primarily on the real, the physical and the observable; its strength is the ability to organize facts as they are presented. It is said that a good journalist must be able to explain "who, what, when, where, why and how." Concrete thinkers are not ready for this lofty profession since their thinking is best suited for "who, what, where and when" but less equipped to handle "why and how."

Rarely do concrete thinkers approach a question by analyzing all solutions; rather, they respond to the first or second conclusion derived from piecing together the available clues. Because of this predisposition to hastily choose one solution, rather than to investigate all possibilities, concrete thinkers are easily lured into viewing only one side of an issue or basing their conclusions on only a small particle of the total evidence. Hence, *concrete thought lacks comprehensiveness.*

General and abstract meanings often escape the concrete thinker. For example, if you ask a six- or seven-year-old to interpret the proverb "You can lead a horse to water, but you can't make it drink," the response might make you cringe. The child may say that you shouldn't force animals to drink, that horses naturally locate water, or some such literal response. Hypothetical problems also confuse concrete thinkers. "If horses had six legs could they run faster?" Many kids draw a blank to this kind of question because it requires them to hypothesize something they know is false. They are likely to reply "Horses don't have six legs." Or, more likely, "What a stupid question. Horses don't have six legs."

Despite the fact that concrete thinkers are capable of reasoning from the general to the specific (deductive reasoning), and as well, from the specific to the general (inductive reasoning), their overall powers of logic are weak because they *do not know how to assemble evidence impartially.* They arrange evidence in a way which best confirms their premises. When data support their hypotheses, concrete thinkers show a good deal of "objectivity" — or so it may appear to an outside observer. As soon as the evidence goes against the hypothesis, however, concrete thinkers may reject it. With the advent of formal thought, the adolescent finally accepts the basic maxim of scientific thought: evidence determines the truth of an hypothesis.

In summary, despite great advances, the middle child's thought is limited by the following shortcomings:

1. thought is primarily directed toward the real and overlooks the ideal;
2. thought is primarily directed toward the present; the long range implications of ideas are not given thorough consideration;

3. thought is directed more toward organizing facts than toward discerning where facts come from; little mental energy is spent validating the origins of information; the concrete child is greatly influenced by authority and uses it to authenticate information;
4. thought lacks comprehensiveness; the child rarely formulates alternate hypotheses; and
5. thought is rigid, because the child is not able to double check the process by which he derived a conclusion.

We shall now turn our focus to the advances in thinking which typify adolescents. Yet, while doing so, we shall keep in mind that one of the most potent features of egocentrism is its ability to encourage the adolescent thinker to abandon the rich complexity of formal thought for the structured simplicity of concrete thought.

The thinking of adolescents: formal thought

Formal thought leaves its mark on the entire intellectual enterprise of adolescence. The following breakthroughs in intellectual style highlight the mental advances brought into being by formal thought.

The first feature of formal thought is *it becomes more abstract*. The facility for dealing with hypothetical and theoretical ideas expands considerably with the onset of formal thought. Abstract thought fosters an awareness of, and a responsiveness to, the **ideal**, the **improbable** and the **nonphysical**; as a result, rumination is less bound to the narrow conclusions of childhood, even early-adolescence. Mental preoccupation with the soul, eternity, eschatology, axiology and epistemology is commonplace even for youngsters unsophisticated in these advanced conceptual enterprises.

The second feature of formal thought is *it becomes more comprehensive*. When solving intellectual problems children do not usually recognize that an unexplored possibility may be as correct as the more obvious possibility. Adolescents are more thorough — they look at more sides of an issue, and are less likely to be duped. Their thought is more comprehensive, and less susceptible to errors of omission.

The third feature of formal thought is *it becomes the object of its own action*. The adolescent discovers that mental conclusions do not have their own life, but rather, that they owe their existence to mental processes. Hence, they recognize that a thought may be borne of rich or poor parentage. Formal thought increases comprehensiveness, and as well, it expands one's powers of hypothesizing, and, adolescents *apply these abilities to their own thought process*.

Introspective thought yields many dividends, not all of them pleasant. Notably, it fosters a certain quality of self-doubt inherent to the awareness of contradictory perspectives. "For the first time the adolescent can take himself as an object, evaluate himself from the perspective of other people with respect to personality, intelligence and appearance . . . Now that the adolescent can, so to speak, look at himself from the outside he becomes concerned about the reactions of others to himself" (p. 102, Elkind, 1974).

A fourth feature of formal thought is *it becomes propositional*. A proposition is any statement capable of being believed, doubted, or denied. Propositional thinking investigates ideas beyond reality as presently understood.

Adolescent political thought, for example, undergoes important changes because of the increased ability to create and examine propositions.

> Ordinarily the youngster begins adolescence incapable of complex political discourse . . . By the time this period is at an end, a dramatic change is evident; the youngster's grasp of the political world is now recognizably adult. His mind moves with some agility within the terrain of political concepts; he has achieved abstractness, complexity, and even some delicacy in his sense of political textures; he is on the threshold of ideology, struggling to formulate a morally coherent view of how society is and might and should be arranged (Adelson, 1972, p. 106).

In significant measure, the sophistication of political thought derives from an increased capacity for propositional thought. And, as we shall see in the next chapter, it greatly facilitates the propensity for "idealistic reform."

A fifth feature: *Thought becomes more future-oriented.* Inevitably the future works its way into the thought patterns of adolescents because, as they approach adulthood, they face decisions which influence the rest of their lives. Their ability to hypothesize allows them to consider numerous possibilities, and the ability to think propositionally allows them to assess the combinations and permutations inherent to the options. Take note of the interesting blend of self-protection and future evaluation of an 18-year-old who recently became a mother:

> But one thing I'll never do is get married. No way. Too much divorce in my family. My mother's been divorced twice, my uncle twice, my grandmother twice. I've learned that marriage just doesn't work. I'll have plenty of boyfriends, but no husbands. Women got to be careful of men. The reason I don't let my baby's father see our son is because he's not helpin' support him financially. If the father wants rights, he's got to live up to his responsibilities. No responsibilities, no rights. I won't let no man just barge in here and start ordering me around whenever he damn pleases. Not with me. I'm not one of those girls! No man's gonna beat me or push me around. My girl friend couldn't say no to her boyfriend and I found her all bloody and beat up with her blouse torn off. Any man who raises a hand to me is gone, and I mean fast! (Frank, p. 96).

The capacity to analyze the future nourishes identity formation and, ironically, identity crises. "It must be clear that without the skills of hypothesis-raising, conceptualization of the future, logical problem solving, and the ability to anticipate consequences of an action, *work on identity formation could not really begin.*" Likewise:

> Without the capacities of formal thought, identity would be tied to the observable, the readily measurable or manipulable dimensions of experience. But with the door of abstract reasoning opened, *identity becomes a vision of what might be possible as well as of what has already been experienced.*

Because of formal thought there is a chance to conceive of an identity that is a unique integration, a new combination of past, present, and future that takes a person along a new course (Newman & Newman, p. 366).

In conclusion, we can state that, in their entirety, the mental advances of formal thought lessen the grip of egocentrism on the adolescent thought process because formal thought encourages the thinker to:

- Go beyond the real to deal with the ideal;

- Go beyond the physical to deal with the hypothetical;

- Go beyond fragments to deal with wholes;

- Go beyond "what is" to investigate "what if";

- Go beyond the present to examine the future.

How egocentrism is overcome

The conquest of childhood egocentrism

The constraints imposed by nature upon the child's thinking apparatus are not as binding as might appear from what we have thus far discussed. The child "outgrows" most facets of egocentrism; equally important, the child is nudged away from it by the force of evidence. By merit of thousands of mini-experiments, from the teachings of parents and siblings, from the results of simple trial and error, and from hundreds of others encounters with the real world, children gradually outgrow, outlast, and ultimately lessen, the grasp of egocentrism on their thought process.

David Elkind, whose research has greatly enhanced our understanding of egocentrism, once penned: "To the child there are no problems of epistemology." By this he presumably meant that children are not concerned with the origins of knowledge, or with the verifiability of information. Rather they accept information as fact, even when the facts are really opinion, conjecture, prejudice, or propaganda. Their mind does effectively differentiate the data it receives, nor does it impose demands for verifiability or objectivity upon it. This insight has proved extremely helpful in our ability to understand the limitations of the child's intellect, and as well, the types of errors to which it is so consistently prone.

It has been argued that the most important factor in the decline of childhood egocentrism is social communication. That is, the perpetual give and take of living in a social context, the endless confrontations with siblings or parents holding different perceptions inevitably forces upon the child a view of things which are not available to the child simply by merit of his or her own faculties. The process is succinctly described by Flavell: "In the course of his contacts (*and especially, his conflicts and arguments*) with other children, the child increasingly finds himself forced to reexamine his own percepts and concepts in the light of those of others, *and by so doing, gradually rids himself of cognitive egocentrism*" (p. 75).

Being confronted with alternate ideas, perceptions, and explanations holds great "expansion value" to the child's narrow thought process. "The crucial factor in overcoming childish egocentrism is the *appearance of dissonant information* in verbal exchanges with other persons." Without such dissonance the impervious child has no tendency to realign or correct faulty perceptions. Hence, "the *occurrence of communication conflicts* is a necessary condition for intellectual decentration" (Looft, p. 76). (It is also one reason why pampered children are so slow to develop a frame of reference outside of themselves).

When all goes well, then, egocentrism is overcome on two vital fronts: (1) intellectually, with the differentiation between one's own preoccupations and those of others and (2) emotionally as the child gradually recognizes, compares and reconciles the feelings of others with his or her own feelings.

The conquest of adolescent egocentrism

> *When I was a boy of fourteen my father was so ignorant I could*
> *hardly stand to have the old man around. But when I got to be twenty-*
> *one, I was astonished at how much he had learned in seven years.*
> Mark Twain

Egocentrism begins to be overcome when the adolescent starts to effectively counter-check, and to verify, the thoughts which present themselves to consciousness. "Present themselves" is critical here. Younger children accept the conclusions their mind presents to them without awareness that what is presented is a function of the thought process itself. Children treat mental conclusions as, so to speak, facts of nature. They simply are. And what they are, is. Thoughts are not double-checked, re-calculated, or re-inspected because the child does not grasp the relationship between process and product. Which is to say that he or she really does not understand how conclusions work their way to the top of the thought chain.

Adolescents know better. They have learned that conclusions do not spring from nowhere; they recognize that conclusions result from a thought process prone to error, and that conclusions can be wrong because of mistakes in the thought process. As a result of this fundamental insight into their own mental apparatus they begin to double-check and to verify conclusions. From this moment adolescents begin to live in simultaneous harmony with, and opposition to, their own thought process. The dialogue which inherently flows from these opposite stances creates standards for the thinking process, and the quality of these standards, in great measure, determines the balance of power between egocentrism and formal thought in the life of the adolescent.

The significance of egocentrism is measured by two critical manifestations. The first is its power to influence the adolescent to accept ideas and beliefs which are false. The second is its power to influence the adolescent to reject ideas and beliefs which are true. Of course, it goes without saying that adolescents, like the rest of us, make mental errors. No one is exempt from this human fact. As far as egocentrism is concerned, the issue is the extent to which false ideas are accepted or true ideas rejected *because of how these ideas affect the person who is thinking about them.* It is here that egocentrism finds its power: in the ability to convince the thinker that one idea is false and another true because of how it relates to "me," how it flatters or frightens "me," how it agrees or disagrees with what "I" want, with what "I" hope for, with what "I" need.

Guidelines for assessing the decline of egocentrism

In terms of day to day behavior within the adolescent's world we suspect that *egocentrism is lessening its grip on the global thinking process when we observe the following trends.*

1. When the adolescent can recognize and respect the rights of others.

2. When the adolescent begins to perceive adults as individuals who have their own individuality and their own unique history, and not merely as part of the "other."

3. When the adolescent accepts that it is impossible for another person to completely understand what it is like "to be me"; that my subjective centre cannot be completely or unfailingly apprehended by others; therefore, to mis-read or mis-understand "me" is an inevitable perceptual fact which does not derive, as is so frequently inferred by younger adolescents, from defects within the perceiver.

4. When the adolescent attempts to explain his or her motives by taking the frame of reference of the other person, and not demanding that the other person always fit into their frame, or see things only from their point of view.

5. When the adolescent describes his or her inner feelings and private experiences without a sense of "emergency"; with the realization that the listener has parallel feelings and experiences; when the *personal fable* begins to lose its power.

6. When the adolescent accurately anticipates the actions and reactions of others. (To make accurate predictions about others one cannot be locked into one's own egocentric perspectives, one must be able to see things from the perspective of the person whose behavior is being predicted). Such perspective-taking signals a weakening of egocentrism.

7. When adolescents are able to recognize when they are and when they are not the object of conversation; when they can accurately determine when their behavior is noticed by others and when it is not; when they are able to accurately envision themselves within their larger social context; when they are able to ascertain when their role within the larger context is "major" and when it is not.

8. When the adolescent is able to arrive at a social gathering without excessive self-consciousness; to join a group without assuming that his or her arrival is closely watched, or carries an emotional significance which it does not.

It can be stated with great certainty that very few *early* adolescents ever attain such mastery of the egocentric element within their thought process. Some *middle*-adolescents master several of the above, but rarely all of them. Among *late*-adolescents and young adults, however, we notice a far greater mastery, which serves the vital function of transporting these individuals beyond the narrowing, contaminating influence of egocentrism.

Some concluding comments on formal thought, egocentrism and the adolescent ability to think clearly

Formal thought is the most advanced of all known thought processes during the adolescent years. Its constructive potential is awesome; ironically, so also is its capacity for distortion. Formal thought does not exist as a constant in the adolescent's thinking patterns — it fluctuates with startling unpredictability, ebbing into childish concretism on some occasions and flowing into advanced intellectualism on others.

At least three points need to be highlighted if we are to grasp the relationship which exists between the pillars of intelligence and the shifting sands of emotivism which characterize adolescent thinking.

First, formal thought does not automatically sustain itself. That is, once set in operation no guarantee assures that it will stay in operation. For formal thought to remain "in gear" it must be practiced, disciplined and trained. We do well to remember that one of the "purposes" of formal thought is to understand reality as it is, and this, unto itself, is no prize in the adolescent scheme of things because as-is reality frequently is unpleasant, unflattering, and all too often, painful. Furthermore, formal thought is obligated to the first rule of science, namely that unsupported hypotheses must be rejected. This contributes considerable grief to any individual (of any age) whose social perceptions are anchored in fictions, absurdities or any world view which the person desires to maintain, not reject.

Second, for the majority of young people, formal thought is exercised most enthusiastically when it *counters unwanted information, or when it investigates data flattering to the investigator*. Egocentrism guarantees that formal thought is used to self-advantage whenever possible. Both of the these built-in processes, at least as they are manifested during adolescence, guarantee that the thought process is not only prone to error, but that it is prone to the most serious kinds of errors, namely: self-deception and intellectual censorship.

Third, during adolescence (especially early-adolescence) formal thought is used awkwardly, even clumsily. Formal thought requires considerable practice, considerable coaching, and, considerable patience before it is deployed with much efficiency.

chapter three

Egocentric Distortions

The belief that one's own view of reality is the only reality is the most dangerous of all delusions.

Paul Watzlawick

The broader meaning of egocentrism

In the previous chapter we looked into the "traditional" understanding of egocentrism; drawing upon the pioneer work of Piaget, Inhelder and Elkind, we presented the important features of egocentrism, and demonstrated how they permeate the thinking process. We emphasized that with age and experience all mental systems become more sophisticated, eventually culminating in what is known as "formal" thought. As a result of these mental advances, egocentrism loses much of its controlling influence on the thought process, and, in turn, on behavior.

This view of egocentrism is not the whole story. As we shall try to make clear, egocentrism influences a far wider spectrum of thought and fantasy than any of the pioneer psychologists, including Piaget, recognized, and this influence spreads well beyond the structural thinking process. In this chapter, we shall pursue our investigation of egocentrism with an eye to its upper limits; that is, to its capacity *to act as a perceptual filter and as an intellectual censor.* I shall try to impress upon the reader that egocentrism screens, distorts and rearranges a vast array of data processed within the adolescent mental apparatus. Egocentric censorship is one of the defining features of adolescent thought, especially among those youth who are excessively preoccupied with their own interests, qualities and entitlements. And, if we are to believe the professionals who work with youth on a daily basis in our society — this includes a great percentage of young people.

Egocentrism is weakest when perceptions are determined by the characteristics of the object perceived rather than by the needs of the perceiver. Hence, the opposite of egocentrism is thought without bias, without prejudice, and unmoulded by vested interests. In a nutshell, it is honest and accurate. Voltaire once suggested that truth is "a statement of facts as they are." As we shall see, understanding "the facts as they are" is an extremely difficult achievement for adolescents.

Cognitive distortion

The early investigators of egocentrism, especially Piaget and Flavell, were aware of the fact that intellectual distortions are born of egocentrism. Piaget claimed:

> With the advent of formal intelligence, thinking takes wings and it is not surprising that at first this unexpected power is both used and abused . . . Each new mental ability starts off by incorporating the world in a process of egocentric assimilation. *Adolescent egocentricity is manifested by a belief in the omnipotence of reflection, as though the world should submit itself to idealistic schemes rather than to systems of reality* (1967, p. 63, my italic).

One ready example of what Piaget calls the "omnipotence of reflection" is the tendency of adolescents to behave as though they are able to "read" other people's thoughts, especially when these thoughts are central to the adolescent's fears or anxieties. Hence, when fighting with mother, the adolescent girl is convinced that she knows exactly what mother is thinking; or when worrying about a girlfriend the adolescent boy believes he knows exactly what is going through her mind, what course of action she is planning, why she did this or did not do that. These unwarranted inferences, so commonly made by adolescents, derive from their earnest belief that they know exactly what is transpiring in another person's mind. Hence a boy hits his girl friend because he knows with certainty that she is "thinking about" being unfaithful, or screams at his mother because he "knows absolutely" that she thinks he is a failure.

The idea that one can "know" the workings of another person's mind derives from a rather convoluted process:

> The adolescent, now capable of abstract reasoning, can formulate thoughts about thoughts . . . the person often uses this ability to think about others' thoughts . . . further, the adolescent starts thinking about what others are thinking of the adolescent him/herself; and finally . . . the adolescent is thoroughly convinced that what he/she thinks the other is thinking is, in fact, exactly what the other is thinking. *In other words, the adolescent believes he or she knows what is going on in another's mind* (Enright, Lapsley, & Shulka, 1979, p. 687).

Ironically, advanced thought patterns make the adolescent susceptible to a wide range of preposterous ideas to which the child's less developed intellect is not attracted — the belief that one can read another person's thoughts being only one example. One of the ironic qualities of adolescent thought is that advances in the intellect, not regressions, are the primary source of thought distortions.

Assumptive realities. Earlier we discussed the child's tendency to confuse hypotheses about reality with reality itself. Among mature thinkers, when the available data do not support a hypothesis, the hypothesis is dropped, or at least investigated further to determine if it is worthy of being accepted. Children, as a rule, do not follow this procedure. When data do not support their hypotheses they simply distort or discard the data. Thus, an eleven-year-old boy who believes that he is the best baseball player in the 5th grade, and predicts that he will be the first player chosen when teams are selected, may not alter his belief even when he is chosen last. He may simply distort the data with a few unprovable interpretations, i.e., "The other players are jealous of me," "I really didn't want to play on this team." The point here is that the hypothesis is not rejected because of contradictory information. Adolescents, in contrast to children, are more able to face evidence as it presents itself, and as a result, re-work their beliefs. "Maybe the coach is right. I'm not as good as I thought." Nothing heroic here; it is simply the realignment of beliefs to fit the data, a normal indicator of mature thought.

However, some ideas become so entrenched within the youngster's mind that he or she believes they fit reality perfectly even when they do not. This is what Elkind calls an assumptive reality; that is, "assumptions about reality that children make on the basis of limited information and which they will not alter in the face of new and contradictory evidence" (1974, p. 79).

Assumptive realities are not the same as delusions, even though they resemble them in their mis-reading of reality. The significant difference between assumptive realities and delusions, according to Elkind, is that "assumptive realities derive, at least originally, from new cognitive abilities and lack the systematization and narcissism of true delusions." Perhaps even more relevant, however, is that "assumptive behavior engaged in by children is often entered into in the spirit of 'fun' or 'play' which suggests that at some level of consciousness, the child is aware that he is operating *according to a convenient fiction*" (1974, p. 80, my italic).

Despite these qualifiers, assumptive realities are, in effect, mental sets which falsify reality, and, as such, they are one of many "scramblers" which distort the thought process.

These assumptions about reality may hold considerable influence on thinking habits. For example, the teenager's belief that sexual intercourse will not result in pregnancy even though, for people in general, it frequently does;

or that speeding in the automobile will not result in an accident even though, for people in general, it frequently does; or that even though Jimmy treats girls in general like dirt, he will treat me (because I am unique) like a goddess. False beliefs flower from false assumptions, and, with great consistency during adolescence, lead to self-destructive or counter-productive behavior.

Social distortion

In the practical use of our intellect, forgetting is as important as remembering.
William James

Egocentrism subordinates facts to desires. And, as William James suggested in the preceding quote, this can be executed as efficiently by forgetting unwanted facts as by remembering desired ones. However, as James also suggested, facts are rarely forgotten in their totality; usually they are merely distorted, bent, or otherwise realigned into a more digestible form. Important realities are simply too vital to be completely forgotten. The "art" in mental distortion, therefore, is not simply to forget, but rather, to rearrange.

For each of us an integral part of our identity is our understanding of how we live our lives, how we meet challenges, how we live up to expectations. This "court record" of our personal lives, something of a mental transcript of past actions, is a perfect example of how we rearrange our history through selective forgetting and selective remembering. The court record of our own lives is not kept with hardened objectivity; our egocentric self records our day-to-day life in such a way that our role in events is usually elevated beyond its rightful station. Here is how Goleman, whose ideas are integral to this chapter, stated it:

> As the central observer and recorder of life, the self stands in the role of historian. But impartiality is not one of its virtues ... The past is remembered as if it were a drama in which self was the leading player. *The self fabricates and revises history*, thereby engaging in practices not ordinarily admired by historians (1985, p. 97).

Adolescents, more than either children or adults, edit their personal court record in flattering ways. The end product is often a fictionalized version of their past achievements and a romanticized version of their present accomplishments.

A further distortion occurs when adolescents exaggerate the reactions of others to them, as when they claim, "I really blew him away with that remark," impervious to the fact that school counsellors hear bizarre stories each day of their working lives. Adolescents, especially younger ones, easily accept the notion that you saw them at the coliseum (when 10,000 other people were also in attendance), that you remember what clothes they were wearing, the person they were with, the style of their hair. And, of course, their egocentric willingness to participate in any conversation in which they are the central character makes them the unwilling dupes of older, and slightly less egocentric, peers.

Adolescents routinely believe that their own actions account for chance happenings, or that they influence the outcome of events in which they play only a very minor role. Hence, a teenage athlete may interpret his joining the basketball team as the reason for its recent win streak, even though he only plays two minutes per game. A Grade Ten cheerleader once told me (when I was a high school basketball coach) after an especially painful defeat, that the star player played poorly that day because he was worried about *her* upcoming math test!

Tragically, many teens believe that they are the reason that their parents divorced, that their expenses led the family to bankruptcy, that their failures are the cause of their father's depression. This propensity to falsely envision oneself as the causal factor in human events is nearly universal. Even runaway "street kids" are likely to blame themselves for the terrible things that happen to them on the streets, and sometimes for the tragic home situations from which they are fleeing:

> No matter which social class street kids come from, they tend to feel responsible for the crimes others perpetrated against them. Even non-street kids from privileged families . . . assume that family breakdown is their fault (Webber, p. 31).

The irony of egocentric distortion is that it works in all directions. It doesn't serve only to reduce anxiety as is the case with defense mechanisms. It may distort reality in such a way that it actually increases anxiety, as when we wrongly assign blame to ourselves. Or, conversely, it may increase pleasure as when we take credit for successes we don't deserve.

EGOCENTRISM AND PSYCHIC THEATRE

> *All the world's a stage, And all the men and women merely players,*
> *And one man in his time plays many parts . . .*
> Shakespeare, *As You Like It*

The roles we play and the dramas we act in our daily lives are a source of awe, and perplexity, to all of us; but, to adolescents they are much more than this because frequently they cannot separate the roles they play from their own unfolding and somewhat unknown selves. In these settings, the stage is not a metaphor for life; it is life. And, without question, the task of coming to "know

thyself," and the responsibility of formulating a coherent identity are complicated in the extreme if the subject does not know when it is being itself or when
it is performing a role; or, equally perplexing, when the self cannot tell when
it is performing before a real or an imaginary audience.

The Imaginary audience

Adolescents are absorbed in a unique brand of egocentrism which causes
them to believe mistakenly that other people are paying attention to them when
they are not, are fascinated with them when they are not and experience
emotional reactions to them when they do not. Concurrent to this, adolescents
are living through a period of their lives when they undergo a dramatic increase
in the power, the urgency, and the "thrill" with which they experience their
own selves. Since their self-experiences are so powerful, their thinking is, quite
incorrectly, stamped with the presumption that the people in their environment
somehow also are attuned to these intense self-experiences. As a result, they
take on an exaggerated self-awareness and a heightened self-consciousness
that resembles the hyper-self-consciousness which adults assume, for example, before an important job interview. That is, they mould every sentence, and
manicure every expression. Again, like the adult in the job interview, a keen
eye is focussed on every reaction of the interviewer. Just as the adult is "on
stage" performing for a real "audience" in the job interview, so the adolescent
lives on a daily stage performing before an imaginary audience of peers,
parents and passers-by. One 20-year-old boy, describing his adolescence made
these comments to me: "I was obsessed with the thought that everyone was
always watching me. I was always conscious about what I was doing, just in
case someone was watching and would sometimes do things just because
someone was watching (or so I thought)." A young woman described a similar
theme in her adolescent life:

> I always felt I was being compared to other girls, that they watched how I
> walked, ran, sat down, how my clothes fitted, and the type of clothes I wore.
> At the same time, I was very athletic, but was conscious of what I looked
> like on the court in comparison to other girls. This, of course, hindered my
> playing ability and my performance was often not what it potentially could
> have been. I even thought that if people were talking or laughing when I
> walked in a room they had to be talking about me.

Generally speaking, this form of egocentrism results from the failure to
differentiate between the processes and products of others' thinking and the
processes and products of one's own thinking. This lack of differentiation
convinces adolescents that others are as concerned with their thoughts and
feelings as they themselves are. The heightened self-consciousness encour-

aged by this misperception (please note that everyone becomes self-conscious when they believe others are watching) gives them the sense of always being viewed, always being evaluated, sometimes applauded, sometimes scorned.

However, the imaginary audience is more than mere mental constructs, and it is wrong to think that audiences come into existence only because of advances in the adolescent's intellectual ability. These audiences evoke fantasies and fears which are fueled by conscious needs and unconscious cravings. They also have a strong affective component which may elicit intense pleasure or deep remorse, or simply quiet satisfaction. Here, in the words of a 14-year-old boy, is classic imaginary audience material, blended with fantasy and personal fable imagery:

> I dreamt that one afternoon I walked out on our porch headed for the swimming pool when I observed . . . bleachers with some 2000 spectators sitting and waiting for me to swim. I was so taken aback by this event that I decided to favor them by walking on the water. My repeated success in performing such a feat brought the audience to its feet, then its knees in admiration and homage (Thornburg, 1982, p. 106).

The imaginary audience holds all the pleasure and pain of a real audience; the difference, of course, is that one is fictional and the other real. And, for many youngsters the most important task of adolescence is learning to distinguish one from the other, a task which most youngsters master. As Elkind puts it: "The imaginary audience . . . is progressively modified in the direction of the reactions of the real audience" (1967, p. 1,032).

The personal fable

One of the more fascinating outcomes of the chronic egocentrism of adolescence is the "personal fable": the adolescent's belief that he (or she) is a totally unique person whose experiences are more emotionally profound, whose thoughts are more intellectually advanced, and whose fears are more fearful than anyone else's. As a result of this special status, no other person can comprehend the pain of their suffering, no one can grasp the profundity of their convictions, or fathom the depths of their love. The personal fable elevates the adolescent's sense of uniqueness into the stratosphere.

From their perch of elevated specialness they see things that others cannot, understand relationships that baffle others, and experience passions of love and hate far beyond the capacities of their friends, teachers, and most assuredly, of their parents. The personal fable is the *par excellence* example of self-centred egocentrism. Like the imaginary audience, it tends to be outgrown; yet, while running its course it influences decision-making, especially decisions which require a calculated assessment of outcomes; Will this action lead to pregnancy? Will this action lead to accident? Will this action send me to jail? Will this action cancel my ability to get a job? Such questions affect the course of one's life, and they are questions which the youth of our culture do not answer with admirable efficiency.

The imaginary audience and the personal fable endure with such persistence for several reasons, one of which is that adolescent thought is so influenced by affective logic. In contrast to inductive or deductive logic, which operates on reasoning and comparative objectivity, affective logic is a sequence of judgments in which the *connection between one judgment and another is largely emotional.* "Susan was cold toward me today. She is trying to hurt me." Or, "I received a 'D' in Mr. Wilson's class; he must really hate me." Affective logic binds ideas by their emotive connection; its value lies in its ability to energize emotions and desires, not in its capacity to locate the truth.

Some early and middle adolescents whose lives are filled with anxiety and pain, and who are not especially good thinkers to begin with (most adolescents are not good thinkers no matter what contemporary educators say) *use affective logic as their primary thinking mode.* For these youngsters sound reasoning is in perpetual scarcity. Their decisions are made on the basis of their imaginary audiences, their personal fables, and their fictionalized "as-if" images, the logic of emotion not of reason. This is not to say that young people do not possess formal thought. They do. Nor is it to say that they do not think inductively or deductively. They do. It is to say, and this strikes at the heart of the matter, that egocentrism is so powerful in some young selves that, under certain circumstances, it completely overtakes the rational forces in their thought process.

All in all, when thought outcomes are not diligently counter-checked by the formal thinking process, they often amount to little more than "wishful thinking," where thought, in effect, has been guided by wishes and desires rather than by an objective consideration of the facts.

Parallel to, but independent of, affective logic is a further feature of the personal fable: the belief in one's indestructibility, in one's immunity from the consequences of certain selected actions. I say "certain selected actions" because virtually no adolescents (except the most severely disturbed) believe in their complete indestructibility or total immunity. Rather, distortions of indestructibility or immunity usually apply only to specific domains. A teen may openly admit that her house could burn down, that her father could contract cancer, or that she could be kicked out of school if she skips one more class. However, when an unknown risk, such as the probability of having a car accident while driving impaired, *bears upon an immediate desire*, distortion is likely to occur. Hence, the adolescent who has been drinking and now wants to drive to the dance is more likely to conclude that an accident will not occur as a result of this action than would a friend who does not want to go to the dance. Egocentrism does not distort everything — only that which presses upon one's desires, needs or beliefs.

Here, in the words of a 15-year-old mother, is a splendid example of the mixture of heroic uprightness and childish naivete so typical of the adolescent mind struggling for truth while locked into its own egocentrism:

> Here's to all those doctors and teachers who said I couldn't raise a baby at my age, let alone graduate from school early. I had to prove to all of them, my grandmother, other teens, that not all teens are dumb and ignorant about makin' good choices for themselves. I love proving people wrong, I was gonna be a good example. I knew all about raising children. I had stored up in me all this knowledge about babies and with my own baby I felt I could apply it to my own instead of always telling others what I know. When I was seven, my cousins were having babies. I've been around babies all my life. *I'm still the same person I was before I was a parent. Only thing that's changed is that I have a baby. Same ol' me, though* (Frank,1983, p. 76).

Numerous fables of indestructibility and immunity cluster within the adolescent experience. Some of the most common include:

- Pregnancy will never happen to me.

- Car accidents will never happen to me.

- Drug addiction will never happen to me.

- Alcohol addiction will never happen to me.

- The police will never arrest me.

- Marriage problems will never happen to me.

- The usual consequences of behavior do not apply to me.

Interestingly, virtually all adolescents fully recognize the objective existence of what their fables are denying. Most young people have a friend, or parent, suffering the consequences of one or more of these calamities. These human tragedies are not denied in their totality, and to perceive adolescent denial in this way is to miss the overall picture; rather the adolescent recognizes these tragedies as objective facts of human life, but, and this is vital, *as realities which, in all likelihood, will never happen to me.* The final word is the key word. When the words "me" or "I" enter the sentence in any important or critical way, egocentrism strengthens its grips and narrows the focus of thought, often with such force that it overpowers impartial thought. This reflex in the thought process — the tightening and narrowing of thought when "I" or "me" is introduced into the data — is, unquestionably, one of the greatest sources of intellectual contamination during the entire adolescent period.

Typically, the personal fable thrives in special alcoves where the adolescent does not want reason to prevail. For example, almost all pregnant teens report being "surprised" or "shocked" at finding themselves pregnant. When asked why they thought they would avoid pregnancy a stunning range of fables and fictions emerge. For example:

a) the belief that they did not have sex often enough to become pregnant

b) the belief that they did not experience an orgasm, therefore, could not conceive;

c) the belief they were "too young" to become pregnant;

d) the belief that they would not be "caught" during high risk days (even when they understood the ovulation cycle);

e) "forgetting" to use birth control; and,

f) the belief that it just couldn't happen to "me."

Upon close inspection, one discovers that these fictions are not acquired beliefs picked up from friends, parents, or even from TV; they are not learned, or even imitated — rather, they are fictions personally contrived to deny unwanted data.

Many adolescents whom I have interviewed over the years possess a compromise fable which Elkind, Enright and others have not reported. Their thought process is characterized by a semi-distortion in which they openly admit to the *possibility* that, for example, drug addiction might happen to them, or that they might be involved in a car accident. At the same time, however, they conclude matter-of-factly that they will escape the consequences of what, when it happens to others, is a disaster. Thus even though others might be killed or maimed in the car accident, they would not; or, even if they do become addicted to drugs, they will overcome it when they choose to do so, and then lead a normal life, perhaps even an enriched life because of the "unique" experiences they will encounter in their downfall; or, even if pregnancy does occur, it will result in a happy child, a happy marriage, or a happy life as a single parent. In essence, the adolescent concludes that bad things happen to others, but not to "me." Such is the egocentric triumph within their thought process.

The Idealistic reformer

The difference between a good man and a bad one is the choice of the cause.
William James

Without a revolutionary theory there can be no revolutionary movement.
Vladimar Lenin

Idealism. It is a commonplace observation that adolescents are influenced by their idealism, and that much of their behavior and thought is based on an ideal conception of things as they should be. Idealists strive to achieve their ideals and to live by them, even when they are impractical or unpopular. For adolescents (and, of course, for adults as well) there exists an inherent attraction to ideas that feed egocentricity. Perhaps nowhere is this attraction more enigmatically manifested than in the ideas concerning social reform held by the "idealistic reformer," a phenomenon first described by Inhelder and Piaget (1958).

Idealistic reformers *attempt to transform society in order to better satisfy their own needs,* often without taking into account the needs of others, or the needs of society. In other words, they want to impose their own views on society. Idealistic reformers assume that their dreams and plans are motivated by what ethicists call "right action," by which is usually meant action for which no alternative possible under the circumstances is better. It is simply the most fitting action for the situation.

The egocentric foundation to their ideas and their reforms, however, is betrayed by their intolerance toward anyone who disagrees with their necessary reforms, or by their belief that anyone who disagrees is "out to get me." In our culture idealistic reform is a socially accepted form of self-assertion, and it is experimented with by many youth for a wide range of reasons, many of them admirable and dignified. It is especially prevalent among university students.

Sometimes, however, idealistic reform is little more than an excuse for rejecting some disliked feature of one's society, one's school or one's family. It is claimed that Lenin once observed, upon reviewing the incredible range of citizens attracted to his social reforms: "Revolution attracts the best and the worst from society." In our present society, where virtually all young people spend five days a week in school, where no important or meaningful jobs are available, and where parents are landlords, we find a fierce desire for reform: any reform. Among some of these youngsters (and it is not at all easy to distinguish them from peers who are motivated by a genuine concern for social issues) the real motivation seems to be venting anger, obtaining recognition, or any of a host of "deficiency" motives. Putney described a similar phenomenon among troubled adults, and as is so often the case, normal adolescent traits bear a resemblance to neurotic adult traits:

> A sure symptom of this neurosis is the effort such individuals make to be certain that other people know about their unorthodox views as soon as possible on making their acquaintance. They are prone to whipping out their opinions, apropos of nothing at all, merely to flaunt them publicly. Because they value the unpopularity of their ideas, they are unlikely to do much to further general acceptance of these views, regardless of their protestations. They are more interested in shocking than communicating (p. 61).

Quite obviously, not all "idealistic reformers" fit the above description, but enough do to merit our consideration.

From what we have thus far discussed, it is clear that idealistic reformers are a bewildering mixture of egocentricity and selfless devotion to humanity. Their sense of mission and their aggrandizing interpretation of their own actions encourage them to overlook their inconsistencies and impracticalities. Perhaps they, more than any other group, embody the extreme qualities which Anna Freud described as being typical of adolescents in general. She believed that virtually all adolescents are characterized by a vast array of polar opposites in behavior and emotions. Take special note of these extreme qualities which she attributes to youth:

> Adolescents are excessively egoistic, regarding themselves as the centre of the universe and the sole object of interest . . . They form the most passionate love relations, only to break them as abruptly as they begin them. On the one hand, they throw themselves enthusiastically into the life of the community and, on the other, they have an overpowering longing for solitude. They oscillate between blind submission to some self-chosen leader and defiant rebellion against any and every authority (1966, p. 137-138).

And while these characteristics, in all probability, do not accurately describe the majority of youth in our culture, quite conceivably they provide us with an accurate psychological profile of the idealistic reformer.

The idealistic reformer tightropes real and ideal poles with the anxious urgency of an artist working without a net. And sometimes with the despair of an artist who also knows that, eventually, there must be a fall:

> Elaborate fantasies for utopian societies, pious adherence to religious sects, and enthusiastic involvement in the political sphere are not at all unusual among adolescents carried away by idealistic beliefs about what could be accomplished, or despair about society's current ills. Interestingly, the despair itself is a relatively new attitude toward reality, one that seems to emerge from the ability to think about non-reality (Haviland and Scarborough, 1981).

And how is such a potion brewed? How can the idealistic reformer hold lofty ideas and compassion for humankind and, at the same time, experience so much despair over human actions? Elkind (1974) offers a few observations, one of which strikes me as especially fruitful:

> For one thing, the young person can conceive of ideal families, religions, and societies and when he compares these with his own family, religion, and society he often finds the latter wanting. Much of adolescent rebellion against adult society derives, in part at least, from this new capacity to construct ideal situations. The ideals, however, are almost entirely intellectual and the young person has little conception of how they might be made into realities and even less interest in working toward their fulfillment (p. 103).

Perhaps this imbalance between the adolescent's extended capacity for idealistic formulations and limited exposure to real experience makes for hostility toward the imperfections of others, and for impatience with the "human" element in idealistic reforms.

THE DYNAMICS OF EGOCENTRIC DISTORTION

> *Egocentrism in the cognitive structure of the adolescent makes it difficult for the individual to differentiate between his own highly idealistic thought processes (how things ought to be) and the real world (how things are).*
> Rolf E. Muuss

Here I would like to discuss several types of egocentric distortion which come about in the course of everyday perceptions. These distortions are not pathological, nor are they indicators of neurosis. They come into existence because of the unique ways that egocentrism imposes itself on the adolescent thought process.

Egocentric projection. The extending of one's thoughts, feelings, or desires to the outer world of events and actions is egocentric projection. It differs from childhood egocentrism in a very important way: the adolescent possesses the ability to "pull-in" the egocentric projection and give it a reality check. Adolescents are not completely at the mercy of the egocentric process as are children because, to use Piaget's language, the child "is *egocentric through ignorance of his own subjectivity*." Children simply cannot, with any consistency, overrule their own egocentric processes. And even though children lack the ability to distance themselves from their egocentric projections, adolescents are able to do so, and frequently do. Unfortunately, adolescent reality checks frequently are neither comprehensive nor systematic, and in the final analysis, some egocentric projections, because they are not objectively scrutinized by formal thought end up being identical to the unchecked, reflexive projections of children.

Egocentric projection is not always flattering to one's self-esteem, and in this way differs from the classic defense mechanism of projection. Egocentric projection can be either flattering or deflating, depending on the prevailing state of consciousness. Hence, if an adolescent is feeling guilty, he is likely to project that his parents are ashamed of him, or that his girlfriend hates him. Adolescents often fail to look for indicators which verify this projection because in egocentric projection one *automatically assumes that the subjective state of another parallels one's own.*

When teenagers reflexively (I use this term to convey a spontaneous, unreflective quality) act out their inner moods, for example, their giddiness or silliness at being shuffled into the principal's office, one of the many things they learn is that adults do not always share (or even tolerate) "inappropriate" moods. However, *when egocentric projection is sufficiently strong,* as it frequently is, the adolescent is essentially impervious to (but not necessarily defiant of) adult displeasure. This distinction between imperviousness and defiance is not minor. Both are easily observed in any adolescent-authority relationship. The dynamics, however, are totally different, as is the remedy. Here I do not want to discuss adolescent defiance, distrust, or rejection of authority (see the chapter on Negative Identity for an overview of these topics); rather my concern is with imperviousness: *being impenetrable by merit of unawareness.* This is the feature of adolescence which is so thoroughly maximized by egocentric projection. Far more than modern psychology acknowledges, the real issue for many adolescents is not defiance, anger, or even anti-authority, but rather, it is imperviousness — the condition of unawareness so complete that the actions and feelings of others simply do not register, hence, they do not affect one's behavior.

Egocentric transformation. Egocentric projection is the extension of one's mood or thoughts onto the outside world. *Egocentric transformation* is the reverse: it is the realignment of incoming information so that it fits one's mood, thoughts, or desires. Hence, if one's inner emotional state is anger, incoming perceptions tend to be perceived within the circumference of that anger. When such an interpretation of outside events can pass the scrutiny of the intellect (which is sometimes critical and sometimes not, like the customs officer at the border crossing) then it is accepted by the adolescent as an honest perception justified by the objective factuality of the situation.

Egocentric transformation, when all is said and done, is the imposition of one's personal agenda, however loose that term may be defined, on data as it comes into awareness.

. . . we are usually unable to turn our own viewpoint off completely when trying to infer others'. Our own perspective produces a clear signal that is much louder to us than the other's, and it usually continues to ring in our ears while we try to represent another's point of view accurately through this kind of noise, *and the possibility of egocentric distortion is ever present* (Flavell, 1977, p. 124-125).

In its harmless manifestations egocentric transformation is merely a variant of self-centredness. However, *as a mental habit* it assumes considerable importance when it yields evaluations of reality which are consistently self-concerned rather than other-concerned, and consistently false rather than true.

Webber, who spent two years interviewing adolescents, relates a telling tale of harmless, though typical, egocentric transformation. In preparing to conduct an interview with a young man, one of dozens whom she interviewed for her book, she had gone to great lengths to explain to him that in her book no names would be revealed, that anonymity would be maintained throughout, and that, in disappointing fact, because of time and space constraints, most of the youngsters she interviewed would never even be included in the book. After these ground rules had been carefully established and agreed to by the young man, an interview followed. Upon its conclusion a friend of the young man arrived on the scene; he was introduced to the author with typical egocentric panache: "This is the lady I told ya about that's writing a book about me" (p. 9).

Egocentric speech. First, it should be made clear that adolescents are gifted speakers and conversationalists, especially when compared with children. Their command of the rules of conversation (known as pragmatics) is commendable, as is their capacity to convey exact meaning, and extract precise messages from the people with whom they are communicating. They take their turn in conversation far better than children, and are able to recognize when trying to speak might be lost in the hubbub of confusion or distraction. They know how to use questions to convey commands (Why is everyone talking so loud at the dinner table?); how to deploy articles such as "the" and "a" in ways to enhance understanding (She is *the* person to see if you want a job.); and how to tell stories, jokes and anecdotes to entertain guests of varying age levels.

Parallel to these great advances in social language is a form of selfish speech which exists on a plane of its own which I call "egocentric speech" for reasons that will soon be apparent. Egocentric speech bursts on the scene in surprising flashes which may last only a few seconds, or, as is the case for some adolescents, it may become the dominant mode of communication.

Egocentric speech is the espousing of ideas without much concern for the exact meaning of what is spoken. This is to say that during adolescence egocentric speech (much like egocentric speech during childhood) ventilates emotions or releases tension more than it expresses specific ideas. It is speech in which "I" have the say, and in which "I" usually is more important than the "say." In egocentric speech self-assertion and self-affirmation are the undisputed motives, even though the adolescent is rarely aware of this. As a result, egocentric speech often resembles proclaiming more than speaking.

Egocentric speech is sometimes little more than vitalized narcissism, the expression and assertion of oneself through the melody, or power, of language. At other times it is a way of laying claim to an unsatisfied desire, or an unmanageable impulse, through the articulation of words related to it. As if by ringing word circles around them one actually embraces the desire or manages the impulse.

Another variant of egocentric speech, quite removed from what we have thus far discussed, is what I call "pronoun contamination." That is, when the adolescent, by dwelling excessively on the pronoun in the sentence, completely misses its meaning. Since the adolescent selectively attends to references pertaining to the self ("I," "me," "mine," "my") pronoun contamination is a fairly common occurrence. A few examples may render greater clarity. "My what beautifully crafted leather sandals you are wearing." "Yes, I am. I wear them when I'm in a good mood." This reply, so typical of early adolescent conversation, deflects the focus away from shoes (the original starting point of the comment), and whatever feature about them that elicited attention, and places the focus upon "me," the wearer of the shoes, and secondarily on "my" mood. Not infrequently, the adult who initiated the conversation may continue with a further comment, such as "Where did you buy those sandals?", only to receive, "I call them my mood shoes. I wear them when I'm in a good mood." The conversation partner will encounter greater success when he or she accepts the manipulation and strikes up a conversation about the person's mood. Since this is a topic of egocentric concern, the sandal wearer may visit at length on this topic.

Or, consider this: "Your father is very displeased with you because you skipped school yesterday." "Yes, I know. He's always angry about something." Here, the reply transforms the focus from my skipping school to father's anger.

Pronoun contamination realigns meaning so that the "I," "you," "he," "she" or "me" within a sentence preempts the intent, or transforms the focus, of the sentence. On the utilitarian side of things, this phenomenon does provide the formula for engaging egocentric individuals in conversation: simply make them the object of discourse, for that is what their egocentrism is clamoring for in the first place.

Some summary observations on the impact of egocentrism on the adolescent thought process

The error built into most egocentric thought is the unflinching belief that whatever applies to me also applies to the outside world. Hence, we observe one of the most prevalent outcomes of the adolescent thinking process, an outcome which produces considerable insight and, considerable error: the belief that self-truths are universal truths.

By definition, egocentric thought is prone toward mis-reading the objective universe — especially the social universe. This does not mean it cannot produce excellent ideas or brilliant hypotheses. Not only is this possible, it is standard fare in adolescence, where we routinely see the outcome of advanced, sophisticated thought existing side-by-side with primitive, poorly defined thought. Egocentrism does not destroy the raw power of human intelligence; it merely channels it into domains where needs and cravings, not reason, are sovereign.

The end result of our investigation leads us to conclude that the most profound effects of egocentrism are manifested in three critical domains of the adolescent thought process:

1. egocentrism encourages adolescents to perceive things not as they are, but as they wish them to be;

2. egocentrism encourages adolescents to perceive things not as they are, but as they fear them to be, and;

3. egocentrism encourages adolescents to perceive things not as they are, but as they have been trained to believe they will be.

chapter four

Narcissism

> *. . . the concept of narcissism remains elusive and obscure, even*
> *though it appears eminently accessible . . . Narcissism is a difficult*
> *idea that looks easy — a good recipe for confusion.*
>
> Christopher Lasch

The myth of narcissus. Narcissus was a physically perfect young man and the object of desire among the nymphs, for whom he showed no emotional interest. When he reached the age of sixteen his path was strewn with heartlessly rejected lovers, for he had a stubborn pride in his own beauty, and a ceaseless fascination with everything that pertained to himself. One nymph, Echo, who could no longer use her voice except in foolish repetition of another's voice, loved Narcissus deeply and one day she approached him only to be rudely rejected. In her shame and grief she perished, fading away, leaving behind only her responsive voice. The gods, in deciding to grant the nymph's wish for vengeance, decided that Narcissus must also experience the pain of an unreciprocated love. One day, while looking into a clear mountain pool, Narcissus viewed his own image and immediately fell in love, thinking that he was looking at a beautiful water spirit. Unable to tear himself away from his own image, and unable to evoke any response from the reflection, which disappeared when he attempted to embrace it, he grieved until death. When the nymphs came to bury him, he too had disappeared, leaving in place a flower.

Although some controversy exists as to whether Freud explicitly chose this myth to articulate the nuclear ingredients to narcissism, there is no doubt that many of the features associated with narcissism are present in this now famous myth: arrogance, grandiosity, self-centredness, obsession with the visual, and a juvenile fascination with surface appearances. I find the narcissus myth an excellent catalyst for discussing the themes which inevitably present themselves in a study of adolescent experience.

The general usage of the term "narcissism"

Narcissism is a preoccupied fascination with oneself which lives as "an infatuation with self so extreme that the interests of others are ignored, others serving merely as mirrors of one's own grandiosity" (Alford, p. 2). Narcissism can also be understood, however, as the force within the personality which strives to orchestrate the outer world so that it nourishes and flatters the inner self.

What differentiates the overly narcissistic individual from the rest of us is not selfishness, *per se,* but rather, the tremendous quantity and the irrational quality of this selfishness. Narcissists, and here they share so much with so many adolescents, have great difficulty granting to others the rights they desire for themselves; they never seem to learn the secret of giving without losing, of obtaining without depriving.

Narcissism gravitates toward praise and admiration. Conversely, narcissists are repulsed by people, events, activities and symbols which, in any way, detract from their selfish self-centredness.

Most theories of narcissism accept that the primal selfishness of human beings is never completely eradicated; it is only subdued, detoured, or denied. Because narcissism accompanies all strata of our experience, and influences so much of our actions: "The goal of maturity is not the abandonment of narcissism . . . but the integration of narcissism with the various stages of . . . development" (Alford, p. 55). In adolescence, this integration of narcissism with the self is a difficult and taxing proposition. Especially in cultures such as ours where youth are given a special, though essentially irrelevant, social status in which one of their requirements is to experiment in a wide-ranging fashion with self-awareness, self-understanding, self-improvement, self-expansion and self-justification. The struggle for legitimate, sturdy selfhood is complicated in serious measure by the cravings, the impulses, the fears and the diminishments that come with narcissism.

Why use narcissism as a theme in adolescent behavior?

Although many scholars now recognize the important role narcissism plays in the adolescent drama, this is a fairly recent turn of events. Textbooks of adolescent psychology, devoid of soul and passion as they are, rarely include more than a paragraph on narcissism. However, despite the tendency for many psychologists to neglect this topic, I find narcissism a rich area of investigation for several reasons.

First, narcissism is anchored in self-experience. The concept of narcissism recognizes that the young person's self is grandiose, inflated and exaggerated while at the same time fragile, vulnerable and minimal. Recognizing these opposites *as inherent properties of the self* help us to better understand the polarities of mood and the extremes of behavior which typify so many young people.

Second, the concept of narcissism provides insight into the selfish obsessions of conformist, "law and order" adolescents. These youngsters are difficult for psychologists to understand since their behavior is other-directed and outward-focussed, yet it displays a fundamental selfishness similar to the more flamboyant versions of narcissism. Both the "flamboyant" and "subdued" forms of narcissism originate from a common source: an empty, unnurtured, self which has little connectedness to meaning or morality outside itself. These youth do not reject society's customs and conventions; yet, because they possess no genuine self-direction, *they are alienated from themselves, and ultimately, from society and its values.*

Third, narcissism provides a theoretical springboard from which to investigate the icy detachment and untouchable quality of many youth; their defiant isolation and their cold, contemptuous attitudes. Furthermore, narcissism speaks well to some critical emotional facts of adolescence, especially the personal fable, the imaginary audience and exaggerated feelings of entitlement, none of which are, it seems to me, effectively explained, or even sufficiently emphasized, by current theories of adolescent behavior.

Fourth, the social and physical facts of moratorium life add to adolescent narcissism. In our culture the young people have very little access to worthwhile activities, and almost no opportunity for dignified self-expression. On the other hand, our society provides a wide range of options for carnival showmanship, street corner theatrics, defiance, negation and other forms of juvenile self-assertion, which are narcissistic in character, and which effectively isolate youth from the important machinery of society. As well, our consumer society encourages all of us to define ourselves in terms of what we own rather than what we are, and to evaluate others by their appearance rather than their substance — all of which contribute to the narcissistic style.

It is of more than passing interest to us that J. Satinover (1987), after searching for a term to encapsulate the narcissistic profile so prevalent in Western Culture, settles on "Puer Aeternus" — the *eternal adolescent.* In describing the pre-eminent features of this narcissistic syndrome Satinover utilizes a vocabulary historically associated with adolescence:

> It is a personality, on the one hand characterized by poor adjustment to . . . demands, a failure to set stable goals, and a proclivity for intense but short-lived romantic attachments, yet on the other hand by noble idealism, a

fertile romantic imagination, spiritual insight and frequently, too, by remarkable talent (p. 86).

Narcissism is a source of the necessary inflation each of us require to stay afloat in a competitive culture; it also protects us from being drowned in anonymity, lost in the crowd, forgotten. Under certain circumstances, especially when one is neglected or isolated, narcissism is the core of defiance, of opposition to that which minimizes me, myself, or that which is mine.

Adolescence is a time of life when narcissistic impulses attain considerable ascendancy, when they blend with sexual impulses into new cravings and expressions, when they integrate with aggressive impulses, with strivings for perfection, with self-love and with self-hate. The implications for an investigation of adolescence are nothing less than tremendous!

The psychoanalytic understanding of narcissism

Self-love, my liege, is not so vile a sin as self-neglecting
Shakespeare, *King Henry V*

Sigmund Freud

Freud saw narcissism as the turning of love away from the world and inward upon the self; this inward turning of love creates an excessive self-absorption that destroys the ability to selflessly relate to others. Freud also believed that each of us begin life in a blissful state he called "primary narcissism." In this state no distinction exists between self and world, hence no painful tensions from unfulfilled desires, and no experience of frustration. It is a primitive emotional state in which, somehow, the infant psyche is bestowed with a grandiose inflation, and with feelings of being perfect and powerful. From Freud's original ideas on narcissism emerged the psychoanalytic notion that the infant is fused with the mother and the world in a condition of narcissistic wholeness and bliss. A blissful state indeed, but one that is short-lived, and one which many of us (according to psychoanalysts) spend our adolescent and adult years trying to re-capture. (It must be pointed out, however, that there is no way to prove or disprove this pivotal psychoanalytic assumption; that is, there simply is no way to verify that the infant, in its earliest psychic state, exists in blissful, perfect harmony with "mother and the world," or with anything else. To reject this assumption, which Lasch mistakenly calls a "discovery," is to reject the psychoanalytic foundation of narcissistic theory. However, since the concerns of this book are with behavior more than with theory, this point does not halt our investigation of narcissism and its impact on adolescent experience).

Primary narcissism is not a perversion nor is it a defect; rather it is the first stage of psychosexual development where the child's pleasures are concentrated within the self and the body. Eventually, much of the child's primary narcissism is abandoned in favor of ego development, and in time, the child replaces self-love with love for others. But the love received from others is never as profound and never yields the narcissistic satisfactions of one's original, primal self-love.

As the infant develops it separates its own self from its surroundings and from this separation a primitive sense of tension differentiates *into the experience of need for others.* As the infant grows:

> needs put pressure on the developing ego to acquire the skills necessary to fulfill the need, and so the ego adapts to object-reality. All the energy that in infancy was bound exclusively to the subject in this way slowly extends out and becomes bound up in the subject's pursuit of objects. The process is essential to normal development (Satinover, p. 87).

All narcissism represents the struggle to regain the forever lost, grandiose feelings of the primitive self.

The euphoria of these primitive emotional states can never be completely regained. *The best any of us can hope for are fleeting episodes of euphoric self immersion, and periodic flashes of primal grandiosity.* The narcissist, being both more brazen and more frightened than the rest of us, is relentlessly driven by the desire to nourish the primitive self and to regain its euphoria. Of course, this can never be. The world has no interest whatsoever in being subordinated to narcissistic impulses, and, accepting this fact of life is a most vital step in the emotional development of the adolescent.

Some psychoanalysts do not accept Freud's premise that narcissism derives from self-love, rather they start from a different angle, claiming that narcissism originates as a hatred for the outside world. From this perspective, the narcissist is incapable of relating to the outside world because in that relationship internal hate will escape and will bring to it the punishment of a hostile environment. This understanding of narcissism improves our understanding of the intermittent hatred, and the enormous quantity of free-floating anger which characterizes the narcissism of so many young people.

Two fundamental questions focus our discussion of narcissism: (1) Is narcissism a form of genuine self-love, or is it a deflection of self-hate? (2) Is the self-centredness of narcissism caused by a grandiose, hedonistic self, or, at the opposite end of the continuum, by a minimal, fragile self struggling so desperately to establish itself that it can never, even for a moment, let go of its selfish concerns? These two basic questions guide our understanding of narcissism, and as we shall see, Karen Horney did not agree completely with Freud on either of these critical points.

Karen Horney

Karen Horney resisted several of the classic Freudian formulations concerning narcissism. Her clinical observations did not support Freud's libido theory, which claimed that self-esteem is a desexualized form of self-love, and that persons tending toward overevaluation must be expressing self-love. She concluded that the basis to neurosis was not one of instincts but of self-attitudes, and, furthermore, *that narcissism is best understood as unrealistic self-inflation.*

In *New Ways in Psychoanalysis*, (1939) Horney put forth several concepts which speak to the relationship between narcissism and adolescence. To her, narcissism means that "the person loves and admires himself for values for which there is no adequate foundation. Similarly, it means that he expects love and admiration from others for qualities that he does not possess, or does not possess to as large an extent as he supposes." And, in a tacit acknowledgment of the differences between healthy and neurotic narcissism she claims:

> It is not narcissistic for a person to value a quality in himself which he actually possesses . . . These two tendencies — appearing unduly significant to oneself and craving undue admiration from others — cannot be separated. Both are always present, though, in different types one or the other may prevail.

Horney assumed that exaggerated self-aggrandizement is the consequence of disturbed relationships in early childhood (as is true for the psychoanalytic understanding of virtually all emotional ailments). Her emphasis, however, was based on the child's alienation from others provoked by grievances, fears and anxieties. Hence, the narcissist is someone whose emotional links with others are brittle, and who suffers a loss of the capacity to love. Self-inflation (narcissism) is the child's attempt to cope with the loss of the "real me" under conditions "of parental coercion in which the child suffers impairment of self-sufficiency, self-reliance, and initiative" (Cooper, p. 120). The overevaluation of self becomes a substitute for undermined self-esteem; the overvalued self becomes the "real me."

Karen Horney described three persistent consequences of narcissistic self-inflation.

> First, decreasing productivity because work is not satisfying for its own sake. Work is never an end, it is always a means to obtain money, hence "conscientious workmanship" falters.

Second, excessive expectations as to what the world owes the individual without effort or contribution on the part of the individual. That is, "society owes me," or "school owes me," or "parents owe me."

Third, increasing impairment of human relations due to constant grievances, confrontational styles, and overriding feelings of entitlement (Cooper, p. 121).

(It is interesting to note that even though these observations ring true to modern ears, and sound somewhat like a list of grievances brought forth by a school principal, they were first outlined by Karen Horney in 1939).

In the attempt to make clear her divergence from Freud, Horney concluded that "As a consequence, the correlation between love of self and love of others is not valid in the sense that Freud intends it. Nevertheless, the dualism which Freud assumes . . . contains an odd and significant truth. This is, briefly, that *any kind of egocentricity detracts from a real interest in others, that it impairs the capacity to love others*" (1939, p. 100).

Criticisms of the various theories of narcissism

Some psychologists don't like the term "narcissism," finding it entirely too vague and imprecise. Wursmer (1987), for example, referring to narcissism, claims: "That concept has become so broad that it covers almost everything and thus has lost most of its usefulness" (p.74). Cooper claims: "Few concepts in psychiatry have undergone as many changes in meaning as has narcissism . . . It has become increasingly apparent that the term is so burdened with the baggage of the past that it has perhaps outlived its usefulness" (p. 117-118). For some critics it simply describes too many different levels of abstraction about the self, and provides too many behavioral outcomes. Pulver, for example, concluded that the term narcissism, over the past decades, has been used to describe (1) a sexual perversion; (2) a mode of relating to objects; (3) a developmental stage; and, (4) self-esteem.

Few scholars, however, have been as critical as Gendlin, who in "Philosophical Critique of the Concept of Narcissism" claims it is a "catch-all category" into which psychoanalysts dump everything other than the ego (1987). Gendlin also claims that psychoanalysts have variously described mathematicians as narcissistic because they spend so much time alone; poets and artists as narcissistic because their expression exceeds rational ego-forms; spirituality as narcissistic because of its "oceanic feeling," a feeling which Freud claimed he never experienced (p. 271).

Despite the differences inherent to this concept, and despite the philosophical objections to the broadness of the concept, virtually all theorists accept

Pulver's observation that "the concept of narcissism is one of the most important contributions of psychoanalysis" (p. 91).

One of the premises of this book is that narcissism, and the cluster of behaviors and emotional states associated with it, exists as a powerful force within the adolescent community. The theories which explain narcissism, especially those which explain its origins, unfortunately, have no such powerful force. As Alford emphasizes: "There is, of course, no theory of narcissism as such, but only theories or partial accounts." (p. 67).

The purpose of these chapters, then, is to describe the various ways in which narcissism is linked to the adolescence experience.

Postscript

Perhaps we should now go back to the very beginning of this chapter and reexamine Christopher Lasch's observation: " . . . the concept of narcissism remains elusive and obscure, even though it appears eminently accessible . . . Narcissism is a difficult idea that looks easy — a good recipe for confusion."

In the next three chapters we shall examine some of the consequences of this elusive, obscure concept as they manifest themselves in adolescent selfhood. In Chapter Five our focus will be on how narcissism diminishes the adolescent self, especially in the ways it encourages a narrow protectionism, and a fear of confronting fearful or unflattering aspects of the self. In Chapter Six we shall examine how narcissism influences adolescent friendships and relationships. In Chapter Seven we shall take a look at what I call "the corrupted self" — when the characteristics of narcissism become so exaggerated that the individual becomes emotionally disturbed.

chapter five

Narcissism and the Diminished Self

The narcissist is preoccupied with self, not because he or she has a
clear sense of a self to be imposed on the world, but because of deep-
rooted anxiety and insecurity that comes from not having much of a self.

J.P. Hewitt

In the previous chapter we discussed some of the basic themes of narcissism. In this chapter we shall look into the ways narcissism diminishes and reduces the adolescent self. Few topics can be of greater concern to the student of adolescent behavior, for it is during this period of life that the self must grow, expand and enrich itself if it is to effectively negotiate the more complex and more demanding responsibilities of approaching adulthood.

Heinz Kohut is a psychoanalyst whose theory of narcissism is based upon the primary fusion theory of early infancy. He is one of the most influential of a new generation of psychoanalytic writers who place great emphasis on the self, and whose ideas are generally referred to as "self-psychology." Kohut is perhaps the most widely known contemporary psychoanalytic writer on narcissism (Hamilton, 1982, p. 41).

According to Kohut's theory of narcissism (1971, 1977), to reach adolescence in a condition of emotional strength the self must have two basic needs nurtured on an ongoing basis: the "need to be mirrored" and the "need to idealize." The need to be mirrored refers to children's wishes (cravings) to have their actions, their efforts and their creations acknowledged, praised and admired. The vital "mirrors" are parents, especially the mother. Children also need to idealize, and this is expressed in their admiration of and identification with adults more competent and more powerful than themselves.

All too often, however, the child is insufficiently mirrored by the mother, and the father removes himself emotionally or physically from the child resulting in a *damaged self*. The failure to be mirrored (acknowledged, praised, admired), and the failure to idealize (to form identifications with powerful or competent adults) stunts mature development. This diminishment expresses itself in many ways, however, among adolescents it consistently shows itself

a) in feelings of inadequacy,

b) in apathy,

c) in the refusal to develop one's skills and abilities, and,

d) in contempt for one's self and for those one loves.

For many young people these are the predominant experiences in their struggle for selfhood.

The *ideal* self, on the other hand, is characterized by genuine self-esteem and sturdy self-confidence, by vigor and assertiveness — what Kohut calls the "autonomous self." These youngsters are solid in their sense of security, hence they are not driven to receive the praise of others, nor obsessed with their favorable reactions. They enjoy the acceptance and the goodwill of peers but they are not emotionally dependent on it. In essence, their self was thoroughly and adequately mirrored in childhood, and their need to idealize was satisfied by wholesome, reassuring interactions with parents. These are the traits of a nurtured, gratified narcissism. Most youth, however, are not "autonomous selves"; most, if not all, possess "nonideal" personality features which play vital roles in the day-to-day drama of adolescent existence.

Kohut's self-psychology speaks to the factors which contribute to a coherent self, and, as well, to those which produce a diminished, minimal self. In Kohut's psychology the overriding factor in disorders of the self is a failure in empathy; this failure creates a series of relentless hungers which the individual futilely attempts to satisfy through obsessive cravings.

Narcissistic hunger

Three patterns of narcissistic hunger draw our attention:

1. mirror-hunger;

2. ideal-hunger;

3. alter-ego hunger.

Mirror hungry youth are young people who are "famished for admiration and appreciation, feeling an inner sense of worthlessness deriving from parental frustration of the need to be admired and appreciated. Consequently, the mirror-hungry personality leads persons to display themselves incessantly" (Maddi, p. 303).

Mirror hunger nurtures *exhibitionism,* and the insatiable need for recognition and admiration. For mirror-hungry youth the social world becomes a stage where their daily performances may be applauded by appreciative or, even better, awestruck spectators. Unfortunately for their emotional well-being, mirror-hungry youth do not build credits for received praise. That is, the praise they receive from others does not carry over from day to day or event to event. Like oxygen, it must be replenished constantly, and the act of replenishment becomes automatic rather than exhilarating. Hence, while praise is constantly craved, its receipt never satisfies.

The self-conscious energy so typical of mirror hungry adolescents is expressed through many forms of exhibitionism, sometimes in outrageous gestures of self display, but most typically, in *parading*. Teens attain a certain affirmation from strutting and promenading themselves before the eyes of real and imagined beholders. Parading manufactures recognition, the plasma of narcissism.

Wursmer (1987) claims that the narcissistic self secretly wants "to overpower the object by the magic force of his expressions, of his or her looking, talking and thinking; the subject wants to fascinate, charm, spellbind, grip, mesmerize, magnetize, or subjugate the other and merge with him or her." There is much to be learned from this message because the motive driving much seemingly pointless adolescent behavior is the wish to fascinate, to charm and to *entice peers into one's own centre.*

In the teen world, especially in the school setting, one generates social reactions by being observed, a fact which sets in motion a typical parading ploy. The adolescent locates a setting where it is acceptable to make oneself visible, i.e., the school library. By parading before desired eyes the adolescent invites a range of reactions. The intent is to invite flattering reactions while at the same time to reserve the right to reject anyone for any reason. In this way parading solicits attention, and attracts observers (the desired effect) while giving to the parader complete rights of rejection; this heady mixture caters to the adolescent's need for power and control, while flattering the need to be recognized, hence, nurturing the illusion that one is desired.

In our culture it is expected that adolescents will learn to distinguish those reactions which are stimulated by parading and exhibitionism from those which are based upon genuine concern. Unfortunately, one of the hard facts to report after studying adolescents for over 30 years is that many youngsters so hunger for acknowledgment of *any kind* that they simply do not differentiate audience reactions.

Ideal-hungry youth "are forever in search of others whom they can admire for their prestige, power, beauty, intelligence or moral stature. They feel worthwhile only as long as they can look up to someone because it was specifically in the area of the idealizing need that they were frustrated in childhood" (Maddi, p. 303).

The hunger for affiliation with the powerful, the beautiful, or the highly intelligent is a driving force in "ideal-hungry" youth. They also hold a fascination with idealistic reform, and they tend to glorify certain selected heroes. As we shall see in the next chapter, the desire to attach oneself to prestigious peers is an important factor in adolescent friendship patterns.

The search for someone to admire yields mixed returns because adolescent choices are so "hit-and-miss." Their decisions backfire, for example, when the person they admire does not live up to their expectations, or worse, is exploitive or punitive.

Every narcissism originates as a deficiency, and even though this deficiency is channeled into an admired person, the admired person is never the true issue. The true issue is the need to attach to someone greater than oneself and through this attachment attain greater power and confidence. As a result, *admired persons are fairly interchangeable* as long as they satisfy the deficiencies which called them into existence in the first place.

Alter-ego hungry youth "can experience a sense of self as real and acceptable only when they relate to others who slavishly conform to their opinions, values and ways . . . Once again the void cannot be filled, and the alter-ego hungry person discovers that the other person is not himself or herself and consequently feels estranged" (Maddi, p. 303). These youth were frustrated in both their mirroring needs and their idealizing needs and, as a result they continue their restless search for friends and companions to replace their own empty self. Ironically, many of these youth attract companions, followers, "friends" with little difficulty. Their hunger for others is so ravenous that they cultivate techniques to bring peers into their embrace. The young people they attract are themselves so hungry for love, affection and acknowledgment that they gladly participate in the exchange. For them, any embrace is better than no embrace.

The hungers described by Kohut demonstrate that narcissism is motivated by deficiencies which eventually produce obsessions and cravings, which, in turn, call into existence a cluster of self-protecting and self-inflating mannerisms. It is these very self-protecting and self-inflating mannerisms which are the defining behavioral features of adolescent narcissism.

The minimal self

Christopher Lasch's description of "the culture of narcissism" and his overview of "the minimal self" have added significant new insights into our understanding of the relationship between youth, culture and narcissism. And even though his commentary is not directed immediately to youth, his ideas cast light on the empty roles and meaningless involvements of their lives. Moreso even than Kohut, Lasch's understanding of narcissism emphasizes the disconnectedness of the self from society, and its failure to develop any measure of genuine autonomy or legitimate individuality.

Lasch (1984) describes a narcissism for which the most conspicuous feature is "the loss of self." This loss results in a "minimal self" constructed out of classic narcissistic qualities, most notably: self-centred grandiosity, unrealistic expectations of entitlements, and a pendulum self which swings alternately between self-love and self-hate.

In this portrayal of modern narcissism, young people do not merely lack commitment to family ties or to communal life, *they lack the strength of self, and the justified self-pride that can allow them to actually make a commitment.* Despite their self-centredness, they have only a minimal self; or, to more accurately summarize the logic of minimalism: the minimal self, fearing its brittle boundaries will shatter, protects itself with a relentless self-centredness. In the words of Hewitt:

> The narcissist is preoccupied with self, not because he or she has a clear sense of a self to be imposed on the world, but because of deep-rooted anxiety and insecurity that *comes from not having much of a self* (p. 50).

This is not a narcissism of grandness; the minimal self is really little more than self-obsession grounded in anxiety. "The contemporary narcissist suffers, in short, not from selfishness or excessive individualism, but from the loss of self and from the incessant anxiety that loss causes" (Hewitt, p. 47). Narcissism, as understood by Lasch and the minimalists, is obviously not the mere pursuit of pleasure, as we typically associate with hedonism, but rather *it is the frenzied search for any involvement or stimulation which provides an underdeveloped ego with some sense of itself, some empowerment, some affirmation.*

Narcissists obsessively pursue ego nourishment because they cannot sustain a sense of themselves without it. They attempt to fill the void of their own emptiness with the very self that lives within the emptiness. The narcissist's sense of worth is bound to praise received from people who are not valued for anything other than their praise. People are, to them, little more than essential suppliers of emotional goods.

> Notwithstanding his occasional illusions of omnipotence, the narcissist depends on others to validate his self-esteem. *He cannot live without an admiring audience.* His apparent freedom from family ties and institutional

constraints does not free him to stand alone or to glory in his individuality. On the contrary, it contributes to his insecurity, which he can overcome only by seeing his 'grandiose self' reflected in the attentions of others, *or by attaching himself to those who radiate celebrity, power, and charisma* (Lasch, 1979, p. 10, my italic).

From this minimalist stance they evolve lifestyles of selfish aggrandizement and self-centred gratification which ultimately come to represent the core of their personal meaning. Their sense of identity is impoverished because they have no allegiance to any kind of dignified social system capable of directing their lives, or of lending meaning to it. And while it is true that they believe in their society and their country, in theory at least, they could as easily accommodate to any other society or country as long as it nourished and gave direction to their minimal self. Societal beliefs, and this is a critical point, are not based upon a coherent ideology, rather, they derive from self-protection. Narcissists are not ideologues in the sense that they believe in something greater than themselves; ideology is simply a means by which to nourish or advance the self, and when all is said and done, this is their deepest and most urgent motivation in life.

An *optimal self*, because it possesses coherent direction and has the ability to honestly share itself with others, lessens the obsessive need for self-aggrandizement. The *minimal self*, is so lacking in genuine identity that it is only through the praise and admiration of others that it can verify itself. Hence, the minimal self maximizes narcissism, and narcissism, because of its selfish narrowness, minimizes the self.

The minimal or narcissistic self is, above all, a self uncertain of its own outlines, longing either to remake the world in its own image or to merge into its environment in blissful union. The current concern with 'identity' registers some of this difficulty in defining the boundaries of selfhood (Lasch,1984, p. 19).

Minimalism, despite its selfish base, encourages conformism — to be too different places the self at risk. Our culture, of course, encourages dependent conformity; through it the school and the family operate most efficiently. Yet, it is precisely in this emotionally shallow world of school conformity and family conventionality that many narcissists find a comfortable, flattering niche.

From the picture thus portrayed, we see a minimal self retreating into itself in a futile attempt to nourish itself. And since there is no future in psychic cannibalism, the adolescent pursues continuous self-stimulation to supplant the very emptiness of that self.

The minimal self, and the brand of narcissism which accompanies it, are difficult to immediately comprehend. One reason is that these adolescents tend to be conformists rather than individualists, rule followers rather than rule breakers. Theirs' is a subdued, unobtrusive self-centredness without flamboyance or excessive fanfare. It is a contained, non-defiant narcissism in which the adolescent complies with the rules of the family and the school, gives the impression of being genuinely concerned with others, and follows the rules which regulate social intercourse. But from within the imperatives and cravings are narcissistic, and the plans these youngsters silently draft for their forthcoming adulthood are sparked by only one ambition: self-gratification.

In addition to their bland conformity these youngsters are also characterized by a well integrated system of defenses which Wilhelm Reich called "character armor." By this he meant the system of defenses that enable adolescents to assume certain roles in interpersonal relations they could not otherwise sustain. For example, a high school student may conceal hatred of school, or contempt for its depersonalization, and yet play the role of the model student. Such well developed character armor allows the student to appear outwardly as "well-adjusted" (which may be completely true) but it as easily can hide the youngster's compelling narcissistic motivations. This indeed is the profile so effectively peddled to youth on TV and in the movies: the outwardly adapting, socially accommodating individual *whose underlying motivations and desires* are little more than the classic narcissistic triad: grandiosity, power and entitlement.

Narcissism, self and behavior

In a thoughtful discussion on "the narcissistic course," Ben Burstein makes several comments germane to our discussion.

> Narcissistic personalities have a very intense interest in their selves—so much so that they often can see others only as extensions of themselves, or existing for the purpose of serving themselves. With this definition in mind we can rephrase the question of the narcissistic course. We can ask: "Why do these people need to have so high an interest in themselves?" Perhaps the answer is that they cannot take themselves (their selves) for granted; they constantly need to confirm their selves (Nelson, 1977, p. 17).

It is this need to constantly confirm the self which so clearly defines the motivation of the narcissistic adolescent, and it is the pursuit of peers who will serve as "confirmers" that so clearly defines the actions of the narcissistic adolescent.

Narcissists seek relationships with rather predictable themes. After all, their motives are egocentric rather than allocentric, their need to receive is far more advanced than their willingness to give, and their capacity for intimacy is not nearly as developed as their skill at shallow diplomacy. With these defining features it is easy to see that their relationships must run along well prescribed lines:

> It is definitely a two person relationship in which, however, only one of the partners matters; his wishes and needs are the only ones that count and must be attended to; the other partner, though felt to be immensely powerful, matters only insofar as he is willing to gratify the first partner's needs and desires or decides to frustrate them; beyond this, his personal interests, needs, desires, wishes, etc., simply do not exist (Nelson, 1977, p. 104).

According to Erich Fromm, (1964) the narcissist's perceptions of reality are such that everything belonging to the self is highly valued and everything belonging to another person is devalued, minimized or ridiculed. One's clothing, physique, intellect, method of getting to school, everything, is superior to others. Such incessant preoccupation with oneself is an acknowledged feature of narcissism.

The themes of adolescent narcissism also parallel what Karen Horney called "neurotic claims" — the distorted belief that one's extraordinary personal qualities, or intrinsic specialness, elevates them a position of entitlement and superiority. As well, since they are so special, they need not prove or demonstrate their worth; by merit of simply being themselves they deserve not mere acknowledgment, but praise and adulation. In this we see the classic narcissistic belief system:

a) the belief in my singular specialness and uniqueness (which for many teens is even further magnified by the personal fable);

b) the belief that my specialness does not need to be earned or proved;

c) the belief that my specialness makes me superior to everyone; and,

d) the belief that my specialness entitles me to special treatment.

We do well to remind ourselves that all claims which emanate from the narcissistic core, no matter how preposterous they appear to others, or how they may infringe on the rights of others, seem completely legitimate to the person from whom they spring.

The awareness paradox. One of the many paradoxes of narcissism is that it simultaneously enlivens self-awareness and deadens action-awareness. The sensation of one's own feelings and emotions are felt with a powerful, unmistaken clarity, sometimes with a force of, quite literally, trembling excitement. Concurrent to this heightened self-awareness (perhaps because of it) the individual undergoes episodes with only minimal awareness of his or her actual behavior. In sum: Some youngsters, for example, do not seem to know what they are doing when they are doing it; they are, in a very real sense, "disconnected." Teachers encounter youth each day who, when confronted with a wrong doing simply claim they didn't do it. Or, yes they did it, but they couldn't help it; or, yes they did it but they didn't know they were doing it; or yes, they did it, but so what. Sometimes they simply disown what they have done. Such denial produces a very unwelcome mixture of self-alienation and social defiance.

> The student of today is deeply unaware of the need to be cooperative with others, either students or teachers. He doesn't even seem to be in touch with being cooperative with himself; *some students appear to be unconscious of their very actions* (Nelson, p. 67).

The refusal to take responsibility for one's actions, and the constant denial of one's own actions are but two of many, many problems school teachers encounter in their attempt to educate narcissistic youngsters:

> The teacher enters upon his career as relatively sane and as well balanced, presumably, as anyone else in the humanistic professions. But after a time he also undergoes a metamorphosis. *For no teacher can be exposed to over 100 narcissistic personalties each day without some alteration in his character*, and the degree of his frustration operates in direct ratio to the zeal with which he enters upon his task (Nelson, p. 70).

A parallel phenomenon is the belief that *when intentions are not bad, neither is the behavior that follows*. ("Hey, I didn't mean anything by that.") When confronted with a wrongdoing, these youngsters claim that their behavior wasn't bad because they didn't intend to do anything bad. They act "as-if" their motives are actually more important than their actions — something they never tolerate in others. Such behavior-deadening was dramatically conveyed by a sixteen-year-old boy I once interviewed in a youth detention centre. He was incarcerated because he shot, with a hand gun concealed in his jacket, another teen. He told me it was unfair that he had to serve time because he didn't intend to shoot him. The young man I was interviewing intended to shoot a member of a rival gang, but " . . . this other dude just started shoving and gettin' involved where he didn't have any right being. I shot him but it was no big deal. I didn't even mean to shoot him. If I shot 'D.,' like I wanted to, then they would have a case. Just cause some guy gets in the way. Its really more like an accident. I don't think I should do time for that."

Narcissists defend their unacceptable behavior with "I didn't plan to do what I did, therefore, it can't be bad."

Some consequences of the diminished self

Several conclusions present themselves to the researcher who investigates adolescent narcissism, the first of which is the theme of this chapter — it diminishes the self.

Narcissism focuses the self excessively and thereby diminishes it. Many students of adolescent behavior are initially befuddled when confronted with this irony — that the narcissist's self which governs so much of what the person does, and monopolizes so much of what the person thinks can also be "diminished." This apparent contradiction is resolved when one recognizes four basic principles of the narcissist's inner workings.

First, the narcissistic self is grounded in a perfectionalized image of itself rather than in its actual operations; therefore, in many regards, it is a "false" self which does not have the range of a true, authentic self.

Second, the narcissistic self is remarkably vulnerable to anyone who will nourish or flatter it. Narcissists "flow" to gratifiers because they live in a perpetual state of emotional deficit where their needs for approval, admiration and adulation are never completely satisfied. The self is thus diminished because it cannot escape beyond the narrow perimeter created by those who flatter it. The narcissist leads a diminished existence because he or she is a prisoner to needs which demand constant nourishment.

Third, narcissists seemingly are never in control of their own lives because, in a very literal sense, their self "has" them more than they "have" a self. This is readily apparent in their universal pleas: "I couldn't control my self." "It just came over me." "I just had to do it?" Ultimately, it is their lack of genuine freedom in regards to their own self which defines, and causes, their human diminishment.

Fourth, narcissistic youth are diminished in their interactions with peers and adults because they perceive all criticism as an attack on their person. Like agoraphobics, who remain hidden within their homes to avoid threats from the outside world, the narcissist's fear of criticism shrinks them into a narrow shell which protects them against "attacks" from the outside. This reaction inevitably diminishes the range of human relationships they can experience and share.

Narcissistic youngsters are quite inept at reading the intentions of others, hence, what a parent or teacher considers a statement about "appearance," or "study habits," they perceive as an insult or as an attack. Teachers who interact with these youngsters discover that criticism must be carefully monitored so that it will not be taken as character assassination. Narcissists cannot accept comparative judgments (even favorable ones), *concerning their own creations*; they resist any description of their faults, and they react emotionally to all disapproval.

Their most consistent response to criticism is anger (which younger peers often mistakenly perceive as heroic anger — one of many reasons that narcissistic teens prefer younger companions). Usually, however, their anger exists as *narcissistic rage* — the aggression directed against those who fail to support their fantasies of total control.

All of these features combine to produce a style of life which is emotionally impoverished and behaviorally diminished.

Narcissism encourages generalized, free-floating selfishness. Whether understood in its original psychoanalytic meanings of primary and secondary narcissism, or, in a more extended manner, the common trait shared by all narcissists is a "style" of self-protecting self-ishness. And while one might rightfully say that "You must love yourself before you can love others," it is readily apparent that narcissists love themselves instead of others. The underlying motivation for this selfishness is unclear, but virtually all theorists claim that it derives from the painful anxiety of lost love, or from the smoldering, resentful anger of being insufficiently loved.

Erich Fromm described the selfishness of narcissism as:

> A state of experience in which only the person himself, his body, his needs, his feelings, his thoughts, his property, everything and everybody pertaining to him are experienced as fully real, while everybody and everything that does not form part of the person or is not an object of his needs is not interesting, is not fully real, is perceived only by intellectual recognition, while affectively without weight and color (1973. p. 87).

Perceiving one's emotional interests as prior to all other interests sets in motion a sequence of events in the lives of narcissists which, in simplified terms, goes like this:

- I want

- I deserve

- I have the right

- I get hurt

- I get revenge

Narcissism impedes moral development. Morality, by definition, requires the alignment of one's actions and beliefs with a principle or a standard greater than oneself. Such an alignment is inherently difficult for narcissists since they tend to make decisions about moral rightness (or wrongness) according to how they affect the self. This is not to say that narcissists are immoral, or that they believe that concepts of right and wrong do not apply to them; rather, it is to say, that, by merit of their psychological makeup, narcissists choose moral viewpoints which favor their own emotional interests. Their morality is egotism blended with pragmatism; hence, when any given morality is self-serving it is clung to with a strong sense of righteousness, however, when it no longer is self-serving, or even worse, when it is condemning of one's actions, it is abandoned.

Narcissism distorts the thought process. Narcissists, like children, bend information to fit their desires. This bending does not occur in all areas, but it consistently occurs whenever emotional needs are at issue. The narcissist's understanding of why people behave as they do is contaminated by projection and denial. Frequently they simply ignore what doesn't fit, and in this regard they are living examples of what in legal circles is called *ignoratio elenchi* — the ignoring, rather than the ignorance, of a contention. Ignoratio elenchi is the intellectual style of all narcissists regardless of age, intellectual power, or social skill because their *style of thought* requires them to ignore data which takes them out of their own fascination with themselves.

Further, narcissism distorts perception by focussing excessively upon the self and passing over everything else. Here is how Fromm describes it:

> A person, to the extent to which he is narcissistic, has a double standard of perception. Only he himself and what pertains to him has significance, while the rest of the world is more or less weightless or colorless, and because of this double standard *the narcissistic person shows severe defects in judgement and lacks the capacity for objectivity* (1973, p. 148).

In this chapter I have tried to describe some of the ways narcissism diminishes the self. In the following chapter we shall look into its influence on adolescent friendships and relationships.

chapter six

Friendships and Relationships

*Narcissistic personalities have a very intense interest in their
selves — so much so that they often can see others only as extensions
of themselves, or existing for the purpose of serving themselves.*
Ben Burstein

The above quote is taken from a thoughtful and informative essay, "The Narcissistic Course," by Dr. Ben Burstein. Several themes are discussed in this essay, foremost among them being the selfish, self-centred quality which pervades all narcissistic behavior. Burstein's observation introduces this chapter because our concern here is with narcissistic properties and how they influence the young person's needs for friendship, companionship and love.

Narcissism, quite obviously, does not exist with equal force among all people — young or old. In fact, the differing degrees of narcissism which exists among individuals is a significant factor in all human interactions, but nowhere are its effects more profound than in friendships, relationships and romantic involvements of adolescents.

As I tried to make clear in Chapter Four, narcissism provides a necessary inflation which many youth require to meet the challenges of a world which can easily swamp them. However, when narcissism assumes excessive proportions it tilts the young person's natural need for self-assurance and self-reliance into an over-bearing craving for self-centredness. This exaggeration of the narcissistic quality within the personality results in what usually is meant by the terms "narcissist" and "narcissistic."

Narcissists (young people with high quantities and qualities of narcissism) are not emotionally disturbed, nor do they need therapy. Excessive "normal" narcissism, just as, for example, excessive competitiveness or excessive frugality, is not a psychiatric ailment, rather it is part of the human condition, and as well, of "the adolescent condition." The form of narcissism which is thought to be a psychiatric disorder (pathological narcissism) is discussed in the next chapter.

These introductory comments are designed to inform the reader that the actions and emotions described in this chapter refer to those commonly observed among "normal" adolescents.

Narcissists share with all other youth a desire for friendship and companionship; it is unfair to claim that they do not need friends every bit as much as other teens. The difference is that among the highly narcissistic the need for friendship exists in more impulsive surges, and it satisfies a completely different set of cravings. Remember, narcissism as a force within the personality guides the individual into relationships which aggrandize the self. Hence, the motives which propel narcissistic relationships invariably are self-serving, and as such, they are weakly concerned with the needs and rights of the relationship partner. In addition, even though narcissistic youth very much want to have relationships with peers and lovers, they hold expectations of giving and receiving that inevitably lead to dissatisfaction. Problems with "giving" and "receiving" undermine all narcissistic relationships because narcissists know how to receive, but they are, in a very literal sense, afraid to give.

Speaking in rather general terms, we observe two different types of narcissistic friendship patterns. In the first type, one of the partners lends cohesion and stability to the relationship by serving as a "confirming psychological mirror" to the other. In the second type, the narcissist merges with the strength, prestige, or visibility of the partner, and in so doing, gains power from the strength of the friend. These patterns follow the same principles established in childhood "when a parent's empathic understanding of the child either lends needed support to its sense of self . . . or, when the parent's apparent greatness infuses the child's feeble sense of self with power, value and cohesion" (Wolf, 1977, p. 214). From these two fundamental principles (1) an attraction to those who mirror, and (2) an attraction to those who possess idealized strengths, all narcissistic friendships are motivated.

In the past, several of my graduate students (who work professionally with both "normal" and "disturbed" youth) have resisted the notion that narcissists could ever be good friends because their selfish core opposes honest reciprocity. The resistance of these students is predicated, I believe, on the assumption that adolescent friendships exemplify the best in bonding or companionship. Few beliefs are further from the truth. Adolescent friendships are sometimes molded from necessity, sometimes from desperation, sometimes from emotional hunger, and sometimes from the dignified core of a beautiful, sharing self. But, unfortunately, there is virtually no way to clearly determine which is which when dealing with adolescents.

The pursuit of admiration and the denial of shame are primary motivations in the emotional lives of narcissists. (One of the defining characteristics of narcissists is that they desire admiration more than respect). Over the course of time they become mini-experts in the pursuit of admiration and the denial of shame, and they use this expertise to solicit peer mirroring, and to attach themselves to the powerful friends they so desperately need in order to feel worthy. This expertise in peer manipulation is especially evident among socially skilled youth whose abilities are prized by peers who themselves hunger for praise, recognition and love. Narcissists, by merit of their need to feed their own chronic self-absorption, acquire skills in social navigation that most of their agemates simply do not possess.

Shy youngsters keep their "self" hidden until it is pursued, sought out; yet when someone takes the effort to seek it out, it is freely given, even when the seeker is merely pursuing the gratification of his or her own needs. These reserved youngsters need to be praised and coddled before they feel safe enough to give themselves to another. "A self . . . aware of its existence, its capacities, ambitions, skills and values often stays hidden until it finds some-one . . . to whom it feels safe to reveal its potential goodness or uniqueness" (Harwood, p. 74). For many youngsters these glorious moments of self disclosure and subjective sharing first occur with a narcissistic partner who has encouraged, usually for private gain, their migration away from their unshared enclosures. Hence, narcissists "open" their friends in order to have their own self exalted, but this opening is often so profound an experience that the friend attributes its special quality to the narcissistic partner and holds a deep gratitude which may manifest itself as friendship, love, adulation, or with surprising frequency, subservience.

As part of my ongoing research with adolescents (which began in the early 60s) I have interviewed dozens of early-adolescent girls (ages 12-15) who are pregnant, or who have recently given birth. Many, certainly not all, of these girls (young women) have relationship stories which hold a special relevance to narcissism. It is not rare to meet a young mother who does not talk to the man (boy) who fathered her child because she feels betrayed. The stories hold a remarkable consistency — at least in their general outlines. The boy is often one or two years older, and during early- or middle-adolescence this amounts to a tremendous developmental advantage. At the beginning of the relationship the boy praises, pursues and woos the girl with an earnest aggressiveness. The girls, with a stunning consistency, perceive these actions as "love," or some such lofty experience, whereas "eroticized fascination" usually describes the relationship more honestly. The girl perceives the boy's persistence as an interest in her — even when she has been "forewarned" by her girlfriends, her mother, and sometimes, the boy's friends. Their involvement becomes sexual, she becomes pregnant, he becomes gone. She feels betrayed; she trusted him and he turned out to be fraudulent. Her feelings of betrayal eventually turn to an anger which is expressed in the refusal to see him.

The narcissism, of course, is not only within the male. The girl cannot distance herself from the praise, from the admiration, from the eroticism. And, usually, these girls refuse to pay attention to their own reality checks. They "know" that love is not what is happening, yet they will not admit this to themselves. Their assessment of the relationship is "elevated" by their egocentrism. To further emphasize the narcissistic element in such relationships, many of these young mothers, while deploring their mate's desertion, also sing his praises, foremost of which was his willingness to praise them. And this point should not be lost in our evaluation of adolescent relationships, for it is in the primal act of praise and flattery that many, many adolescent relationships are forged and sustained.

A fifteen-year-old mother living with her parents in rural Washington put it this way: "He was a liar most of the time, but he made me feel good. He was always nice to me so I can't be too mad at him." Her best friend, age sixteen, also has a baby. Of her boyfriend she said: "I'm glad I didn't have to marry him but I wouldn't want to have never met him. He was a nice guy, just not dependable. I kinda thought this (becoming a parent) might happen, but I never thought too much about it."

A seventeen-year-old living in inner city Portland offered this assessment of her "love" relationship: "I loved it when he was nice to me. I don't know if I ever loved him, even though I told everyone I did. I just liked his always wanting to do things for me, and his always saying nice things about me."

THE DYNAMICS OF ADOLESCENT FRIENDSHIP

Intimacy

From the start it must be made clear that much of what typifies adolescent friendship is different from what emotionally mature adults think of as genuine friendship or honest intimacy.

> Intimacy . . . requires . . . a clearly formulated adjustment of one's behavior *to the expressed needs of the other person* in the pursuit of increasingly identical— that is *more and more nearly mutual-satisfactions.*

I have highlighted two phrases in this well-known quote from H.S. Sullivan to emphasize that in the intimacy relationship there must exist a concern for the *genuine* needs of the partner, and for *mutual* satisfactions and gratifications. Unfortunately, it is in these very demands for honest reciprocity and genuine concern that adolescent relationships are frequently lacking.

Adolescent relationships are typified by a range of narcissistic qualities, perhaps the most noteworthy being the fear that in giving one risks losing. This fear, unto itself, virtually precludes genuine love relationships, since "intimacy is the ability to fuse your identity with somebody else's without fear that you are going to lose something yourself" (E. Erikson, cited in Evans, 1967, p. 48).

Intimacy requires a fairly solid sense of personal identity, for it is, after all, one's identity which is shared in intimacy. This poses a special problem for adolescents because in their very lack of identity they hunger for an intimacy which will, in effect, *help them to create an identity*. Such pseudo-intimacy, anchored as it is in a shifting and incompletely formed identity, is doomed. Once again, our understanding is enhanced by Erikson who observed how the challenge of intimacy strains the adolescent character by posing a fundamental conflict between "I" and "Thou"; a conflict which frustrates narcissistic centredness and which also taxes the tentative adolescent identity.

> As the young individual seeks at least tentative forms of playful intimacy in friendship and competition, in sex play and love, in argument and gossip, he is apt to experience a peculiar strain, as if such tentative engagement might turn into an interpersonal fusion amounting to a loss of identity and requiring, therefore, a tense inner reservation, a caution in commitment. Where a youth does not resolve such a commitment, he may isolate himself and enter, at best, only stereotyped and formalized interpersonal relations; or, he may, in repeated hectic attempts and dismal failures, seek intimacy with the most improbable of partners. For where an assured sense of identity is missing, even friendships and affairs become desperate attempts at delineating the fuzzy outlines of identity by mutual narcissistic mirroring; to fall in love means to fall in love with one's mirror image, hurting oneself and damaging the mirror (Erikson, 1968, p. 167).

In those rare, grand instances when youthful intimacy blossoms it is a beautiful sight, and an even more beautiful experience. In adolescence, unfortunately, it is a rare experience. Egocentrism, narcissism and an incompletely developed identity all conspire against it.

Motives which underlie adolescent relationships

Adolescent friendships do not always evolve from lofty motives; sometimes they are based on little more than mutual admiration. Not mutual admiration in the sense that "We both admire each other's qualities"; rather,

"I like her because she likes me." Friendships based upon such egocentric "mutual admiration" serve to relieve feelings of inadequacy and inferiority as much as anything else.

Much of what I am trying to convey here has been well presented by Edgar Friedenberg in his classic work *The Vanishing Adolescent*. At one point he observes:

> Groups of juveniles are not friendly; and strong-felt friendships do not commonly form among them, though there is often constant association between members of juvenile cliques. They are not there to be friendly; they are there to work out a crude social system and to learn the ropes from one another. To some extent they behave like the gang in an office, jockeying for position within a superficially amiable social group (p. 44).

Adolescents search out companions who perceive their failings or limitations in a favorable light. With the passage of time youngsters whose friendship starts from this unspoken agreement may develop a profound desire to be with one another because in each other's company their defects become virtues and their weaknesses become strengths. This pattern is what Putney (1964) calls *reciprocal rationalization.*

One can easily determine when reciprocal rationalization is the basis for an adolescent friendship. Each person is drawn to the other; each person wants to be in the other person's presence, yet their togetherness always contains an element of tension and a residue of hostility. "Each is drawn to the other because he is trying to justify behaviors or beliefs about which he is extremely dubious" (Putney, p. 98). The heart of the relationship is that each friend is trading approval and support in return for the other's. This is an alliance of emotional convenience, and even though almost all adolescents use the term "friendship" to describe these relationships, they tend to harden their appraisal after they have attained a more honest view of their motives. Typically, this occurs during late adolescence or early adulthood. Most university students candidly admit that many of their adolescent friendships, especially those of early and middle adolescence, were self-serving and narcissistic.

Part of the reason is that adolescents are so insecure in their own personhood that they are incapable of reading the behavior, and assuredly the motives, of others. This holds serious consequences because at the heart of friendship lives a clear knowledge of exactly where one stands in relation to the friend. Without this clarity there is no friendship in the dignified sense of the word. Karen Horney was among the first to observe that in such a state of uncertainty the insecure person may call his partner friend "but the word has lost its meaning. Any argument, any rumor, any misinterpretation he puts on something the friend is saying, doing, or omitting may arouse not only temporary doubts but shake the very foundation of the relationship" (1950, p. 296).

In sum, genuine friendship requires both a self-knowledge and a maturity of identity which is lacking (actually, still forming) in many youngsters. Their situation is really a form of *emotionalized affiliation*, by which I mean a relationship, an affiliation which generates powerful, genuine emotions but which may not as yet answer the requirements of friendship or love. However, learning to distinguish such forms of emotionalized affiliation from love or friendship is a major task of adolescence, and a critical achievement in the formation of a mature personal identity. As with so many youth issues, however, it is necessary to point out that many youngsters fare poorly with this distinction, and, as a result, forge into adulthood with no clear sense of the difference between energized emotionality and reciprocal love. Perhaps no group of individuals is less capable of recognizing this distinction than highly narcissistic youth.

One of the most potent forces in sustaining adolescent friendships is the phenomenon of *particularization* — the equation of a particular means of satisfaction with the need itself. That is, the mistaken belief that the friend with whom an experience is shared *is the cause of that experience*. Rather than attributing the cause of the experience to a feature of their own such as their inner feelings, their warmth, or their sexuality, it is attributed to the partner. As a result, their partner takes on qualities and attributes far beyond to which they are entitled. Particularization is one of the major reasons why young friends and lovers over-estimate the abilities, the qualities, even the mortality, of their partners.

Young people are remarkably attracted to the idea that the best within their nature cannot surface on its own, and that it must be elicited by another person. They also are inclined to believe that only one person can bring these feelings into existence, and that this one person is wonderful beyond anything to which they are entitled. Of course, to lose this person would be an emotional disaster which must never, ever occur. The young, as often is true for the very elderly, are inclined to believe that only one person can create love in their world and make their lives meaningful and when that person is gone so also is love and meaning.

When a young person profoundly and passionately experiences himself or herself only with one particular person, that relationship can attain a life-and-death urgency. Thus, if the lover or friend is lost, if the relationship is broken, the adolescent experiences an overpowering loss, for in losing the person one has forever lost the experience. So at least it appears. And, in turn, the grief suffered by the wounded youth is justified by the unspeakable tragedy of the situation. When such an outlook is further enlarged by the personal fable, especially the belief that "my love," "my friendship" is more profound than anyone can possibly know, the stage is set for the adolescent's willingness to make any sacrifice for his or her partner. And from this fabled scenario emerges many of the adolescent's most heroic acts of loyalty, fidelity and selfless giving.

The power of particularization in adolescent relationships is made even more powerful when it is reinforced by *fidelity*. In Chapter Nine I discuss fidelity in far greater detail, so for the moment I would like merely to point out that fidelity refers to the desire to give one's loyalty and one's allegiance to someone or something greater than oneself. Fidelity is the predisposition to be faithful to someone, to make a commitment to something, to believe in someone.

Adolescents need friends who honestly describe their actions and their motives, that is, they need accurate mirrors. However, the pressures of peer life weigh so heavily on some youth that what they crave (not the same as need) is not an accurate mirror but rather a flattering mirror. In the real world of adolescent friendships one of the basic functions of friends, or at least certain kinds of friends, is to be a flattering mirror, even if it means being a false (distortional) mirror.

In the course of time, these flattering mirrors (even the false ones) become indispensable to the flattered friend, and from this relationship evolves a mutual emotional dependence which the flatterer perceives as proof of his or her importance ("he needs me"). This mutual dependence between the flatterer and the flattered is invariably perceived by adolescents as deep friendship, and in a certain sense it is; but in an equally certain sense, it is not. As this arrangement endures each youngster learns to give approval and support for the other in exchange for the same consideration. This alliance is even further bolstered by a "non-aggression pact," their solemn agreement to do nothing to hurt or embarrass the other.

As adults know (often because of what they learned during adolescence) such pacts rule out blunt observations, or unwanted candor, that might lead to hurt feelings, or to a loss of status. In far too many adolescent relationships honest criticism is regarded as nothing more than a hostile attack. Those readers who, in their own lives, have experienced genuine intimacy know how counterfeit, how shallow, and how empty such "mutual admiration" relationships eventually become. For a remarkable number of young people, however, this brand of "flattery friendship," or "mirroring friendship," anchored as it is in basic narcissism, represents the peak of their human relationships. It is the best relationship they have thus far experienced, and for some, it will be the best they ever will experience. These youngsters know virtually nothing about reciprocal, honest, constructive relationships, and as a result, they have no basis in personal experience for thinking anything other than the egocentric, self-aggrandizing thoughts created by their personal fables.

Peter Blos points out that it is not uncommon for adolescents to use friends in make-believe relationships in order to work through developmental changes in the personality. He claims that these fantasy relationships "lack a genuine quality; they constitute experiences which are created for the purpose of disengagement from early love objects" (1962, p. 97). These "friends" serve as representations more than as persons; their primary function is to provide reassurance in the face of the adolescent's separation from parents. And, even though Blos speaks from a tradition (psychoanalysis) which does not go to great lengths to empirically verify major hypotheses, ample evidence in the world of teen behavior supports such a viewpoint.

Blos also refers to "a type of friendship selection that is motivated by the desire of the adolescent to possess an admired quality, by proxy, through the friendship" (Lapsley, 1988, p. 119). That is to say, the motivation for the friendship is not as much for the person who becomes one's friend, but for the psychological bolstering which comes about as a result of the friendship.

The confusion between loving and longing

Adolescents confuse longing with love. This confusion is one which they share with all narcissists who, almost invariably, cannot differentiate cravings from the grander experience of unselfish love.

The adolescent's tendency to confuse longing with love works to the advantage of the narcissist for the elementary reason that so many lonely kids very much want to believe that their longings and cravings really are the same as love. (Some young people have received so little "real" love in their lives that it is questionable whether they can comprehend, either emotionally or intellectually, the difference between loving someone and craving something). These kids become even more vulnerable when narcissists falsely parade longing as loving, or when they insist that craving one another is, in fact, a glorious and grand form of love — an insistence which middle-adolescents are remarkably prone to believe.

> The difference between a strong longing for a person and "love" for this person can be best illustrated by an individual's longing for food. The hungry person longs for food in order to consume it; it represents a necessary object for a drive gratification. In like manner persons may be desired only for the

purpose of one's own gratification. The most evident example is given by a person whose longing for a partner is only sexual, completely disregarding the partner's other needs and interests (Weiss, p. 115).

Of course, the motivation behind longing may or may not derive from sexual desire; the point to be made here is that the person is longed for because of his or her ability to satisfy a need. In essence, narcissists long while the objects of their longing love. In such a relationship the narcissist thrives and the unloved partner withers. Keep in mind that many youngsters know so little of real love, have seen so little of it in their household, and have received so little of it, that they genuinely do not know the difference between "withered" love and flowering love. They will know the difference when they experience genuine love, but until that moment, as adolescents, they simply have no basis in real experience from which to draw a legitimate comparison. Hence, they buy an image of real love, and convince themselves that they are experiencing it, and attribute the greatness of their love to their super-human partner, but, in all too many instances, their experience is self-deception fueled by emotional hunger and the need to be loved.

Self-love, self-hate

In one of the most quoted passages of his landmark essay, *The Ego and the Id*, Freud (1923) observed that

...clinical observation shows not only that love is with unexpected regularity accompanied by hate, and not only that in human relationships hate is frequently a forerunner of love, but also that in many circumstances hate changes into love and love into hate.

Although it seems improbable that such a connection between love and hate could exist with the consistency that Freud claims, there is no doubt whatsoever that such an understanding of love and hate is completely justified as far as adolescent narcissism is concerned. Therefore, I draw the reader's attention to this feature of narcissism which, unfortunately, makes the puzzle of adolescent friendships and relationships even more complicated.

For narcissists the dance of self-love shuffles unpredictably into a march of self-hate. These opposites are so jumbled that one rarely knows with certainty which is which, or when one will assume the rhythm of the other. These opposites exist side by side because narcissistic cravings, when satisfied, produce a grandiose, splendid euphoria; however, these same cravings, when frustrated, produce a hostile self-hatred. Hence, narcissistic lovers who shower affection upon a cooperative partner, become self-pitying, depressed, or enraged when this partner is uncooperative. Their behavior, their mood, even their morality is totally dependent on whether their narcissistic cravings are satisfied or frustrated. And since this cause and effect relationship between behavior and need satisfaction monopolizes their conduct we observe in narcissistic youth pendulum swings in mood and behavior. And many people who share their lives with narcissists find it easier simply to give them the adulation and admiration they obsessively crave than to put up with their self-pitying resentment.

Of course, the self-esteem of all youngsters fluctuates, to a certain degree, in accordance with how well their needs are satisfied in any given day or week. This fluctuation is what Rosenberg calls the "barometric self-esteem." With narcissists we see a totally exaggerated manifestation of this phenomenon; their fluctuations are not mere ebbs and flows of esteem; they become episodes of self-love and self-hate.

To clarify this point, Weiss provides an interesting, though perhaps dated, story of a female patient:

> A young woman patient manifested a strong need for popularity, prestige and admiration. Her demands in this respect were excessive. Whenever the situation allowed her to be the centre of interest she felt very happy. When, however, another girl was more attractive than she and people paid more attention to her rival she suffered immensely. Since it did not occur too often that she was the favored one, she was usually very depressed, and complained that she did not like herself in any respect. In such situations of extreme frustration she did not impress people as loving herself, but on the contrary, as despising herself. It is easy, however, to recognize that her frustration and complaints about herself were the consequence of too strong a narcissistic craving . . . It was extremely important to her to be loved and admired; she had too great an urge to love herself . . . and all these narcissistic demands were frustrated (1950, p. 28).

The implications for friendships and relationships are staggering. For not only is the partner in such bondings unable to know with any certainty the degree to which the narcissistic companion respects the friendship, it is equally impossible to know whether narcissistic cravings will result, in any given moment, in ebullience or anger; and, even more to the point, whether what is paraded as self-love and self-respect is merely impersonated shame or self-hatred.

Echo, Echo

At the beginning of Chapter Four, I briefly introduced the myth of Narcissus, which Freud, and others, used as a starting point in their theoretical analyses of self-love and self-fascination. Narcissus, of course, was the personification of self-conceit — his vanity being such that he used to idle by the brinks of clear fountains to gaze upon the reflection of his own face. His fascination with himself was so complete that he rejected all suitors, and left in his wake the broken hearts and crushed spirits of those who loved him but received no love in return.

But here, our concern is with Echo, for it is she who so strongly desired Narcissus, who pursued him, and yearned for him even after he rejected her and left her to pine away. All of this she did without a hint of love, without even a moment of closeness, and with complete awareness that this was the way which Narcissus treated all women who desired to share his beauty and splendor.

Legend tell us that Echo was a beautiful nymph, fond of the woods and the hills, where she devoted herself to woodland sports. However, one day she deceived Juno, and when Juno discovered it she passed sentence on Echo in these words: "You shall forfeit the use of that tongue with which you have cheated me, except for that one purpose you are so fond of — reply. You shall have the last word, but no power to speak first."

One day Echo saw beautiful Narcissus as he was hunting in the hills. She immediately loved him and hurriedly followed his footsteps. How she longed to address him in the softest accents, and win him to conversation. But it was not in her power. She, therefore, waited with impatience for him to speak first, and had her answer ready. One day Narcissus, being separated from his companions, shouted aloud, "Who's here?" Echo replied in the only way she could, "Here." Narcissus looked around, but seeing no one called out, "Come." Echo answered, "Come." As no one came Narcissus called again, "Why do you shun me?" Echo then asked the same question. "Let us join one another," said the beautiful youth. Echo answered with all her heart in the same words, and hastened to the spot, ready to throw her arms about his neck. But he turned away in anger and disgust. "Not so," he said; "I will die before I give you power over me." All that Echo could say was, humbly, entreatingly, "I give you power over me," but he was gone. She hid her blushes and her shame in a lonely cave, and never could be comforted. Yet, still her love remained firmly rooted in her heart, and was increased by the pain of having been rejected. Her anxious thoughts kept her awake and made her pitifully thin. They say she has so wasted away with longing that only her voice now is left to her.

So Narcissus went on his cruel way, a scorner of love. But at last one of those he wounded prayed a prayer and it was answered by the gods: "May he who loves not others love himself." The great goddess Nemesis, which means righteous anger, undertook to bring this about. As Narcissus bent over a clear pool for a drink and saw there his own reflection, on the moment he fell in love with it.

As I have tried to indicate throughout the course of this chapter, all narcissists require their Echo, that is, they need companions, friends, lovers who will repeat as they say and follow as they command. In the adolescent community this is not nearly as difficult as one might imagine since so many youngsters possess under-developed, even impoverished identities, and, as a result they are magnetized by the charm, the strength, the "maturity," and especially, the initiative of narcissistic peers. As Echo was unable to initiate her own speech, so these youngsters are unable to initiate their own ideas or their own ambitions. Hence, they seek refuge in someone who already has a plan for them. They are the answer to every narcissist's dream, for they so lack direction that they will, in exchange for affiliation and closeness, allow another to navigate their life course for them.

Despite the failure of Echo and Narcissus to connect with one another in myth, they do so with remarkable regularity in the real world. Why? As Hamilton observed: "Echo and Narcissus fit together perfectly; neither is able to initiate and sustain dialogue. Both are consequences . . . She offers nothing which might correct Narcissus' ever-expanding delusions of grandeur" (1982, p. 128). Narcissus, not surprisingly, appears to be almost indifferent to anxiety; he does not seem to feel pain. "Since both self-examination and the voice of criticism are unfamiliar to him, there is little cause for anxiety. Narcissus has never been rejected, his life-style has never been called in question. By a twist of his head, an aversion of his eyes and the turning of his back, a displeasing scene is dismissed" (Hamilton, p. 129). Hence, the narcissist's immunity to the very anxiety which paralyzes their admirers, draws them into his circle.

And while it is obvious that no eternal truth dictates that every Narcissus must have an Echo to spurn, or that every Echo must have a Narcissus to pursue, there can be no doubt whatsoever that this drama is played daily in the adolescent theatre.

Postscript

This chapter has spoken almost exclusively to the less grand and less glorious dimensions of adolescent friendships and relationships. And though this approach does not romanticize youth in the manner to which we have become unfairly accustomed, we do well to remind ourselves that when discussing something as fine as friendship there is no honor, and certainly no honesty, in denying its less noble elements.

What you see is not always what you get in friendships and relationships. The reason being that the hidden, subterranean motives which forge a relationship often are more relevant to its existence than the reasons we create to justify it. Sometimes adolescents are aware of the discrepancy between their motives and their justifications, but frequently they are not. Becoming aware of such contradictions is one of the many adventures in self-discovery which punctuates the adolescent experience.

Several ideas have been presented in this chapter which, hopefully, will help us to better understand some aspects of adolescent relationships which psychologists, educators and parents seem all too often to overlook. In abbreviated form, here are some of the most relevant to our understanding of adolescent psychology.

1. Some young people are too insecure and too frightened to freely share their self with another. For them, relationships are, of necessity, conditional, tentative, "wait and see." Since adolescents are in the process of forming their personal identity they are, so to speak, "in process." Most of what they bring to a relationship, by definition, is susceptible to change and realignment.

2. Because of their insecurity and fearfulness many young people desire a flattering mirror far more than an honest mirror. For them, friends are a means to bolster their self-esteem, and if the "friend" fails in this function, so also does the friendship.

3. One of the many purposes of adolescent relationships is to help them to "learn the ropes" of their social system. Hence, friendships are simultaneously instrumental and personal; functional and intimate; utilitarian and sharing. Especially in early- and middle-adolescence friendships may hold a genuinely pragmatic component. Friends are bonded as people, to be sure, but the bond is welded by many forces other than the human qualities of the friend.

4. Adolescent friendships are acted upon by reciprocal rationalization; that is, giving approval and emotional support to a friend in exchange for the same favor. As well, convincing one's friend that his or her defects are really virtues in exchange for this attitude being reciprocated.

5. Adolescents (especially early- and middle-adolescents) are weak at reading the motives of others, a weakness grounded in their lack of interpersonal experience and their lack of developmental maturity. This weakness contributes greatly to their inability to predict how their friends will react to new experiences, even more importantly, it dims their insight into the unspoken agendas of their friends, and ultimately increases their vulnerability to manipulation and exploitation. Once again, we remind the reader that most adolescents eventually overcome these limita-

tions, and, as a result, grow, mature and continue with their identity project.

6. Adolescents are inclined toward particularization, that is, they believe that the particular person with whom they experience friendship or love, is the cause of it. Hence, to Romeo, Juliet is the cause of their love, and without her he can have no love. It never occurs to Romeo that Juliet is the recipient of his love but not necessarily the cause of it. If Juliet figured it out, she didn't tell.

7. Many adolescents have trouble differentiating emotional cravings from more complex experiences, such as love. Once again, this is especially true during early- and middle-adolescence, and, as well, it is a differentiation made with far greater proficiency in late-adolescence and early-adulthood than during the early teen years.

8. Some young people alternate between self-love and self-hate, especially if during their own childhood they alternately received love then hate from their parents. Since their own internal experience of themselves is polarized, it is not unusual for these adolescents to have relationships completely opposite in character; one which fuels their hatred and another which nourishes their love. For some as yet unknown reason (or, for reasons upon which no agreement exists) this mixture of love-hate relationships seems especially true for young men, and as a result, their behavior and demeanor becomes compartmentalized, with their actions reflecting whichever relationship they are "in." Hence, in one set of relationships they are hateful and angry and in another loving and calm.

All of which contributes to the intricate, and profound, mystery of adolescent friendships and relationships.

chapter seven

The Corrupted Self

In the previous three chapters I have described at length many of the features of normal, "selfish" narcissism. From these descriptions it is clear that narcissistic individuals are gripped with an exaggerated sense of entitlement, and like Narcissus himself, their personality is laced with self-infatuation and fixated upon surface appearances. These characteristics, unflattering as they may be, are not pathological in the psychiatric sense of the word, rather, they are the ingredients of an inflated, though normal, narcissism.

Pathological narcissism, as its name indicates, is the neurotic exaggeration of normal narcissism. *It is corrupting because it destroys the balance every self requires for its own growth and fulfillment, the healthy balance between I and you, we and me, and between self-interest and social-interest.*

Normal and pathological narcissism exist on a psychological continuum; when normal narcissism becomes excessively exaggerated, when it begins to "take over" the personality, it assumes pathological properties, and conversely, when the neurotic manifestations of pathological narcissism lessen and lose their power they begin to resemble normal narcissism. This dialectic relationship is of great significance in our investigation of adolescents, for when, for whatever reasons, normal narcissism escalates, races out of control, the probability of pathological narcissism increases. As Alford (1988) reminds us:

> Although pathological narcissism sounds so sick . . . healthy narcissism shares many of the same characteristics . . . This is explained by a presumption . . . shared by almost all theorists of narcissism that there is a continuum between pathological and normal narcissism, and that even the most extreme manifestations of pathological narcissism are not entirely alien to normal narcissists (p. 70).

Pathological narcissism is not a condition inherent to the normal growth process nor is it a characteristic of the normal personality. Yet, the fact that its pathos derives from exaggerated normalcy can help us to better understand some of the more common obsessions and fixations shared by young people in our culture. As Christopher Lasch concludes:

> On the principle that pathology represents a heightened version of normality, the "pathological narcissism" found in character disorders of this type should tell us something about narcissism as a social phenomenon. Studies of personality disorders . . . depict a type of personality that ought to be immediately recognizable, in a more subdued form, to observers of the contemporary social scene . . . (1978, p. 38).

The relevance of this observation to our investigation of youth in modern culture is clear, if, as Lasch suggests, the symptoms of pathological narcissism *exist in subdued form* in the behavior, the attitudes and the obsessions of the adolescent community.

It is, of course, a mistake to think that we can understand adolescence *in its totality* by looking at pathological narcissism. However, when one is concerned, as we are, with young people's exaggerated sense of entitlement, with their selfish indifference to the rights of others, then pathological narcissism can be a productive, perhaps even necessary, frame of reference.

What is pathological narcissism?

Pathological narcissism has been defined by C. Fred Alford as:

> An exaggerated concern with power and control, the result of which is interpersonal exploitiveness. Typical also is an orientation of entitlement, the notion that one is worthy of great admiration, respect and reward regardless of one's achievements. Pathological narcissism is further characterized by relationships that alternate between extremes of idealization and devaluation. Finally, the pathological narcissist's grandiosity is curiously coupled with great fragility of self-esteem (p. 3).

With this serving as our general guide, we may establish that the most significant features of pathological narcissism include the following:

1. an obsession with power and control which invariably leads to exploitation and manipulation in interpersonal relationships;

2. feelings of entitlement, and demands for special treatment, even when neither have been earned;

3. feelings which alternate between grandeur and unworthiness not only toward oneself but toward one's parents, friends and lovers; and, finally,

4. a self-concept which, under some circumstances, can endure remarkable adversity, yet, under other circumstances, withers and cracks from pressures the ordinary person takes in stride.

A profile of pathological narcissism

The pathological narcissist cannot survive without massive infusions of attention, adulation and admiration. This core of narcissistic grandiosity invariably leads to disturbances in interpersonal relationships, especially tendencies toward exploitation, feelings of entitlement and a lack of empathy. Pathological narcissism, by definition, is a psychiatric malfunction, not a condition of normal development. However, *episodes of pathological narcissism occur to virtually all adolescents at one time or another with varying degrees of intensity. Hence, the features of pathological narcissism can be seen as intermittent features of normal adolescent growth.*

In pathological narcissism the self is so absorbed with itself that seeing the world with objectivity is impossible. The very self-immersion upon which pathological narcissism is founded causes a remarkable overestimation of one's abilities, an over-assessment of one's achievements, and a relentless mis-reading of the interaction between the two. Even though narcissists genuinely believe in their "magnificent heroics," it is not unusual for their feelings of greatness to descend into a pressing anxiety over worthiness or competence. Hence, a student who ordinarily receives 90s may feel like a total failure upon receiving an 80 or 85.

Narcissism, when carried to the extremes we are describing here, inevitably distorts the individual's ideas about how the basic necessities of life are obtained. As a result, they may have notoriously unrealistic goals about possessing unlimited wealth, awesome power, or the kind of prestige accorded only the most important people. These "goals," however, usually are not pursued in any systematic fashion, but they are always romanticized, talked about and idealized. The self of pathological narcissists is so corrupted that they feel entitled to achieve these goals, and to experience the glory which comes with them, whether they actually earn them or not.

Even though these individuals feel completely entitled to receive endless admiration from others they, ironically, possess low self-esteem and a fragile sense of well-being. They respond to criticism with either a cool indifference or with rage. Their emotional reactions to criticism are devastating to the fragile side of their nature, and painful far beyond the disappointments experienced by "normal" adolescents.

Perhaps the most conspicuous feature of the pathological narcissist is an outrageous sense of entitlement. That is, the expectation that "I" am entitled to receive special favors without assuming special responsibilities. That "I" am entitled to the best you, or anyone else, may offer. When confronted by the unfairness of this point of view, or its moral emptiness, they retaliate with a barrage of "You hate me," "Why are you fighting me?," "I thought you were on my side." When young narcissists are challenged by their parents, teachers or friends to explain why their relationships are falling apart they unfailingly blame the selfishness of others. On this last point narcissists differ profoundly from normal youngsters in that they simply do not learn from experience, or from the advice of their friends; they never seem to correct the correctable. In a very real sense, they are failures at the entire process of self-analysis, and this is a failure of major proportions for it is through self analysis that personality weaknesses and character defects are diagnosed, improved upon, and sometimes even eradicated during the adolescent years. It cannot escape our attention that the egocentric immaturities and self-centred fixations typical of early adolescence, and outgrown by most of us in late-adolescence, remain with the narcissist into the twenties and thirties.

Even though it is apparent to impartial observers that their friendships lack dignity and reciprocity, narcissists emphatically deny this. Instead, they claim that the relationship contains *special elements* which the ordinary person cannot comprehend. In a typical use of the personal fable, this is explained by asserting that "my" friendships possess a grandness not known to ordinary people. When the narcissist can no longer deny that the friendship is falling apart (or was never together in the first place) he or she usually projects the cause to the superficiality or the emptiness of the partner, and thereby feels even further justified in rejecting that person.

Narcissists are a study in self-fascination gone awry. Frequently, for example, their obsession with grooming, with physical appearance, with fitness, and with presenting a beautiful body, rather than building confidence within them, triggers a chronic envy of these very features when they appear in others. Part of the problem is that they simultaneously crave and hate the same thing: they love, for example, stylish haircuts when they have one, but hate them when they are "flaunted" by someone else.

The behavior of pathological narcissism

Narcissists cannot cope with the candid "give and take" of normal human interchange. They react to criticism with rage, shame or humiliation; and frequently they hold a hostile grudge against the person who delivered the criticism, no matter how well-intended (or deserved) it may have been. This grudge, with time, may grow into malice or hatred. One of the many painful facts of pathological narcissism is that hateful emotions survive with greater persistence than loving sentiments, *and when these opposites conflict with one another, the hateful element consistently prevails.*

Adolescents who fit the profile of the pathological narcissist are exploitive in their relationships with peers and parents; they consistently take advantage of others to satisfy their own needs or to achieve their own ends. All too frequently they are able to steal, cheat and lie with proficiency and without remorse. Punishment for these sins is perceived as an unfair retaliation by a parent or teacher who "has it in for me." Any attempt to point out the moral inappropriateness of such behavior falls on deaf ears since narcissists believe that their actions have an inherent rightfulness.

Like the rest of us, narcissists possess a wide range of skills and abilities. Nothing inherent to this condition assures one of being a high achiever or a low achiever, dull or quick, clumsy or coordinated. Whatever the talents and abilities of narcissists, one thing is certain: they exaggerate their achievements and overrate their talents. They invariably assess their accomplishments as being far greater than they are. They also are predisposed to falsify experiences and events, *especially when their lies cannot be disproved.* As a result, far more than the rest of us narcissists see a UFO while walking alone at night, encounter an escaped criminal while camping, or receive exciting sexual offers from beautiful strangers. Fantasy, of all sorts, is their constant companion for it is an endlessly renewable source of psychic nourishment.

Expectations are remarkable. Invariably narcissists expect special treatment such as the right to be admitted to a theatre after it is sold out, to be given permission to take an examination late when such permission is granted to no other student. Their sense of entitlement is not based on assumed duties or obligations; narcissists believe they are entitled simply by being "me." A consequence of extreme relevance to the adolescent community (and to society-at-large) occurs when boys believe they are entitled to the affection, loyalty, or sexual favors of a girl they know, or date, or with whom they simply share a classroom. When these entitlements are not received the boy usually pouts, holds a grudge, or slanders the girl who failed to deliver. Sometimes aggression follows rejected entitlements — after all, "I was entitled to it, wasn't I." The most important entitlements, however, are not spoken aloud. They are so firmly accepted as true that acting upon them seems "natural," and going out of the way to articulate them is completely unnecessary. Hence a comfortable smoothness connects expectation with action. After all, why should someone feel self-conscious, or even be concerned about the reactions of others, when taking something to which he or she is entitled?

By now it goes without saying that these emotionally arrested young people require constant attention, admiration, mirroring and stroking. Their self lacks the strength to handle daily pressures without endless reassurance. They often feel agitated in social gatherings when too much time elapses without some praise or special acknowledgment being directed toward them. Since their evaluation of adults is based on being flattered by them, they consistently denigrate adults who are unaware of, or unimpressed with, their presence. Adolescent narcissists are condescending toward, or ridiculing of, adults who don't shower them with special attention. Among peers they may even attain considerable acclaim by their ability to make administrators look like buffoons, teachers idiots, police Nazis, or psychologists neurotics.

Although their insights into the workings of the human personality are developed well enough to solicit the allegiance and sympathy of their companions, narcissists usually are weak at recognizing how others feel *when these feelings bear negatively on them*. The narcissist may become irritated with a friend who failed to provide a ride to school because he was sick that day, or with a parent who drives a friend to the hospital and therefore cannot loan out the car. When their relationships turn sour, when exploited friends complain or simply walk out, when parents tell them they are sick of being their servants, narcissists are usually taken by complete surprise. Unbalanced relationships are so compatible with their selfish nature that it does not occur to them that their partners feel exploited.

Preoccupations and obsessions

All adolescents own personal fables — beliefs which exaggerate their uniqueness and specialness. The lives of pathological narcissists are completely taken over by such fables. With a stunning consistency they believe their problems and circumstances are so unique that they can be understood only by the heroic efforts of special people. (People become "special" by showing a fascinated interest in, or an affection for, the narcissist). These exaggerated, over-blown personal fables magnify their feelings of specialness, the anticipation of entitlements, and their imperviousness to the feelings of others.

Narcissists attribute very special qualities to peers who are interested in them, a remarkably successful ploy in attracting to them socially marginal youngsters with low self-esteem. They may even sign loyalty or friendship pacts, promising to support each other forever. Narcissists tell their friends that they love them, that life without them is unbearable. And, in a certain immediate sense, this is completely true. All too often this message is consumed by younger, naive peers craving confirmation, or merely acceptance. In the adolescent community only the most socially inept narcissists are without "friends" and followers. It is not necessary to be a beautiful Narcissus in order to attract an Echo.

Narcissists are obsessed with people of greatness, whether nuclear physicists or rock musicians, because, by merit of their greatness, they know first-hand the adulation of the masses. These superstars are the vicarious cohorts of the narcissist's self-image and they are worshipped to prove to the narcissist that such worship is, in fact, real. By worshipping the greatness of others narcissists verify to themselves that they are entitled to receive the worship of the lessers who surround them.

The relentless preoccupation with adulation and admiration does, however, take an emotional toll. The constant attentiveness to who is admiring whom erodes away any hope for an objective understanding of human interactions and replaces it with the warping pain of jealousy and envy.

Hence, what we see among these individuals is an entire attitude organized on the principle of resentment:

* resentment that others have what I do not have;

* resentment about having to live in a world which causes such anxious envy;

* resentment that others are not consumed with resentment.

Inevitably, resentment converts to anger, and all too frequently, anger converts to hostility and violence.

Self-concept and self-esteem

One of the many vexing characteristics of narcissists is that they are unable to regulate their own self-esteem, hence, their sense of themselves fluctuates between grandiosity and shame. And even though vacillation between the extremely worthy and totally unworthy is a fact of the narcissistic character, there are considerable differences as to how frequently descents to the unworthy pole will occur, and how long ascents to the worthy pole will last.

In the narcissistic character, the development of the "real" self has never really taken hold. The self-concept, for all intents and purposes, remains under the influence of childhood emotional states and the conflicts attendant to them. The more powerful these childhood emotional states are experienced, and the more primitive the conflicts within them, the stronger the narcissistic component to the personality. The stronger the narcissistic component to the personalty the more unpredictable are the shifts in self-concept and self-esteem.

To sustain the false self upon which the personality rests, the narcissist "sees himself in relation to the world through rigidly held constructs *and assimilates new information into those constructs or ignores it*" (Johnson, 1985). In other words, the narcissist simply fails to process certain data, and as a result, is impervious to anything which contradicts the grandiose self.

The failure of narcissists to discriminate effectively between the cravings of the self and the desires of others renders them particularly prone to exaggerated suspicion, even paranoia, whenever the self-esteem (or the false self) is threatened.

The narcissist's emotional state is dominated by the fear of humiliation. And, while it is true that narcissists invite interpersonal confrontations, it is equally true that they respond best to nurturance and reassurance. In fairness to those who do the nurturing and reassuring, however, narcissists have a seemingly endless capacity to receive reassurance, nurturance, and love without modifying their behavior to any appreciable degree.

Interpersonal relationships

It is abundantly clear that for narcissists extreme difficulty with human relations is the trend, good relationships the exception. The reason for this difficulty is a simple matter of personality dynamics: the narcissist cannot handle relationships based upon honesty and equality, or any form of relationship in which the "give" and the "take" exist in fairly equal portions. Hence, human needs which require such conditions of equality (such as love and respect) are unsatisfied.

Narcissists divide their social world into two camps: " . . . others are viewed in one of two distinct categories: the good people and the bad people. A typical narcissist will take great pains to be identified with the good people and shun the bad . . ." (p. 49, Johnson). As well, narcissists usually have a very well-honed perception of who is "above" and "beneath" them according to various social or physical criteria. And, as Lowen observes: "Narcissistic characters . . . are not just better, they are the best. They are not just attractive, they are the most attractive . . . they have a need to be perfect and to have others see them as perfect" (1983 p. 17). Furthermore, those who are close to the narcissist, i.e., parents, lovers, peers, "are often expected to read his mind and provide gratification without being asked" (Johnson, p. 50).

Postscript

When narcissism attains extreme prominence it corrupts the self with destructive self-obsessions. Despite this unpleasant fact, pathological narcissism is, in essence, an exaggerated variation of normal narcissism — the differences between them being of degree not kind.

The defining features of chronic narcissism include:

1. The inability to receive criticism without painful repercussion to one's self-esteem; the tendency to perceive all criticism as an attack on one's self.

2. Exploitive interpersonal relationships; taking advantage of others, even friends and family, for personal gain.

3. Expectations of special treatment and the total belief that one is entitled to receive such special treatment; furthermore, special treatment has nothing to do with the qualities of the person who is providing it, rather, it is received because of the specialness within me.

4. The inability to accurately perceive the reactions of others to one's self-centredness.

5. Exaggerated and overly dramatic personal fables; fantasies of heroic specialness.

6. Unshakeable feelings of envy and jealousy; resentment at one's failure to attain what others seemingly possess in great abundance.

7. An incessant fear of humiliation; refusal to participate in any activities or to involve oneself in any relationships where humiliation could occur. The belief that anything less than perfection will bring shame and humiliation.

8. The belief that one's social world is divided between good people and bad people; the good one's being those who support or nourish my narcissistic grandiosity and the bad one's being those who resist it.

9. A willingness to fight, oppose, slander, resist, sometimes even do violence to the "bad" people.

chapter eight

Self-Understanding

Nothing is so difficult as not deceiving oneself.
Ludwig Wittgenstein

Psychologists specializing in the behavior of young people are in agreement with the parents who raise them and the teachers who educate them that adolescent's are vulnerable to a surprisingly wide range of irrational opinions and unjustified certainties which interfere with their capacity for honest self-understanding. How these come into existence is not agreed upon by psychologists. Some youth experts believe that young people simply have not learned the ropes, and that inexperience accounts for most of their irrational beliefs — with experience and wise counsel most of them are discarded. There is considerable merit to this point of view, especially when it is directed toward twelve-, thirteen-, and fourteen-year-olds. However, it seems lacking when we attempt to understand older teens, especially late-adolescents who are seventeen-, eighteen- and nineteen-years-old. Other youth experts believe that *mechanisms inherent to the adolescent thought process* produce irrational beliefs and attitudes. Both of these viewpoints are explored in this chapter.

What is not disputed is that false ideas magnify in power once they are transformed from hypotheses into beliefs. After all, an hypothesis is merely an assumption which serves as a tentative explanation; it is an unproved proposition used as a basis for further investigation. A belief, on the other hand, is the acceptance of something as true. Hypotheses are guesses about what might be. Beliefs are convictions about what is — they not only guide action, they initiate and control it. And while many factors contribute to irrationality, one of the most important is the conviction that one's hypotheses accurately describe reality when they do not.[1]

---

1 As part of the background research for this chapter, I interviewed 105 teenagers living in small, rural towns attending high schools (and junior high schools) with less than 400 students. I specifically chose this group of youngsters because most of the young people interviewed for other chapters in this book grew up in urban centres. These rural adolescents, whose quotes are interspersed throughout this chapter, live in Alberta, Saskatchewan, Oregon and Washington.

Like the rest of us, and in some instances because of the rest of us, adolescents are burdened with absurd ideas about how to be loved, how to be popular, how to be successful; about "How I should behave," "Why people don't like me," and "I would be perfect if I could only . . ." But, as I shall try to demonstrate in this chapter, these are most assuredly not the only, or even the most important, irrationalities in the adolescent community.

A quick review of terms will make our task somewhat easier. An "absurd belief" simply means believing an obvious falsity or something which stands in opposition to common sense or reason; something obviously contradictory to accepted truth. "Irrational" refers to that which is contrary to reason or to the principles of logical thinking. And, perhaps even more relevant to our discussion, "irrational" makes reference to *beliefs determined more by one's needs and desires than by the actual situation.* Albert Ellis, one of the pioneers in the investigation of irrational beliefs and the actions borne of them, claimed that "irrational" also includes the tendency to repeat the same mistakes, to be superstitious, intolerant, grandiose and perfectionistic. (Ellis, 1963).

If these terms make you edgy, you are not alone. It is hard to know with certainty when anything is "an obvious falsity," or stands in opposition to common sense. Sometimes common sense itself seems absurd, as most teen-agers will freely point out, especially when confronted with someone who has more of it than they do.

"As-if" thinking

Erik Erikson and Margaret Mead popularized the concept of adolescence as an "as-if" period of life; a time when young people can experiment with various roles "as-if" they were committed to them. Since this is an "as-if" period they are not held fully accountable for mistakes which might be made in learning about these new roles. Adolescents can change their values and commitments as a result of such as-if experiments. In theory, living in a social world with such freedom allows the adolescent to experience a broad spectrum of roles and responsibilities before making the important decisions of adolescence and adulthood.

There is another use of this term: thinking which causes one to act "as if" *an unproved assumption were true.* For example, a youngster assumes that teachers are against him, "out to get me," as a result he behaves in a hostile manner toward all teachers. The adolescent simply categorizes teachers "as-if" they possessed certain characteristics and interacts with them "as-if" they possessed these characteristics, whether they do or not.

"As-if" thinking typically involves a regression to the cognitive patterns of children aged seven to eleven which Elkind calls "concrete operational egocentrism." At this level of intellectual development children have great difficulty differentiating between a hypothesis and a fact, and as a result they sometimes treat hypotheses as if they were facts and sometimes they treat facts as if they were hypotheses. When children have their hypotheses challenged by new information they quickly "bend" it to fit their hypotheses. They believe their thought is imbued with its own logical consistency, hence it does not seem reasonable to them to change it. This primitive thought sequence repeats itself with great regularity during adolescence. It does not, however, occur randomly; it most frequently operates when the adolescent must deal with ideas and facts threatening to the self.

In this chapter I would like to highlight four examples of attitudes and expectations which interfere with self-understanding, and, which lessen the adolescent's ability to achieve a solid and coherent identity. They include:

1. the craving for approval;
2. the craving for perfection;
3. distorting future; and,
4. the expectation of excessive entitlements.

The craving for approval

One belief that works its way into the thought patterns of many young people is that it is necessary to be approved of by everyone. Ironically, for an age group supposedly at odds with adult society, the belief that one should receive the approval of adults, especially parents, is rather common. As one girl put it:

I always wanted to be the best and I would try to show my parents this. When I was 13 I lived on a farm and I decided the best way to get my father's approval would be to help him or tag around with him. All summer I rode tractors, went fencing, and continually followed him around.

With my mother I agreed with everything she said no matter what. I picked out clothes I thought she would like. Well, the next year at school I felt out of place because I then realized that my mother's taste in clothes was much different than my friend's taste.

Another adolescent girl reported:

As a young teen I'd do anything my Mom wanted, just to have her approval; to make her believe I was her best daughter. When she would ask my sister to do something, I would jump to the opportunity of doing it. For example, going to the garden to dig some potatoes for supper. I'd also study real hard for an exam to meet Mom's approval of being an "A" student because that is what she was in school.

Even more prevalent is the belief that all of their peers should approve of and like them. These youngsters crave acceptance and popularity, and if they are socially gifted, they may even obtain a great measure of both. For most teens, however, craving universal approval leads to painful disillusionment. Even craving the approval of one person, if it is a special person, can lead to disappointment.

> I had an obsession for gaining the approval of my parents, particularly my father. I tried to make him proud of me by getting good grades, being a good athlete, and basically trying to do things for him. Unfortunately, he never showed me his approval. So then, I went the other way. I let my marks drop, stopped sports, but still got no reaction. As a result, I stopped trying to gain the approval of anyone by late-adolescence. I no longer cared.

When carried to extremes the craving for approval results in what Karen Horney called the "neurotic need for affection and approval," an indiscriminate wish to please others, and to live up to their expectations. For these youngsters everything centres on the good opinions of others, and the fearful apprehension of their rejection.

Some psychologists, especially social-learning theorists, argue that the quest for social approval is motivated by its instrumental value, that is, as a means to an end rather than as an end in itself. Since most of us tend to reward those people we approve of in far greater measure than those we disapprove of, it is in the best interest of all of us to be socially approved. Social approval is valuable because obtaining other rewards such as friendship, sex or money is based on it; unquestionably, the practical value of social approval motivates many young people. It is doubtful, however, that such a utilitarian view can account for the *craving* for social approval which overpowers so many young people.

A more "dynamic" explanation has been forwarded by Nathaniel Brandon who claims that craving the approval of others is not motivated by its instrumental value but, rather, by a deficiency in self-esteem, and, until one is able to approve of himself or herself, the approval of others will never amount to much.

> One of the characteristics of a self-esteem deficiency is an excessive preoccupation with gaining the approval and avoiding the disapproval of others, a hunger for validation and support at every moment of our existence ... But because the problem is essentially internal, because the person does not believe in him- or herself, no outside source can ever satisfy this hunger,

except momentarily. The hunger is . . . for self-esteem. And this cannot be supplied by others (1979, p. 47).

An important side effect of the obsessive desire for approval is that its absence is experienced as guilt. Since approval-seeking youngsters often do not possess independent judgment about their own value except as it is reflected in the approval of others, they become awash in guilt when they fear that validation from others is not forthcoming. They readily accept that when they are not "approved of" it is because they are unworthy. To correct this situation, that is, to once again become worthy, they turn to these very others for direction and approval. "Their anxious feelings are often experienced as fear of the disapproval of others. Others are perceived as the voice of objective reality calling them to judgment" (Branden, 1979, p. 68). The fear of disapproval (which is not the same as craving approval, but frequently it is the motive behind it) is a common adolescent theme. Here, in the words of an eighteen-year-old boy, is a "typical" adolescent fear of disapproval:

> It's not so much that I wanted to be approved of, really it was more of a fear of not being approved. I was shy and never talked much because I felt that my peers were just there waiting for me to say something wrong or to criticize what I would say. I was always afraid they would reject me, but I don't think I ever wanted their approval.

Craving approval, unto itself, is neither irrational nor absurd; it becomes so only when it takes on self-defeating proportions. "The desire to be validated, confirmed, or approved of, in our being and behavior, is normal. I call such a desire irrational or pathological only when it gains such ascendancy in our hierarchy of values that we will sacrifice honesty and integrity in order to achieve it . . ." (Branden, 1979, p. 46). This sacrifice of one's integrity in exchange for approval is usually, but not always, anchored in a poor self-concept and low self-esteem. Every once in a while, however, it is observed in a youngster who is simply so obsessed with peer acceptance, with membership, or group affiliation that he or she abandons virtually everything else for its attainment. These youngsters are not psychologically damaged in any clinical sense, yet they are relentlessly driven by their cravings for approval. For many of them this irrational quality lessens by late-adolescence or early adulthood, but, for some young people this craving persists into adulthood and becomes a defining feature of their adult personality.

Youngsters consumed by approval want to be surrounded by a familiar world that reinforces their belief in the rightness of the ideas that have been trained into them, often without their own participating thought. Typically, youth who hold irrational ideas about approval have blindly incorporated the social rules and expectations of their group into their own belief network.

One of the more unpleasant outcomes of the adolescent's obsession with approval is a disgust toward, sometimes even a hatred for, individuals thought to be "too different." They are perceived as evil merely because they are different. This belief prospers among youth who themselves possess unmanageable impulses, or who struggle with their own fears of being too different, too far off base, too unacceptable. The belief that differences are evil manufactures a remarkable volume of prejudice and hatred, especially toward groups or individuals already discriminated against by society at large.

A related misapprehension inclines the adolescent to conclude that people who behave differently are inferior. Before we saw difference as evil, here difference as defective. Differences are thought of as moral inferiorities. Many adolescents so hunger for superiority that even when it is satisfied merely by proclaiming someone else's inferiority, it briefly satisfies the hunger.

One final observation concerning young people obsessed with the need for approval: *they are fools for consumerism.* Since their identity is not sufficiently developed to autonomously define themselves they are forced to rely upon the approving judgments of others. Hence the idea which propels all advertising, that the "right" commodities, signified by the "right" labels, will bring instant approval, finds a receptive audience among acceptance craving youth. As with other attempts to gratify cravings grounded in insecurity or inferiority, consumerism usually ends up being more a source of frustration than gratification. As Lasch (1984) perceptively observes: "The state of mind promoted by consumerism is better described as a state of uneasiness and chronic anxiety. The promotion of commodities depends . . . on discouraging the individual from reliance on his own resources and judgments . . . his judgment of what he needs in order to be healthy and happy" (p. 28).

Approval seeking is a culture-wide phenomenon, as is the use of consumer goods to "buy" approval, acceptance, status and a cluster of other affiliation needs. Ours is a consumer culture and the impact of consumerism on the psychological need structure is everywhere observed, perhaps nowhere more blatantly than in the fictionalized lives of approval obsessed adolescents. The effects of consumerism are magnified in the teen world where reliance upon the opinions of others is at a lifetime high while practical experience with the economic world is minimal. The personal fable encourages the perception that their purchases, their goods of consumption, will create reactions which far exceed what they deliver. As well, the "imaginary audience" inclines them to accept the advertising ploy that everyone will notice, even be amazed by, every new purchase and every new acquisition they add to their repertoire. Youngsters who believe this fallacy, and they exist in staggering numbers, find themselves emotionally locked into dependence on consumer goods not so much for the approval they elicit from others, but for approval from oneself — a self convinced that without material goods *genuine* approval is impossible.

> . . . societies based on mass production and mass consumption encourage an unprecedented attention to superficial impressions and images, to the point where the self becomes almost indistinguishable from its surface. Selfhood and personal identity become problematic in such societies, as we can easily see from the outpouring of psychiatric and sociological commentaries on these subjects (Lasch, 1984, p. 29).

The function of goods is to produce illusions, which in one way or another, also perpetuate fictions:

> Commodity production and consumerism alter perceptions not just of the self but of the world outside the self. They create a world of mirrors, insubstantial images, illusions increasingly indistinguishable from reality . . . The consumer lives surrounded not so much by things as by fantasies . . . (Lasch, 1984. p. 30).

And finally, the ultimate contradiction, consumerism weakens rather than strengthens the self-concept:

> A culture organized around mass consumption encourages narcissism . . . a disposition to see the world as a mirror, more particularly as a projection of one's own fears and desires — not because it makes people grasping and self-assertive but because it makes them weak and dependent (Lasch, 1984, p. 33).

The craving for perfection

A decidedly fixed certainty for many young people is that they must not only be thoroughly competent, they must be literally "perfect" if their actions are ever to amount to anything worthwhile. This obsession with perfection shows dramatic increase during the teen years (it is fairly rare in childhood) and it manifests an even sharper upswing during early adulthood. Interestingly, the perfection motive is frequently observed among high-competence people, leading some psychotherapists to describe it as an "executive ailment." School teachers see it in students who fall apart if they don't receive 100 percent, or whatever symbolizes it. Parents see it in kids who won't leave the house unless their clothing, or hair, or makeup, is impeccable. Coaches see it in kids who quit the team when they can't perform perfectly. Teens see it in friends who must win every argument.

Some of these cravings are, admittedly, harmless eccentricities.

> When I was younger I did have on obsession with perfection, in fact, I still do. I always needed to have everything in perfect order to be satisfied. I

needed to fluff my pillows and have my blanket straight on my bed and have it tucked in between my bed and the wall before I could go to bed. I would arrange things on a shelf with the English label facing out (I still do that once in a while). I arranged my money in my wallet in order of value and with the people's heads all right side up. I used to never wear clothes that were unmatched even when I was alone at home.

Harmless obsessions with orderliness or tidiness do not represent an issue of much significance in the world of adolescence. However, the neurotic exaggeration of such obsessions, what Karen Horney called the "neurotic need for perfection and unassailability" is a serious matter. Here one is fearful of making mistakes, of being criticized, and great lengths are taken to appear impregnable and infallible. The youngster searches for flaws in himself or herself so that they may be covered up before anyone else detects them. Their self-concept flounders in chronic feelings of inferiority and insecurity. (Paradoxically, for many youngsters, illusions of perfection protect them from *recognizing their own finite limits*. Their perfectionism is, in essence, a denial of their human limitations.) A phenomenon repeated all too often among adolescent girls is precisely summarized here:

> I thought I had to be the thinnest person in my grade and when I got to school in the morning I would make myself throw-up. I would throw my lunch away so my mother would not find out. After supper I would make myself throw up again. Finally, I woke up and realized I was thin enough, but this was after I kept passing out and felt extremely tired all the time.

For some teens it is catastrophic when events do not unfold exactly as they think they should. Early and middle adolescents are especially inclined to believe that their slightest error invites the greatest possible catastrophe. The anxieties inherent to this misapprehension are magnified by the further belief that one's emotional security and prospects for meaningful relationships are completely dependent upon *being accepted by a limited group of specific people*. As a result, arguments and disagreements among peers assume enormous significance. Early and middle adolescents are especially inclined to believe that if they are rejected, in any way, by their peers they will undergo irreversible social damage. In their eyes, they are lost forever. This, of course, is quite a burden to bear. The painful process of learning that this attitude is essentially false represents, for many youth, a breakthrough in self-understanding.

One of the consistent features of adolescents driven by the need for perfection is their tendency toward self-condemnation. Falling short of their goals leads them to sense doom and ruination; they censure themselves so strongly, and issue themselves such severe reproofs that they literally judge themselves as unfit. Many of these youngsters eventually tire of such self-punishment and learn to "take it easy on myself." Others, however, carry the self-condemnation of not being perfect into their adult years, bewildering their adulthood friends and lovers with an endless array of self-punishing beliefs and self-condemning attitudes.

David Burns (1986) worked extensively with individuals driven by perfection, and, as a result of his investigations, he isolated several features of their emotional disposition. He claims perfectionists have trouble in their interpersonal relationships, and are prone toward powerful shifts in moodiness. As well, perfectionists are sensitive to any form of disapproval because they perceive it as total rejection. In addition, the perfectionist is "vulnerable to a number of potentially serious mood disorders, including depression, performance anxiety, test anxiety, social anxiety, writer's block, and obsessive-compulsive illness . . . Perfectionistic individuals, we find, are likely to respond to the perception of failure or inadequacy with a precipitous loss in self-esteem that can trigger episodes of severe depression and anxiety." Perfectionists also are plagued by loneliness and feelings of emptiness (p. 253-255).

Relevant to our concerns is Burns' observation that the thought patterns of perfectionists are characterized by a series of distortions. According to Burns: "the most common mental distortion found among perfectionists is all-or-nothing thinking. They evaluate their experiences in a dichotomous manner, seeing things as either all-black or all-white; intermediate shades of gray do not seem to exist." The outcome of this thinking pattern is the tendency to think of oneself "as-if" one is a complete failure or a complete success. A second mental distortion of perfectionists is overgeneralization — the belief that when negative events do occur, they *will be repeated endlessly*. Hence, they always fear failure, and believe that if they do not handle every situation just perfectly, that somehow, a disaster will ensue. A third mental distortion is that perfectionists are excessively burdened with "shoulds." For example, when perfectionists fall short of meeting a goal they say to themselves: "I *shouldn't have* taken a rest on Saturday." "I *ought to* know better than to visit too long." "I *must never* phone her again." Hence, failures take on a moral quality which cause perfectionists not only to recognize their failures, but, as well, *to condemn themselves for making them.*

Ironically, despite their high standards, and often high levels of performance, perfectionists tend to see themselves as wasteful of their time and talents. They falsely believe that other individuals achieve their goals and meet their deadlines with little or no effort, with minimal soul-searching, and with few errors. Hence, not only do perfectionists mis-read themselves, they completely mis-read others.

Vocabulary is both a cause and an effect as far as the obsession with perfection is concerned. Adolescent's are prone toward a vocabulary of extremism, and they misuse words such as: never, always, every, none, nobody, everyone, totally, completely, and forever. These words carry such finality that they make any situation appear more grave than it is; and when these terms are taken literally, as they often are among perfectionists, they impose a completely unwarranted urgency. Hence, after a job interview the adolescent claims: "Everyone thought my interview was totally stupid. I'll never get a job anywhere." The same youngster, after being turned down for the job: "Jim told everybody that I didn't get the job. Everybody thinks I'm a total idiot."

Counsellors and teachers learn from experience how vital it is to teach these youngsters that the world does not screech to a halt after one has made a fool of oneself, or when one has been rejected, or when an examination comes back with a failing grade on it. With the accumulation of experience, youngsters learn to better balance private demands with public expectations. Many, however, develop such elaborate defenses that inaccurate perceptions actually multiply rather than diminish during the adolescent years. They eventually become perfection-driven adults who, in the course of raising their own children, serve as a model for this approach to life.

On the other hand, most youth learn from experience, even from their failures and their many imperfections; eventually they recognize, and accept, that no one is perfect, that even their idols are "human," and that error is universal. Such insight is, for them, a profound source of enlightenment which contributes immensely to their self-understanding.

> I always wanted to be as neat as possible with my homework or notes, or whatever I did at school. So I would re-copy my notes at home that I took in school. I would spend hours re-copying. Sometimes I would even re-copy what I had already re-copied. I would spend hours. I finally realized it was just a big waste of time.

Another individual I interviewed summarized his experiences with perfectionism this way:

> It took me a long time to realize that I couldn't always look perfect. No matter how hard I tried. I always thought that if you just tried hard enough you could accomplish anything. Even be perfect. That was stupid. So was I, I guess.

And, finally, distantly remote from all this, comes the defiant proclamation of one self-admitted non-perfectionist:

No way! I hate perfection. I grew up with a younger sister who was a perfectionist about being neat, so I was messy. Perfection takes up too much time. I always enjoyed my time. I am too lazy to be a perfectionist. I like my fun too much to be a perfectionist.

Distorting the future

> *To make children capable of honesty is the beginning of education.*
> John Ruskin

In North American culture one of the most critical demands of the adolescent identity project is to map out a *general* plan for the future. Such maps help immeasurably in the effective management of the resources young people possess, or have available to them. As we shall describe in Chapter Nine, the effective anticipation of the future, the ability to accurately predict and influence some of its unfolding, is a priority of adolescent identity.

Preparing for the future, however, is complicated by the propensity of some adolescents to completely mis-read the economic realities of a capitalist society. In our culture fictional thinking is most likely to occur in three critical areas:

1. the mis-understanding of how wealth is accumulated;
2. the mis-understanding of low-wage employment; and,
3. the mis-understanding of the economics of marriage.

An informative, and sobering, research project conducted by the Canadian Advisory Council on the Status of Women (Baker, 1985) yielded some remarkable conclusions concerning adolescent perceptions. The study investigated adolescent women's aspirations for the future, and as well, their ideas about and their interpretation of that future. Some of the findings were surprising to the authors of this study (by their own admission), but they were not surprising at all to those of us who recognize the adolescent's propensity for unrealistic appraisal of topics which touch upon their self-esteem.

Although about one quarter of the girls in this study said they would probably be housewives at age 30, most saw this is a temporary occupation. The girls did not believe that being a housewife was either physically or emotionally demanding, and, as well, their thinking focussed heavily on the most rewarding or pleasant aspects of this role. This idealized assessment of the future is a typical adolescent phenomenon — especially during early and middle adolescence. (Late adolescents are inclined to analyze the future in more comprehensive "level-headed," terms.)

Few girls in this survey possessed a realistic perspective concerning the low-paying jobs that await them in the work force. Few girls thought about the possibility of having to live through a long period of unemployment, of getting divorced, or having to raise a family without a husband even though these are widespread problems in our culture and ones which most adolescents have observed first hand. The author of this study concludes: "In most of their discussions of the future, there was no unemployment, no divorce, no economic need for the females to work when their children were young." Furthermore . . .

> After interviewing 150 adolescents, we found that many held notions of the future that did not tally with the likely outcomes of their adult lives. Only interesting jobs, adequate incomes, loving husbands, trouble-free children, home ownership, and international travel were on their horizons. Although adolescents are aware on an intellectual level that world peace is in jeopardy, families are breaking up, and many people are living in poverty, *they tend to feel that they are immune to these external forces* (Baker, 1985).

Although the authors did not dwell upon the fact that the adolescent girls in this study manifested selective perception and an imperviousness to first-hand data, they did conclude that: "Young women need a much greater awareness of present realities of the workplace, of the difficulty raising children as single parents, and on the increasing necessity of two incomes if the materials they cherish are to be obtained." (A widespread fiction among teens is that they will be able, somehow, or by some means, to purchase desired goods such as new cars or new furniture, for which they simply do not have sufficient funds, nor do they have any kind of strategy for obtaining these funds).

In essence, these young women's perceptions of the future were colored by egocentric projections which override the objective information readily available to them. And while it is tempting simply to view these thought patterns as harmless features of an idealistic mind, it is a temptation responsible adults cannot indulge because the decisions adolescents make with regard to pregnancy, dropping out of school, and drug use effect not only them, they exert a profound impact upon the social and economic fabric of our entire society. One cannot escape the realization that the thinking habits of young people, especially as they evaluate and calculate the future, are directly related to their ability to survive decently in it.

It can be argued, and usually is by youngsters embroiled in fictions, that at least they have a dream, a vision, a hope for a brighter future. And who will deny that these are vital images to all youth. Dreams are indispensable to charting one's life — an adolescent without dreams is soul without purpose. Sadly, for some youngsters, their dreams and visions are merely deceptions. What they call their "philosophy of life" is all too often merely wishful thinking parading as confident optimism. And like all such fictions, it collapses in the face of an impartial, and far more than the adolescent mind dare comprehend, indifferent, world.

The responsibilities facing *adults* assume even greater proportions when we honestly acknowledge the adolescent's tendency to distort the future. Mis-reading the future, as any financial analyst, government official, or military advisor will attest, is risky business. It causes too many catastrophes in the present!

Adolescents confront many life options which have the potential to radically impact their future, i.e., sexual intercourse, dropping out of school, experimenting with drugs, joining a gang. Our culture encourages experimentation during adolescence, and rightfully so if young people are to benefit from their moratorium experience. Equally true, however, experimentation with a distorted understanding of consequences is terribly dangerous. It is this final matter, the tendency to distort consequences, which so exasperatingly complicates adolescent existence.

The exaggerated sense of entitlement

Entitlement has two general meanings. The first is to *qualify* to do something. As in, "She is entitled to receive the job because she completed her internship." The second meaning is to make a *claim* that one has the *right* to receive something. It is with the second type of entitlement that we are here concerned. Especially as it manifests itself in the adolescent tendency to demand rights, favors or opportunities to which they, seemingly, are not entitled.

By entitlement, psychologists usually mean the individual's expectation of special favors without assuming reciprocal responsibilities. In government language it means benefits without contributions. In "grandparent" language it means getting something for nothing. Individuals with a strong sense of entitlement expect far more from others than is reasonable, and they demand far more from their school, their government, and their family than can reasonably be delivered.

Taking this into account, what is meant by an "irrational" sense of entitlement? In essence, *it refers to the adolescent tendency to believe that they are entitled to special treatment or special favors without corresponding duties or obligations.*

This exaggerated sense of entitlement holds several parallels with narcissism. Arnold Rothstein observes that narcissists "feel entitled to have what they want when they want it just because they want it . . . They feel entitled to pursue it, no matter how they do so or whom they hurt" (p. 67).

Relevant to our concerns is that exaggerated entitlements encourage dysfunction; they get in the way of self-reliance since they demand that others look after me, give me special treatment, locate jobs for me, make school interesting, easy and fail-proof. The majestic "I" is entitled to special treatment, special subsidy, special everything.

When one is entitled to receive, someone else must provide. Hence, adolescents obsessed with entitlements frequently perceive others merely as providers. Once young people perceive their peers, and the adults they interact with (teachers and parents) primarily as providers of needs, they have acquired a perception which radically impedes not only self-understanding but, as well, other-understanding.

Part of the explanation for the widespread entitlement among the young is that the two most important institutions in their lives, their families and their schools, have given a wide range of benefits to them but have set few requirements for how they ought to function in return. There is little doubt that in our present society adolescents live under a regime of social values that allows them to make demands on family, school and society-at-large far more than vice versa. It is, perhaps, from this tradition of being able to make demands without having to accept corresponding duties and responsibilities that irrational and exaggerated entitlement springs (Mead, 1986).

As we shall see in Section Two, an exaggerated sense of entitlement impedes in a very profound way the formation of an identity in which the rights of others are valued and respected.

Self-deception

Self-deception is a human trait which exists in perplexing twists among the young. Not only does self-deception here contain its universal ingredients of deceitful trickery and false appearances, they are magnified by the developmental fact that during adolescence the self which is deceiving itself exists as an incomplete and constantly changing entity. Therefore, it is quite possible that what exists as a self-deception at age fourteen, for example, is not a deception at all at age sixteen.

Self-deception, quite obviously, is not a completely negative phenomenon; if it were it would be a far scarcer commodity than it is. Among adolescents, self-deceptions often enhance self-esteem and, in doing so, serve several useful functions. As Martin points out:

In bolstering self-esteem, self-deception may provide the confidence necessary for coping effectively. It might also help us in other ways to cope with difficult realities. Like blinders on a horse, self-deception sometimes enables us to move forward unhampered by distress. By narrowing vision, it may prevent us from being overwhelmed by sheer multiplicity of stimuli. In sustaining our hopes, it can evoke our energies. And in fostering our faith in other people, it can support friendship, love and community (Martin, 1985, p. 7).

Despite Martin's optimistic tone, self-deceptions usually manufacture more hardship than they are worth. However, in the world of adolescence it is difficult to know with much certainty when anything — even self-deception — is going to have value because anything which bolsters esteem, or lessens feelings of inadequacy, always has some value to a teenager.

Here I would like to discuss two phenomena which play important roles in the adolescent's struggle to attain an honest self-understanding: rationalization and blind spots.

Rationalization

My specialty is being right when other people are wrong.
George Bernard Shaw

Of all self-deceptions rationalization is perhaps the most widely used, typically it is the least harmful, and it is so widely understood that the core of its definition is part of our folk wisdom.

Freud's famed biographer, Ernest Jones, introduced the term "rationalization." To him, rationalization meant that we find acceptable reasons to justify an action which was motivated by something completely different — and usually less noble. In general usage, rationalization refers to protecting our self-esteem by finding socially accepted reasons for our behavior and to the tendency to cushion failure or disappointment with a platitude.

Rationalization is a confusing term because its "rational" prefix inclines us to think it is an objective process. It is not. Objective reasoning discovers *real* reasons — rationalization merely invents *acceptable* reasons. The teenage boy who justifies his daily run on bikini beach because sand is a better running surface than the school track (which is five miles closer) gives us reason to suspect rationalization. So also does the teacher who formerly opposed extra-curricular activities because they are "juvenile," but now that they bring extra pay, believes that they are good for students.

Rationalizations provide acceptable explanations which pass for truth, but which exist to justify some aspects of one's self-esteem. We all have been taught to provide explanations for what we do, and we enjoy hearing ourselves give them. We all desire to justify what we do, especially when we fear that we have done the wrong thing — an occupational hazard of adolescence.

Rationalizations, however, are often doubted or rejected, therefore, to be effective they must be defensible. If I claim that attendance in my university class is high because I am an excellent lecturer, and a student points out that "It's high because you grade on attendance," my rationalization has lost credibility. Since rationalizations are challenged, and often rejected by the listener, we find that conceptually organized, articulate individuals execute them most effectively. Or, on a completely different plane, rationalizations are likely to be effective when the people who receive them are passive and accepting — flattering mirrors rather than accurate mirrors.

Perhaps the most common rationalizations are "sweet lemons" and "sour grapes," and most readers have heard examples of each since breakfast. Sweet lemon is when one concludes that "What I've got is what I want." Sour grapes is when one concludes that "What I missed wasn't worth getting." The adolescent community with its unfulfilled hopes, unrealized ambitions and shackled fantasies is filled with both of these rationalizations.

The act of rationalization is made easier by the fact that every behavior has several motivations, not merely one, so that we have "good" as well as "bad" reasons for any given action — rationalization points out the good reasons while pushing into the background the bad reasons.

For individuals who work with adolescents on a daily basis, especially teachers, rationalization is an issue of special importance because of its relationship to lying. Adolescents are especially prone to lie when they live according to idealized images and all of the "shoulds" associated with those images. Karen Horney explained it this way:

> It is a commonplace that one lie usually leads to another, the second takes a third to bolster it, and so on till one is caught in a tangled web. Something of the sort is bound to happen in any situation in the life of an individual or group where a determination to go to the root of the matter is lacking. The patchwork may be of some help, but it will generate new problems which in turn require a new make-shift. So it is with neurotic attempts to solve the basic conflict: and here as elsewhere, nothing is of any real avail but a radical change in the conditions out of which the original difficulty arose. What the neurotic does instead — and cannot help doing — is to pile one pseudo solution upon another (1945, p. 131).

Blind spots

*Truth, like light, blinds. Falsehood, on the contrary, is a
beautiful twilight that enhances every object.*

Albert Camus

In physiology, the blind spot is the gap in our field of vision that results from the way the eye is constructed. At the rear of each eyeball is a point where the optic nerve, which runs to the brain, attaches to the retina. This point lacks the cells that line the rest of the retina to register the light that comes through the lens of the eye. As a result, at this one point in vision there is a gap in the information transmitted to the brain. Here the blind spot registers nothing, and the perceiver perceives nothing.

In psychological parlance "blind spots" refer to areas within a person's beliefs, attitudes or perceptions which are resistant to change through objective information or rational arguments. Blind spots protect us from unwanted data, resulting "in an incapacity to bring attention to bear on certain crucial aspects of our reality, leaving a gap in that beam of awareness which defines our world from moment to moment" (Goleman, p. 15). For young people this "gap in the beam of awareness" is of monumental significance, especially when it blinds them to the relationship between sexual intercourse and pregnancy, or from recognizing the link between alcohol consumption and automobile accidents, or between dropping out of school and obtaining a decent job.

As with all protective structures, blind spots lessen anxiety by trimming attention, and by sealing off painful experiences. Attention-dimming is the trademark of all young minds because "brightening" illuminates far too many unpleasant facts. Blind spots prevent them from seeing unwanted information, thinking painful thoughts, and experiencing anxious feelings. Blind spots are especially valuable to youngsters who live in environments so painful that it becomes necessary for them to deaden their pain through the warping of awareness. Blinds spots are the par excellence "dimming device," and in their own way contribute to the unawareness, the imperviousness, and the "fog" of adolescence.

Blind spots prevent the adolescent from perceiving their performance weaknesses (such as poor academic achievement), their behavioral shortcomings (such as temper tantrums or undependability) and their character limitations (such as intolerance, prejudice, lying). Blind spots do not merely touch up unwanted information — they obliterate it.

Fortunately, adolescents frequently own up to their blind spots when confronted by peers or respected adults. For some youngsters opening oneself to, and honestly accepting, previously denied data represents a profound turning point in their personal lives. Some Christians even believe that such an expanded awareness, the ability to confront what was previously too painful for the mind to perceive, is actually a form of grace, as is so poignantly expressed in the hymn *Amazing Grace*: "Was blind, but now I see."

Summary

In this chapter, I have highlighted only a few examples of how the adolescent's capacity for fictional thinking encourages self-deception and impedes self-understanding. The intellectual foundations and the emotional underpinnings to these thinking patterns are overviewed at length in chapters 2-7. From these investigations it seems clear that teens are influenced by a cluster of thinking habits which complicate the quest for self-understanding.

Quite obviously, no one claims that adolescents should be completely rational in their thinking or emotionless in their behavior. The message of this chapter is that adolescents, in the course of executing the thought process inherent to their developmental age, are inclined toward fictions and self-deceptions which makes more difficult their struggle for self-understanding and personal identity.

Five such patterns occupied most of the energy of this chapter.

1. the craving for, and the dependence upon, the approval of others;
2. the obsession with perfection;
3. the tendency to distort, even falsify, expectations of the future;
4. the belief that one is entitled to an excessive and unrealistic array of psychological and material benefits without having to earn them; and,
5. the tendency to avoid painful aspects of reality and to rationalize personal actions.

Because so many young people are inclined to incorporate these patterns into their belief structure, it seems reasonable that part of the adolescent experience should counter and negate these absurdities. How this challenge can be met, it seems to me, is the heart of parenting, teaching and rehabilitating young people in our era.

Preface to Section Two

The Struggle For Identity

The themes of Section Two are rather straightforward. The first theme is that adolescents must struggle to attain a sturdy, worthwhile identity. The second is that for many young people the struggle for a worthwhile identity leads to "confusion" — a confusion which may become the most important reality in their day-to-day life.

In Section One great lengths were taken to define, and to elaborate upon, the forces which govern how young people think about themselves, and, on how these forces frequently encourage a self-protecting narrowness. In Section Two the focus is on how young people define and "identify" themselves, and grow beyond what they are.

Identity is especially difficult for youngsters who, in their understanding of themselves and in their relationships with others, employ a thought process which is overly egocentric, and live an interpersonal style which is excessively narcissistic. It will be left to other investigators to determine the incidence, or the percentage, of youth who fit this profile. However, if one can take at face value the observations of front line professionals such as junior high and senior high school teachers, junior high and senior high school counsellors, social workers, probation officers, drug counsellors, drug rehab workers, teen-pregnancy professionals, school dropout counsellors, and the entire cadre of adults who work with "at-risk" youth — the messages are singularly clear and direct. The young people these adults work with are uniformly egocentric rather than allocentric, narcissistic rather than sharing, and direct their lives through personal identities anchored in unrealistic expectations. We are rapidly recognizing that in North America the ingredients of a healthy, worthwhile identity are sorely missing in far too many of our young people.

To understand how identity goes askew we must possess a general understanding of "normal" identity. This is the ambition of Chapter Nine — to provide the reader with the defining features of healthy adolescent identity.

One of the most widely recognized "confusions" of adolescent identity — especially in moratorium societies — is the identity crisis. The investigation of identity crises will be the focus of Chapter Ten.

Perhaps the least understood identity problem, but in the 90s rapidly becoming one of the most relevant, is negative identity. That is, when identity is consumed by negativism and negation. This will be the focus of Chapter Eleven.

Chapter Twelve discusses the important, and pervasive, role played by conformity and conformism in the adolescent identity process. Chapters Thirteen and Fourteen deal with several topics typically overlooked in contemporary investigations of the adolescent identity project: turning points, games, worth and alienation.

chapter nine

The Nature of Adolescent Identity

"Who are you?" said the Caterpillar.
Alice replied rather shyly, "I-I hardly know, Sir, just at
present — at least I know who I was when I got up this morning,
but I must have changed several times since then."
Lewis Carroll, *Alice in Wonderland*

Identity does not come automatically to you or I, and most assuredly, not to adolescents; it is worked for and struggled with, and it undergoes advances, regressions and plateaus. Even those young people who are highly conforming, whose identity is so similar to that of their parents, must work to attain and maintain their identity. The failure to "work" on identity results in a wide range of calamities, some of which are described in the forthcoming chapters. This labor-intensive quality is one reason why I, and other commentators, use the term "project" when writing about adolescent identity. This need to work at and struggle with personal identity, assumes great significance in North American culture because so many youngsters simply do not know how to focus their identity quest, and do not receive constructive assistance from adults in their attempts to fix their direction. Equally true, many adolescents do not receive moral or spiritual guidance in their pursuit of self-definition; hence, much of their identity project is simply wasted, lost, or comes to nothing; or even worse, leads to a negative, self-destructive identity.

The focus of this chapter is *on the composition of identity, on what identity means, and on how identity is achieved.* When all is said and done, nothing is more relevant to the adolescent experience than to nurture an identity capable of mastering the social demands and the moral responsibilities of adulthood.

The nuclear ingredients of identity

Adolescent identity has been the object of systematic psychological investigation for less than fifty years, having been introduced by Erik Erikson in his landmark essay "Ego development and historical change" (1946). Yet, even in this short period of time, we have discovered many commonalties to the identity project.

Young people achieve identity as they invest themselves in, and commit themselves to, a relatively stable set of beliefs. The minimal commitments necessary to achieve a sense of identity include a set of values and beliefs to guide one's actions, and a set of career goals which helps to formulate one's occupational options. In broader terms, adolescent identity is also influenced by each individual's intrinsic characteristics; by identifications with other people who are admired and who influence what the person should become and do; and by societal values to which a person is exposed while growing up in a particular country, community and subcultural group (Kimmel, p. 418).

As identity attains consistency it becomes evident to the adolescent that he or she is similar in some ways to most people, yet different in some ways from all people. When identity is not fully developed (as usually is the case during adolescence) individuals may not believe in their distinctiveness, and, as a result, depend upon others to confirm or verify this important ingredient to their identity.

Healthy identity modifies and adjusts to new experiences, new demands and new responsibilities, hence we say that identity is an ongoing process which retains its adaptive and changing character. Identity during adolescence (except for those youth who have foreclosed) is continuously changing, growing, realigning, and redirecting itself. Identity is by no means a uniformly "positive" project, it includes shameful, punitive and, other negative elements: "Mixed in with the positive identity, there is a negative identity which is composed of what he has been shamed for, what he has been punished for, and what he feels guilty about . . . Identity means integration of all previous identifications and self images, including the negative ones" (Erikson, 1959, p. 67).

Therefore, when we discuss identity:

a) we are recognizing the uniqueness of every individual and the singular patterns of personhood;

b) we are recognizing the continuity of identity despite changes which take place within it;

c) we are recognizing a unique totality leading to a differentiation from all other people;

d) we are recognizing the sameness of essential character which resides within a given individual; and,

e) we are recognizing that its attainment is a project which requires organized effort and purposeful direction.

Taking all of the foregoing into account, what then do we mean when we say adolescents "have" an identity? J.P. Hewitt has assembled the basic themes into one paragraph with commendable cogency. He claims "to have an identity" means:

> To maintain a balance between similarity and difference in the face of individual development and changing social conditions, so that one can assimilate to the self demands for change or adjustment, but also fulfill an inner desire for constancy. It is to be a whole and complete person, and not fragmented into roles and ruled by scripts. It is to be connected with others and yet true to oneself. It is to participate in a variegated and often fragmented social life and yet to maintain continuity and integrity. *Persons with identity, we are apt to say, know who they are, what they are doing, and where they are going* (1989, p. 152, my italic).

Continuity and differentiation

Identity is challenged by two deceptively simple demands: attaining consistency and attaining individuality. Neither is an easy matter.

The sense of oneself as a unified being, that is, as a person whose behavior has consistency, predictability and unity is what we mean *by continuity of identity*. Continuity is the persistent sameness of character that allows us to be the same person from day to day; what Erikson calls "self-sameness." It is unity across time.

That continuity is necessary to a coherent identity is self evident. When I promise to pick you up at the airport next Saturday, it is assumed that I will be there (unless something unforeseen occurs) because the connective links between myself on the day of the promise and myself on Saturday are so strong that one naturally expects that I will be the "same" person next Saturday as I am today. Even those adolescents experiencing an identity crisis who daily wonder and worry about "Who am I?", almost never doubt that they will be the essentially same wondering, worrying person tomorrow as they are today.

> All of our familiar ideas regarding the assignment of personal responsibility and all of our concerns about our own future prospects appear to rest upon the certain conviction that, *despite acknowledged changes, we do somehow remain persistently ourselves* (Chandler & Ball, 1990, p. 150).

Continuity, unto itself, cannot create an identity. One must have more than consistency; one must as well stand out from the crowd, be different, singular, special. In most theories of identity, this necessity is embraced by the concept of differentiation.

Differentiation is simply the process by which we become different from others. This concept is of special concern to us because adolescents strategically work on their differentiation process; the choices they make and the actions they choose, contribute greatly to the specific features their differentiation will take. In this regard, they actually create and mould their own identity.

Every identity project requires one to establish an unquestioned individuality. This requirement is more difficult than meets the eye because the options for meaningful individuality are so limited for teens in our culture, while the demands upon them for conformity, compliance and sameness are extensive. Consequently, some gestures of individuality amount to little more than surface symbols, trendy haircuts, or subculture symbols of defiance. These stabs at individuality serve several purposes, but here we shall focus only on one: the need to differentiate oneself from adults, from younger children, from the gaggle of lesser peers with whom one competes. The more the better since the purpose is to "identify" oneself *by the specific ways in which one is different from others*. Such gestures of differentiation not only "distinguish" one from others, they heighten one's sense of specialness, and help to garner the attention of peers who are themselves hypersensitive to individuality. This is why Kroger, in her overview of differentiation, claims: "The means by which we differentiate ourselves from other people in our lives constitutes the very core of our experiences of personal identity" (p. 6).

One of the many expectations of the adolescent identity project is to create a workable balance between differentiation and continuity. Youngsters who forge an identity heavy on conformism, conventionalism or foreclosure place high premium on *continuity*. Whereas, youngsters whose identity is heavy on individualism, the unconventional, the eccentric, place a high premium on *differentiation*. No matter how the ledger is tilted, toward continuity or differentiation, the relative potency of one over the other goes a long way toward establishing the identity patterns which direct the adolescent's unfolding life.

Experimentation with differentiation and continuity is tied in with the peer experience, especially in cultures such as ours where teens spend virtually all of their social time in the presence of one another. This closeness generates considerable emotional pollution because the Social Darwinism which governs it inclines most adolescents to fear revealing any view of themselves which is uninviting, unattractive or rejectable. They are genuinely afraid that siblings, peers or adults will exploit (or ridicule) their social weaknesses. I focus upon this unflattering reality because in adolescence self-concept is unalterably linked with peer acceptance; not being accepted is, in many respects, not to be. Paradoxically, despite their piercing fear of rejection, many youth do not have any clear understanding of what it is that they want accepted; they do not as yet know their social strengths or their psychological weaknesses. In a literal sense, they present themselves to the open market then await appraisal, some of them to be pleasantly surprised that peers consider them interesting, attractive, influential, or fun to be with, others to be dismayed that peers find them dull, easily outwitted and overly impressionable. Such is the cost of attaining individuality in an adolescent community.

Why is adolescence "the age of identity"?

Identity is not finalized during adolescence, nor does any valid reason indicate that it should. Adolescence, however, is the age when identity assumes its adult outlines, when it becomes noticeably less childlike, and when it attains the strength and autonomy we associate with adult character.

A "full-blown" identity requires us to envision ourselves not only from the frame of present abilities and circumstances but also from the panorama of an unfolding future. Such an identity begins to take hold when one attains a unified reconciliation of past history, present realities and future possibilities. In the life span, adolescence is the first developmental stage when the individual is able to meet these requirements. It is, most assuredly, not the only period, but it is the first. James Marcia, who more than any contemporary, has investigated and operationalized Erikson's ideas on adolescent identity, states it this way: "Although precursors to identity exist in prior developmental stages, *adolescence is at least the crucial, and perhaps the critical, period* for the formation of the first full identity configuration (1987, p.165). If identity is not achieved during adolescence, and it usually is not, we are not necessarily looking at major damage: "Unsuccessful identity resolutions at late adolescence do not necessarily mean that an identity will never be constructed . . . Identity status at late adolescence represents only a first answer to the identity question" (Marcia, 1987, p. 165). Hence, when we speak of adolescence as the age of identity, we are speaking of the solid beginnings of mature identity, but assuredly, not the final product.

To attain a convincing sense of self, we must be able to distinguish how we are like all people, like some people, and like no other person. We must be able to see ourselves in terms of family and society, in terms of group affiliations, but within these configurations, isolate our own uniqueness and privacy. We must be able to make decisions about aspects of our character we want to expand, about limitations we want to improve, about deficiencies we want to eradicate. These evaluations require, in Piagetian terms, the intellectual capacities of "formal thought," and in calendar time this means adolescence.

Identity demands not only the ability to make hard judgments, but also that we judge the very people who are judging us; in essence, judging judgments and judging judges.

> . . . identity formation employs a process of simultaneous reflection and observation, a process taking place on all levels of mental functioning, by which the individual judges himself in the light of what he perceives to be the way in which others judge him in comparison to themselves and to a typology significant to them; while he judges their way of judging him in the light of how he perceives himself in comparison to them and to types that have become relevant to him (Erikson,1968, pp. 22-23).

Expanding intelligence, in conjunction with the unfolding body, sets the stage for adult identity. A stage set not merely in our own century but, as surmised from the written record, so it has been set in all eras, in all societies, throughout all recorded history. (I have never encountered one substantive example from anthropology, history, ethnography or any branch of the social sciences where a society bestowed the privileges and responsibilities of adulthood to its members as a whole — not merely some select special group as was the case with the Pharaohs in Egypt — at any age other than adolescence. In calendar time, between ages twelve and nineteen. For these reasons and many others forthcoming, I view adolescence as "the age of identity").

The moratorium

Erik Erikson coined the term "psychosocial moratorium" to mean a period in the young person's life between the juvenile incompetencies of childhood and the full responsibilities of adulthood. In Erikson's words:

> By psychological moratorium, then, we mean a delay of adult commitments, and yet it is not only a delay. It is a period that is characterized by a selective permissiveness on the part of society and of provocative playfulness on the part of youth, and yet it often leads to deep, if often transitory, commitment on the part of youth, and ends in a more or less ceremonial configuration of commitment on the part of society (cited in Fuhrmann, 1990, p. 359).

The moratorium provides a period of sanctioned and protected experimentation to help young people assume major life obligations and make substantive personal commitments. "The moratorium of the adolescent is defined as a developmental period during which commitments either have not yet been made or are rather exploratory and tentative" (Muuss, p. 72).

The demands of living in a technological society are sufficiently complex that most young people do not attain a solid sense of reality without a period of comparatively free time to explore, examine and sort out their personal milieu. This adventure in self discovery is the important business of the moratorium, and for the most part, society keeps "hands-off" during this time:

> Adolescence is a period in which society takes a relatively hands-off posture, allowing the adolescent to experiment behaviorally and attempt to find himself and his place. The hands-off posture refers to the laxness of society in enforcing rules on adolescents that apply to adults, as well as a general attitude that diminishes responsibility of adolescents relative to adults. The functional reason society takes this stance is *to give adolescents time to mature and experience so that when it is time for them to enter the adult world, especially the occupational world, they will be ready, emotionally and educationally* (Manaster, 1989, p. 163, my italic).

Experimentation is the key. Adolescents are expected (not all of them do) to experiment with social roles, interpersonal relationships, political ideologies and with the self and its swirl of perplexities. Experimentation has attained such emotional and social significance that most experts now define adolescence as a period of life when a wide range of experimentation is necessary simply to be able to understand the array of life decisions required in our culture.

> If adolescents, while experimenting with moratorium issues, have sufficient opportunity to search, experiment, play the field, and try on different roles, there is a very good chance that they will find themselves, develop an identity, and emerge with commitments to politics, religion, a vocational goal and a more clearly defined sex role and sex preference. These final commitments are frequently less radical than some of the tentative and exploratory commitments during the moratorium (Muuss, p. 84, 1988).

 With regard to the struggle to achieve a solid identity, we do well to keep two points in mind. The first is that all genuine identity must be achieved in action. One may think, fantasize, or organize interminably, but eventually, identity must be tested and actualized in action. The second point is that "direction," the focussing of action, is as important to personal identity as any of its many components. "Action" and "direction" are critical in cultures such as our own because to cultivate worthy identities youth must have decent opportunities to test the best within themselves in a challenging, demanding environment.

Know thyself

> *Do not change me! I want to be true to myself.*
>
> Henrik Ibsen

The Delphic saying "Know thyself," which Socrates introduced into Greek philosophy with such force that it even today remains a guiding principle of self understanding, holds special relevance to our understanding of adolescent identity. By "know thyself" I assume that Socrates wanted us to know our inner workings with sufficient honesty to make important decisions about the conduct of our lives and to not merely follow rules made by others; and that, to make these decisions we must have insight into our capabilities, our purpose, perhaps even our destiny. And, of course, this is the very stuff of identity.

Identity is an answer to the question, "Who am I?" An answer which requires a certain unity among the elements of one's past and the expectations of one's future. And since a link exists between the answer to this question and the content of one's identity, it comes as something of a shock when we learn that many young people do not know themselves well enough to answer the basic question, "Who am I?" Though most youngsters claim they want their real self to shine, they do not know what their real self is, this is especially true for early and middle adolescents. They may desire to be more like a best friend, an envied enemy, or a parent, than to be like themselves. It is unfair to think that adolescents "know" themselves in any comprehensive sense. Yet, even though they cannot answer the questions with absolute certainty, they remain haunted by them, and impelled to resolve them. "Who am I?" "What within me is most truly me?" "Am I myself responsible for who I am?" "What about me do others like and admire?" "Am I going to amount to much when I am older?" All of these identity questions are part of the Socratic dictate to "Know thyself".

In his investigation of the self's ability to know itself, Toulmin (1977) suggests that "know thyself" includes several different notions, but most importantly:

1. Knowing your own mind: having settled, consistent and realistic intentions;

2. Knowing your own capacities: being able to judge realistically how far you are able to carry through on your declared intentions;

3. Being able to perceive clearly the relations between your own needs and feelings and those of the other people you deal with, particularly those to whom you are emotionally close;

4. Being in command of yourself: being able to match your conduct to your intentions and capacities (p. 291).

These components to self-knowledge are part of the adolescent identity struggle, but few adolescents can meet them with consistency, although some late-adolescents come close. On the other hand, consider those features which Toulmin claims *indicate a failure in self-knowledge.*

1. inconsistency, vacillation and other forms of indecisiveness;
2. unrealistic or inappropriate conduct;
3. since knowing oneself involves understanding the boundaries between your own plans and those of others, the tendency to misconstrue those limits, or to needlessly deny your own plans and wishes represents a significant failure in self-perception;
4. a certain minimal level of self command is necessary; therefore, "any tendency to lose control, blow up, clam up, or otherwise fall apart . . . constitutes a final variety of defective self-knowledge" (p. 306).

From this vantage point we can readily observe that part of the adolescent struggle to "know thyself" meets with success but, some of it meets with failure. And even though we know that with increasing age the focus of self-knowledge shifts from others to the self, in adolescence this shift is still taking place, and as a result the adolescent struggles not only with self-knowledge and self-understanding, but also with self-deception and self-protection.

Introspection and the subjective self. Introspection is the process of examining thoughts and experiences — it is vital to self-discovery and self-knowledge. In his investigations of introspection, Gurwitsch observed that:

Self-awareness permanently and necessarily pervades all of our conscious life, so that at every moment of this life we are aware of the act experienced at this very moment . . . At every moment, we have the possibility of reflecting upon and apprehending the act which we experience (1985, p. 48).

Some adolescents are subject to powerful episodes of self-reflection which may "impose" themselves with startling suddenness. The moods and emotions which accompany these episodes can be as random as the episode itself, therefore the adolescent reacts a bit wearily to them. The products yielded to the intellect also contain an element of randomness; sometimes the process results in genuine insight and triumph, sometimes only in dim perplexity.

An understanding of introspection impresses upon us how much young people actually create their own identities. Self-concept is, after all, nothing more than the set of judgments and ideas, perceptions and attitudes that every person has of himself or herself, and, in very large measure, they derive from the self thinking about itself. Adolescents actively cultivate specific skills and stifle specific desires; they pride themselves in strengths which bring praise and are shamed by weaknesses which bring ridicule. Young people continuously decelerate this habit, accentuate that mannerism, modify this tendency, stabilize that impulse. Just as the architect bolsters the foundation to lend greater durability, or lifts the edifice for greater visual appeal, so the adolescent strives for greater proportion and strength by realigning and reworking the self.

The subjective self is what the adolescent feels, experiences and knows in the most certain sense. It is the "me" who feels and lives the sadness, not the "me" who describes or reports it. It is the agent within which some philosophers call the "existential" self and what some psychologists call the "experiential" self. For our purposes it is the subjective self.

> From the perspective of the self there is a radical change . . . typically characterizing middle adolescents as well as most adults. One can speak now of the *creation of the subjective self,* in that what was formerly simply lived in an unreflected mode . . . now seems to emerge from action, is unified, isolated and differentiated from other internal processes and experienced as a psychological substance in its own right.

As a consequence of the emergence of this subjective self:

> For the first time one seems to experience oneself as having an intimate centre, and this centre is felt as the real part of one's being, the source of one's individuality. It becomes possible, then, to scrutinize this new psychological reality and to create around it a new set of feelings, motives and evaluations (Blasi & Oresick, 1987, p. 81).

The subjective self is immediately experienced in every intentional act, in each act of desiring, knowing and doing. Introspection is the adolescent's way of engaging the subjective self in dialogue, *and much of the identity project is influenced by the outcome of this dialogue.* It is, after all, the only way to truly "know thyself," and as we shall describe in several of the forthcoming chapters, the adolescent's relationship with the subjective self, whether comfortable or painful, harmonious or hostile, becomes one of the most important factors in the entire identity project.

The Future and Identity

The basic direction of the organism is forward.
Harry Stack Sullivan

Never stumble over anything behind you.
Anonymous

There arrives a moment in human development when time to come destines more than time gone. One such moment is adolescence, where the future attains such prominence that being without hope (futurelessness) becomes, for the first time in the life cycle, a pathological condition.

The conflict between teleology and determinism has not attracted our attention thus far, and, here I shall digress only briefly to emphasize its relevance to adolescent identity. Teleology speaks to the fact of being directed toward a definite end, of having an ultimate purpose, especially when these ends and purposes derive from a natural process. Teleology is a belief that natural phenomena are determined not only by mechanical causes but, as well, by an overall design or purpose. Determinism, on the other hand, adheres to the doctrine that everything is entirely determined by a sequence of causes; and, as far as human beings are concerned, that one's choices and actions are not free, but are determined by causes independent of one's will.

Cosmic purposes need not be invoked to account for the adolescent's preoccupation with the future — it derives, in great measure, from the increased mental abilities inherent to formal thought, and from cultural demands to prepare for occupation, marriage and family. With these preliminary comments behind us, I would like to put forward two propositions concerning youth and their connectedness to the future.

First, the more optimistically adolescents are able to envision the future the greater their ability to cope with adversity in the present; conversely, the more negatively they view the future, the more overpowering is present pain.

Second, when the future is filled with promise, or high expectation, the tension of daily living loses much of its destructive power; conversely, when the future holds no promise, present pain simply takes over one's awareness.

Do not misread the message. Youth are not overpowered by the future; they do not spend every waking moment in its anticipation. The message here is more moderate but, nevertheless, crucial. Future time is an essential parcel in the adolescent package; optimal growth does not take place when the future is feared or when it is thought to be unworthy. Youth grow best when they believe that the future will not deny them esteem, productive work or love. When the future is perceived as holding chains but never keys, growth falters. Nothing is more relevant to the adolescent's search for a mature, solid identity than hope for the future.

The unfolding future, and even more importantly, one's perception of that future, is vital to our understanding not only of personal identity but of our sense of history and our relationship to it. Christopher Lasch describes the "survival mentality" of contemporary culture — the absence of interest in the past or the future resulting in a feeble attachment to the present.

> The everyday survivalists has deliberately lowered his sights from history to the immediacies of face-to-face relationships. He takes one day at a time. He pays a radical price for this radical restriction of perspective, which precludes moral judgment and political activity (1984, p. 93).

The survival mentality prospers when the events of one's life fail to hold meaning that can be projected into the future. In a nutshell, the loss of the future deadens the present, and this is a disaster for an identity whose coherence is based not only on what one is, but equally important, *on where one is going.* The adolescent's responsibility, after all, is not to finalize identity, rather, to create the general outlines of a sturdy identity which adjusts to new opportunities and to new frustrations which evolve over a lifetime.

One final comment. The awareness of time, of which the future is but one category, is the basis for the adolescent preoccupation with destiny, future necessity, and that which is divinely foreordained. The future is so real (especially to the late-adolescent) that its vagaries are systematized and ritualized. Hence, the widespread concern with fate, oracles and the powers which determine the future; with theology, philosophy and religion; with fortune and death. In all of these matters the adolescent acquires not only a spiritual awareness borne of advancing intellectual and moral qualities, but as well, blended in with these "elevated" recognitions, a morbid, primal fascination with fate, destiny and death.

Commitment and Fidelity

Commitment is a necessary, but insufficient, component of identity. Progress toward a mature identity requires one to make commitments, yet simply making them does not insure a mature identity — some commitments contribute to growth while others do not. "Ideal" commitments, such as Commitment to a vocation, to one's society and to sharing, intimacy and love help to produce an identity described by Hewitt earlier in this chapter — an identity in which the individual is a whole and complete person, and not fragmented into roles and scripts; where the individual is connected with others and yet true to oneself. As Hewitt noted: "Persons with identity know who they are, what they are doing, and where they are going (p. 152).

Commitment is propelled by fidelity — the desire to give one's loyalty and allegiance to someone or something greater than oneself. To understand commitment we must first understand fidelity.

In Erikson's understanding of adolescent dynamics, *fidelity exists as a predisposition to faithfulness and commitment.* Therefore, ". . . When you reach a certain age you can and must learn to be faithful to some ideological view . . . without the development for a capacity for fidelity the individual will have what we call a weak ego, or look for a deviant group to be faithful to" (Evans, p. 30). This understanding of fidelity is more open than that held by Marcia, for example, who thinks of fidelity as a commitment to a vocation, or a set of important values, or to a sexual identity. In the broader use of the term (which I prefer) fidelity does not refer to the actual decisions which have or have not been made, or even to the commitments which have or have not been finalized, but, rather *fidelity exists as the impulse to make commitments.* Fidelity is to commitment as sexual desire is to sexual behavior — a pre-existing force which seeks expression. It is precisely this "pre-existing" quality which exerts such great impact on adolescent identity, for by its very nature, it impels youth to make commitments, it inclines them to pledge their allegiance, *it drives them to affix themselves to something or someone.*

Like most adolescent inclinations, fidelity yields mixed dividends, especially to youth whose cravings for loyalty or attachment are not balanced by the ability to assess practical consequences. Fidelity sometimes encourages a commitment to peers, lovers or ideologies, which simply prove unworthy of allegiance. Erikson claims that even "the delinquent adolescent, too, is looking for the chance to conform to some subculture, to be loyal to some leader, and to display and develop some kind of fidelity" (p. 40, Evans).

Fidelity unquestionably increases the adolescent's vulnerability to manipulation and exploitation. As a rule, it inclines youth to overestimate the personal qualities of those people who are the recipients of their allegiance; and, as well, it increases their attractiveness to charlatans, impersonators and narcissists: ". . . the adolescent is vulnerable to fake ideas, he can put an enormous amount of energy and loyalty at the disposal of any convincing system" (Evans, p. 34). On the positive side, fidelity promotes allegiance to the dominant society when it appears worthy of allegiance, and it increases the capacity to sustain love relationships; it discourages egocentrism by focussing one's interest outside oneself; it facilitates long-range planning.

As with many of Erikson's fertile ideas, the concept of fidelity poses numerous theoretical questions. For example, assuming the predisposition to faithfulness or loyalty does exist, how does this predisposition come into existence? Does it have to be nurtured or does it shine "naturally"? Does the concept of fidelity stand the test of lived experience? Are its consequences observable in the lives of adolescents? Do sex differences exist in the matter of fidelity? If so, how? Perhaps in the "object" of its focus, family, spouse, child or occupation.

If fidelity exists as a predisposition in the life of adolescents (and adults for that matter) what is its impact when it merges with another force, or need, such as love, nationalism, religion? Does the concept of "fidelity" help us to explain segments of adolescent behavior which are otherwise not easily explained?

Identity and Identification

The concept of identification comes to us from psychoanalysis, and though originally used to understand the psychodynamics of child development, it is increasingly used to understand identity formation during adolescence. Freud described identification as "the assimilation of one ego to another one, as a result of which the first ego behaves like the second . . ." Among the more commonly observed identifications are the child who identifies with parents and teachers; the early adolescent who identifies with, and takes as his own, the splendor of sports heroes or the charm of entertainment stars; the late adolescent who identifies with the prowess of a politician or the brilliance of a literary figure. Identification brightens self-definition by attaching the greatness of another onto ourselves. There is no doubt that, as far as adolescents are concerned, *positive identifications* ease the identity process, and promote images of adulthood which make its arrival more a cause for joy than sorrow. *Negative identifications* are another matter.

Identification is an irrational mechanism the full scope of which is never evident to the conscious mind. Hence, some identifications are completely unwelcome, as when one identifies with a hateful ideology, or a spiteful, vindictive person. Identification becomes problematic when the connections it forges encourage negative identity or twisted visions of idealistic reform. All youngsters identify with power and competence, but they do not understand either with much fluency. Younger adolescents are especially inclined to identify with surface symbols, and with individuals who appear competent when they are merely defiant. These identifications tend to be discarded as the thought process becomes more sophisticated and the range of personal experience expands. Late adolescents identify with people (or symbols) more in accord with adult tastes, and this is one of many reasons why these two ages are fairly compatible.

I have introduced the concept of identification in a chapter concerned with identity for several reasons, the most notable being that *adolescent identity often hinges on irrational identifications* which contribute not only to confusion and bewilderment, but also to an identity ill-prepared to cope with the demands of adulthood.

Identification can manifest itself in several ways. One form involves carrying over into relations with one person the response patterns that were truthful to another. For example, the child's reaction to the teacher as if she were his mother; or, the adolescent's interaction with comparative strangers in the same manner as with those who love her and give her special entitlements, such as parents.

Identification also manifests itself in seeing another person as an extension of oneself, and, as a result, *seeking satisfaction through that person's pleasure and achievement.* This type of identification exerts considerable influence on adolescent romance and sexuality, and, as well, contributes to their fidelity, loyalty and allegiance. In essence, it is to accept another person so completely that his or her purposes are more important than one's own.

Identification can also take the form of associating or affiliating oneself closely with a group, even to the point of accepting as one's own the purposes and values of the group. Eventually a "group identification" takes hold wherein the individual so strongly feels as a member of the group that he or she adopts totally its ideas, beliefs and habits.

In the process of identification irrational "identities" work their way into the identity project, and there is no way of knowing whether they will turn out to be narcissistic or altruistic, ambition-promoting or ambition-stunting, enhancers of the self-image or destroyers of it. They are significant, yet completely unpredictable, components to the adolescent identity quest.

Identity beyond adolescence

Youth would be an ideal state if it came a little later in life.
Lord Asquith

What is it that makes the identity of one person more mature than the identity of another?

In Kroger's superb critique of Erikson's work, she reports that even this seminal thinker did not provide us with many specific guidelines for evaluating the maturity of adolescent identity. Erikson did speak to this matter in general terms (very general terms), as the following statement attests:

Its most obvious concomitants are a feeling of being at home in one's body, a sense of "knowing where one is going," and an inner assuredness of anticipated recognition of those who count (cited in Kroger, p. 18).

Hence, by Kroger's reckoning: ". . . optimal identity formation should show itself through commitment to those work roles, values and sexual orientations that best fit one's own unique combination of needs and talents" (Kroger, p. 18).

Adolescence is a time of life defined more by preparations than attainments, and this is uncompromisingly true in a moratorium culture which, by the print of its social contract, requires young people to restrain their immediate abilities in order to nurture their future potentialities. Researchers investigating what is variously called "maturity," "psychological health," or "competence" recognize adolescence as more of a starting point than as a finishing point. Abraham Maslow, perhaps the most influential of these researchers, claimed he would not even look at adolescents if he were selecting mature, self-actualized persons to study. His reasoning was that they are simply too immature, too underdeveloped to be considered as acceptable subjects in this type of research. Rightfully or not, most social scientists studying human development assume that maturing continues throughout life. The events experienced, and the identities formulated during adolescence are vital to the unfolding of adulthood, but they do not, unto themselves, account for it.

Having documented the primary themes in the psychological research pertaining to maturity, D.H. Heath (1977) outlined several categories of human growth which continue to grow and mature well after adolescence.

Throughout adulthood we tend to *increase in our potential for symbolization*, that is, for putting our experiences into symbolic form, whether words, music, art, dance or gesture. With advancing maturity the symbol and that which is symbolized dance a dance far beyond the choreography of adolescence.

During adulthood the personality tends *to become more allocentric*, that is, attuned to issues and realities beyond itself. As a result, adults seem better able to focus long term energy on a valued goal. Heath concludes that adolescents are more egocentric, narcissistic, less able to take another's point of view, less willing to walk in another's shoes. In essence, becoming more allocentric entails the increasing ability to take a multiplicity of perspectives toward a problem, the humanization of values, and the development of cooperative relationships.

Attaining increased maturity also means *becoming more integrated*. Coherence and synthesis become more integral to our nature, and as well a certain internal logic to personal values, ambitions and actions begins to manifest itself. In mature adulthood consistency and persistency are behavioral statements of character, not merely the short-term urgencies typically observed in adolescence.

Closely allied is the adult tendency to become *more stable and autonomous*. Stability enhances self-regulation and efficient adaptation. It releases energy for other life demands, rendering the person more able to effectively deal with the problems of life, love and work. The stable and autonomous adult captains the personality with a sure handedness rarely observed during adolescence. This is, in part, a consequence of adults having grown through the strenuous and taxing experiences of the adolescent identity crisis in which they questioned the perceptions and expectations of their culture, and of developing an autonomous position with regard to their society.

And, finally, we note three further distinctions between the identities of mature adults and mature adolescents.

1. Self-concept: maturing persons become more accurately aware of themselves, more able to define and characterize themselves, and more able to see themselves in relation to other people, and other moments in time.

2. Values: theorists agree that maturing persons are more aware of their psychological motives and their ethical values, and that they are more actively involved in formulating and critiquing them, and adhere more consistently to them than less mature persons.

3. Personal relationships: maturing persons become more aware of others and relationships with them, and the role played by others in the dynamics of human relationships. They also better understand how relationships are moulded by circumstance, necessity, desire and other intangibles of human interchange which frequently bewilder the adolescent.

When identity isn't taking hold: identity confusion

Identity confusion is the experience one feels when the quest for identity is derailed, knocked off course, or for whatever reasons, just isn't taking hold. For the majority of youngsters identity does eventually fit, but like growth itself, it may be slow and painful in unfolding. In the following chapters we shall take a close look at some of the more painful aspects of the identity quest. Here a brief mention of identity confusion is called for because a certain amount of confusion is inherent to every identity project.

In his now classic overview of the major theories of adolescence, Muuss observes:

> The adolescent who fails in the search for an identity will experience self-doubt, role diffusion, and role confusion; such an individual may indulge in self-destructive one-sided preoccupation or activity. He will continue to be morbidly preoccupied with the opinion of others or may turn to the other extreme of no longer caring what others think and withdraw or turn to drugs or alcohol in order to relieve the anxiety that role diffusion creates (1988, p. 63).

The "symptoms" associated with identity confusion that Muuss describes are widely accepted among psychologists and other specialists in adolescent behavior. What these experts sometimes fail to emphasize, however, is that for many youngsters this procedure is completely reversed. The adolescent, for whatever reasons, who is overly possessed by fictions and absurdities, who indulges in self-destructive activities, who has an exaggerated sense of entitlements, who is spellbound with the opinions of others, who abuses alcohol or drugs, *may find that these attitudes and behaviors, unto themselves, damage the identity project.* In other words, these behaviors and attitudes do not necessarily exist because of a failed identity, they can be the causes of it. In the adolescent world, pathology is not always the result of a failure of identity, sometimes it is the cause of it.

POSTSCRIPT AND CAUTION

Postscript

Identity is a life-long proposition which owes much of its character to significant moments in the adolescent experience. It is unwise to overplay the finality, or the unchanging quality of these moments, but it is downright foolish to overlook them.

In this chapter, I have attempted to provide the reader with an understanding of the most important ingredients in healthy adolescent identity. Each of these ingredients contribute to the overall identity, and when they fail to take hold their absence leaves the young person adrift in an increasingly hostile and indifferent world without an internal compass.

It seems to me, taking into account the major points in this chapter, that the key ingredients to a healthy adolescent identity include:

a) a fairly solid sense of "Who I am," and an honest recognition of both the strengths and weaknesses of my own individuality;

b) a fairly solid sense of family and community, coupled with a genuine recognition of the need for social cooperation;

c) a stable set of beliefs by which to make important choices and decisions; and a set of values by which to chart one's course into the future; and,

d) a belief in one's ability to cope with life adversity as it presents itself.

Caution

Even though "experts" in adolescent behavior write endlessly about the adolescent experience we usually prefer not to emphasize how little we know with genuine certainty. Most of what we claim to know is conjectural rather than empirical, inferred rather than observed, and correlational rather than causal.

As near as I am able to ascertain, there are no unfailing rules and regulations concerning adolescent identity. The best we can demonstrate after 50, or so, years of research is that young people prosper more under some conditions than others and that they deteriorate more under some conditions than others. Unfortunately for the enterprise of science, young people are so different from one another that, at the human level, it is extremely difficult to predict who will prosper and who will deteriorate in any given situation. Such uncertainty, even though it impedes our investigations of youth, does not paralyze it. It merely forces a certain humility upon us, and it imposes a caution that all honest investigators are obligated to report.

chapter ten

Identity Crises

Although our knowledge about identity crises has increased significantly in the past decades, there is still no clear definition or model of what an identity crisis is . . .

Roy F. Baumeister

The belief that adolescence is a time of identity "crisis" has been with us throughout the 20th Century, being forcefully introduced into modern psychology in the classic work, *Sturm und drang,* by G. Stanley Hall in 1904. And despite complaints from the inventionists (who view adolescence as an invention of sorts), youth has been described *throughout all of written history* as a time of confusion, urgency and bewilderment. The Greeks, most notably Aristotle and Plato, provided written narratives on the flamboyance and emotionality of adolescence. Aristotle, himself, penned:

> The young are in character prone to desire and ready to carry out any desire they may have formed into action. Of bodily desires it is the sexual to which they are most disposed to give way, and in regard to sexual desire they exercise no self-restraint. They are changeful too, and *fickle in their desires, which are as transitory as they are vehement*; for their wishes are keen without being permanent, like a sickman's fits of hunger and thirst.
>
> *They are passionate, irascible, and apt to be carried away by their impulses.* They are the slave, too, of their passion, as their ambition prevents their ever brooking a slight and renders them indignant at the mere idea of enduring an injury . . .
>
> If the young commit a fault, it is always *on the side of excess and exaggeration* for they carry everything too far, whether it be their love or hatred or anything else. They regard themselves as omniscient . . . (Kiell, 1967, p. 18-19; my italic).

And while it seems likely that Aristotle exaggerated both the virtues and the defects of youth, there is little reason to doubt that some basis in fact existed for his compelling observations.

Among the writings of the early Christians, *The Confessions* of St. Augustine being the most celebrated, we read of anguished sexual passion and the torment of relentless, insatiable adolescent lust. In the Age of Enlightenment, the writings of Jean Jacques Rousseau were the most literate elucidation of what we now call "adolescent identity crises."

It is not my intention in this chapter to make the case that every adolescent experiences an identity crisis; the ambition here is far more modest, and that is simply to recognize that for many adolescents identity crises are a fact of identity formation.

What is an identity crisis?

As with most concepts dealing with internal dynamics, a precise, universally accepted definition of the term "identity crisis" does not exist. In general usage, it refers to a temporary condition in which the adolescent is tormented by doubt, shows regressions in behavior, and struggles to make greater sense out of the basic identity question, "Who am I?".

There are many dimensions to an identity crisis, and they do not appear with uniform consistency from individual to individual. For the most part, however, identity crises are characterized by a series of "symptoms" which do not typify youth in general. Most notably:

* by time diffusion rather than time perspective;

* by apathy rather than interest;

* by negative identity rather than role experimentation;

* by work paralysis rather than work ethic.

These symptoms are accompanied by painful, sometimes shattering, emotional experiences, the full range of which are discussed later in this chapter.

An identity crisis can follow several courses, of which the most typical is the effective resolution of the crisis and the continued search for an integrated identity. A second course occurs when the individual experiences so much panic and fear that he or she simply abandons the search for identity by foreclosing upon it. A third course occurs when the adolescent extends the crisis, and the symptoms associated with it, indefinitely, resulting in "identity diffusion" (which is discussed at the end of this chapter).

A further hallmark of an identity crisis is the failure to find someone (or something) to believe in, or to affix one's fidelity, and as a result, the utter frustration of one's belonging and affiliation needs. Yet, despite this, or perhaps because of it, typical to adolescent identity crises is an overidentification with larger than life media inventions (movie stars, athletic heroes, music sensations) and a rejection of parents, parental values, society and societal values.

For intellectual youth (rest assured, all youth are not intellectual anymore than are all adults) identity crises may take on a strong metaphysical or axiological component, that is, a preoccupied concern with the theory of value, the desired, the good. During an identity crisis, the struggle with meaning, purpose, and destiny may be intense and painful. The predicament of searching for ultimate meaning or universal truths with mere, finite abilities weighs heavily upon intellectual youngsters trapped in the discoveries of their own enlightenment.

The jury is out on the consequences of identity crises, especially as they effect long term development and emotional stability. Some experts believe that identity crises represent a profound emotional upheaval, and if they are not brought to reign they may completely disrupt the personality. Other experts, who in the 90s defend the majority opinion, consider identity crises to be a troublesome phase within the identity process which rarely destroy the emotional fabric of young people, nor do they usually necessitate therapy, medication or other intervention measures.

> The identity crisis is a temporary condition in adolescence when the individual demonstrates doubts, regressions in behavior, and a reorganization of identity. Such symptoms are not considered pathological, as the individual still retains feelings of authenticity and the self as a whole is not in total upheaval (Adams, p. 24).

From this perspective, identity crises do not represent a destructive fact of adolescent existence.

It is worthy to note that adolescents are not the only group of individuals to whom identity crises may occur. The basic ingredients of identity crisis, including fear of the future, anxiety in the present, inability to fix direction or purpose, employment apathy, and time confusion, are observed among many groups other than adolescents. Immigrants, for example, often find themselves scratching to survive in a culture totally different from the one in which they were raised, without friends, without parents, without employment, and without the ability to speak the language of their new culture. Discharged military personnel who leave a position of status and importance to be returned to civilian life with no marketable skills, no role to fill, and no emotional support network, identify their situation and themselves, as hopelessly lost. Some retired people whose entire life has revolved around work and achievement find the emptiness, the lack of challenge, and the loss of comradeship almost unbearable, and this, in no small measure contributes to the high suicide rate among the elderly. In most western cultures, the suicide rate for the "over-seventy" population is approximately twice the rate for the total adolescent population, approximately four times the rate of early adolescents, and approximately eight times the rate of early-adolescent girls. (*Canadian Social Trends*, 1988).

The autobiographies of many noteworthy historical figures disclose a turbulent adolescence riddled with crises in self-knowledge, despair, and even periodic inclinations toward suicide. Kiell, who investigated the adolescent turmoil disclosed in the writings of prominent historical figures from previous centuries, provides several intriguing examples of luminaries whose young lives were riddled with despair.

Napoleon Bonaparte, one of the ablest military minds of his century, a capable and powerful political leader, and a dynamic adult personality, experienced numerous episodes of despair. As an adolescent he wrote: "Always alone in the midst of people, I return home in order to give myself up with unspeakable melancholy to my dreams." In equal measure, the French novelist Romain Rolland described his adolescence as "tragic years, unimportant only to those who would have seen nothing but . . . the familiar schoolboy existence of a restless youth. But they concealed the voracious monsters of a deadly despair. Those were the days when I plumbed the very depths of total emptiness." The despair of Napoleon and Rolland reached even greater depths for Havelock Ellis whose adolescent attitude toward life "was embodied in an 'Ode to Death' in which I implored death to bear me away from the world on gentle wings, although at the same time I had no thought of taking any steps to aid Death in his task."

Finally, to further reinforce the fact that despair finds its way even into youth destined for greatness, comes Goethe's confession:

> This uncertainty of taste and judgment disturbed me more every day, so at last I fell into despair . . . I found myself in the completely wretched condition in which one is placed when a complete change of mind is required — a renunciation of all that I hitherto loved and found good. . . I felt so great a contempt for my works begun and ended that one day on the kitchen hearth I burnt up poetry and prose, plans, sketches, and designs altogether, and by the smoke which filled the whole house threw our good landlady into no small fright and anxiety.

The intent here is not to suggest that all great people struggled with identity crises, but it is important to make clear to the reader that they are part of the historical record, that they are not unique to the 20th century, and that they are as real for the great as for the ordinary.

Are identity crises universal?

In the 60s it was generally accepted by theorists of adolescent behavior that identity crises were a necessary, inevitable part of the growing up process. Today, this viewpoint has largely been abandoned for many reasons, some of which are here effectively outlined by Manaster:

> From my own experience . . . the identity crisis — in fact, the issue of identity itself — appears minor to many adolescents. This is not to say that the internal dynamic of integrating new abilities and experiences at adolescence does not occur. But rather that this integration is not so difficult as to be disturbing — it falls within the realm of normal day-to-day coping with life's problems . . . An identity crisis may be normative at Harvard, and among persons such as George Bernard Shaw, Martin Luther and Saint Augustine, whom Erikson wrote about. But it is not so with the common man . . . (1989, p. 159).

Most experts today agree with Manaster's observation, and among them it is accepted that a significant percentage of young people do not experience identity crises. Their path to an adult identity is fairly uneventful; most youth have neither the time, the inclination, nor the complicated mental operations required of an identity crisis. This viewpoint claims that dwelling excessively upon one's identity is a luxury that comes from an extended moratorium, from not having to work every day, and from a narcissistic fascination with oneself that not all youngsters possess. After all, the majority of adolescents finish their schooling when they receive their high school diploma. They are pressed into the adult world. They find a job. They get married. Many of these adolescents do not experience an identity crisis, and, from a developmental viewpoint, no reason exists for them to do so.

> For a great many people, then, the notion of the normative crisis and hence identity achievement may simply not apply; for such individuals there is no problem of identity. The question, "Who am I?" is unlikely to arise in consciousness . . . (Slugoski & Ginsburg, p. 39).

Consider the following excerpt of an interview with a 24-year-old woman, conducted as part of my research on this topic:

> I feel that I have always known who I was. My identity has always hinged on my responsibilities to my family. I come from a very close, single-parent family. My mother always communicated her needs to me. She needed me to help look after my brothers, to help start supper, to help clean the house. She needed me to be an emotional support and a base that she could rely on. She could count on my compliance . . . By the time I reached late-adolescence I continued to be responsible . . . I think that as an adolescent I had too much responsibility to have time for an identity crisis.

One nineteen-year-old, in response to my question: "Did you experience an identity crisis during adolescence?" stated:

I missed out on having an identity crisis. I always had an idea of where I was going and how to get there, and if I didn't, I always knew who I was. I had a solid value system and a pretty black and white view of the world. I think this was my parent's influence. They were always supportive if I wanted to try something new, but I still had a solid foundation to fall back on. My ideas and ways of looking at things changed, but I always had a clear idea of who I was, and what I believed in.

Responses such as these are commonly reported by young adults; by no means are they rare or difficult to come by.

Adolescents who actually do experience identity crises also have their stories to tell, and, in actual fact, these stories are far more likely to be featured on television, in newspapers, hence, in the public mind adolescence is the time for identity crises. There can be no doubt, however, that many youngsters do experience identity crises, and for them (and the people who share their lives) it can be a shattering experience. It is these youngsters the remainder of the chapter spotlights.

Two different kinds of identity crisis

Erik Erikson claimed that he and his co-workers coined the term "identity crisis" in the 1940s to refer to a specific, narrow type of psychopathology they observed among mental patients at the hospital where they worked. The term became accepted, and with popular usage it began to refer to a wide range of existential ailments. More importantly, it began to refer to the private crises of non-disturbed (normal) persons.

Baumeister (1986), who has analyzed the phenomenon of identity from both historical and cross-cultural perspectives, believes that the crises which occur within the identity process are of two types: *identity deficit* and *identity conflict.*

Identity deficit refers to an *inadequately defined self which is character- ized by a lack of commitment to goals and values.* In the absence of goals and values the adolescent lacks consistent, defined motivation, and has no basis for making unified choices and decisions. The outcome of such a deficit in identity is that the adolescent "does not know what he wants to be or how to decide. He questions himself and the world, looking for new sources of meaning, fulfillment, and value" (p. 19). It is to this specific group of symp- toms that most writers refer when they use the term "identity crisis." However, according to Baumeister, another equally important form of identity crisis is observed in the adolescent community, which he calls identity conflict.

Identity conflict differs from identity deficit in both origin and process. In a relaxed manner of speaking one might say that the major problem with identity deficit is "not enough" identity whereas with identity conflict "too much" identity. Identity conflict occurs when the adolescent has firm, yet incompatible, desires and beliefs; therefore, *different components of one's identity exist in a state of conflict with one another.* This person has firm commitments and beliefs which pull in different directions. Individuals who experience an identity conflict are in constant panic because their loyalties, their beliefs, and hence, their choices all compete against one another.

> An example of this would be a person committed to both career and motherhood who is suddenly confronted with an opportunity for promotion that will require a substantial reduction of time spent with her children. Both commitments are important, but one of them must be partially sacrificed or compromised (Baumeister, p. 200).

The key to these different identity crises is commitments. In identity deficit, the adolescent is so tormented by the available options that he or she cannot completely commit to any of them. (If one were *truly* committed to a belief, or a course of action, one would presumably not experience any kind of identity crisis.) In identity conflict, the adolescent makes commitments, holds allegiances, and has a sense of loyalty, unfortunately, they conflict in important ways with one another. Hence, the critical difference: "The identity deficit is a reluctance to give up any options; the identity conflict is a reluctance to betray actual, felt commitments" (p. 200).

Identity deficit

> *You can't plough a field by turning it over in your mind.*
> Saskatchewan farmer

Young people who experience an identity deficit lack solid commitments, yet they are engaged in a struggle to attain them, and it is this very struggle to make important life choices which differentiates them from identity diffused youth — those youngsters who have completely abandoned the struggle to attain a mature identity. This painful struggle to obtain personal values and to make honest commitments is the defining feature of their fledgling identities. Here is how one 21-year-old university student described events and experiences in her adolescence which can be tentatively thought of as a deficit identity crisis.

> I experienced what I would call an "identity crisis" very late in my adolescence, age eighteen-nineteen. I was in my first year, or so, of university . . . Anyway, I felt very alone. I spent many hours alone in my bedroom crying. My stomach pains grew worse and lasted longer. I couldn't eat and got to the point where I was down to 80 pounds. I kept this all very well hidden until one day I lost control and broke down to my mother. You see I got to the

point where I did not know who I was. I didn't know my name or what my purpose in life was. I started to feel as though I was living my life for everyone but myself . . . I confronted my mom with all of these anxieties about expectations and slowly but surely was able to work through them. I quit university (the hardest decision of my life) and joined the work force . . . I'm keeping my fingers crossed.

Another nineteen-year-old described her adolescent experiences this way, which includes several features typical of an identity crisis.

I was unsure what I really wanted to do with my life. This brought about feelings of uncertainty, uselessness and failure. This was intensified as most of my friends were moving on to post-secondary education and doing other things that I thought were better or more important than what I was doing . . . I moved away from home to complete high school, got a job and basically removed myself from those influences that had me feeling the way I did. There I was able to re-evaluate what I wanted to do and who I wanted to be — outside the overwhelming influence of parents and long-time friends.

And lastly, adolescent recollections from a 21-year-old:

I felt very confused about who I really was. Part of me was this calm, intelligent, polite, respectable girl while the other part wanted to be wild, unpredictable, attractive and live life on the edge. I tried to do both. I would play a different role with different people so much that I really didn't know which was the real me . . . I had a hard time dealing with my emotions. My emotions would range from utter happiness, to anger to depression. This variety in emotions showed in my actions as well. I still did well in school, and held down a part-time job. But, I also drank, tried drugs a couple of times, went into the bar underage, and had sex. I had a hard time deciding what was right and what was wrong.

Experiences associated with identity deficit

The descriptions provided by researchers who investigate identity crises, from the psychiatrists who treat them, from parents who live in the same house with them, and from the young people who "have" them are, as one might expect, really quite diverse. The following have all appeared in the psychological literature as describing the subjective feelings which accompany identity deficit.

1. feelings of uncertainty, vagueness and amorphousness;
2. feelings of emptiness, disquietude, isolation;
3. generalized confusion and bewilderment; the feeling of living in a "generalized malaise";
4. preoccupation with great, unsolvable questions; the perplexed sensation of metaphysical bewilderment;

5. feelings of detachment, loss of interest in the ordinary business of everyday life; the feeing of being excluded from everything important;

6. free-floating anxiety, apprehension, hypervigilance; a generalized condition of nervousness brought about by a failure to know "what is going on";

7. continuous and exaggerated self-examination; hyper-introspection; prolonged fascination with one's thoughts and ideas; entrenchment within one's feelings and emotions;

8. confusion, bewilderment, discouragement interspersed with anger and frustration; cynicism and the rejection of societal values;

9. hostility toward parents, authority figures and authority in general.

10. changing commitments and confusion about one's values, beliefs, goals and purpose.

Baumeister believes the common theme to all of these diverse experiences is the pain of coping with conflicts inherent to the moratorium: commitment versus freedom, and choice versus the fear of consequences.

> Emotionally, the person is torn between a *desire for commitment* and *the reluctance to give up any options*. Making a commitment means giving up certain possibilities in order to pursue others. You cannot really develop any of your potential beyond a certain preliminary stage without making a commitment. But by committing yourself you renounce other potentialities, a painful act . . . Adolescence may be the first point at which most people have to face that pain . . . (p. 213).

Hence, the desire for commitment coupled with the fear of giving up one's options sets the stage for the painful drama which Baumeister calls the *identity deficit crisis*.

As for the strong anti-authoritarian attitudes so widely reported among young people struggling with an identity crisis, it should be noted that:

> Identity deficits are often begun by a repudiation of the values and goals one has learned from one's parents. It is widely believed that attitudes toward authority are first shaped by attitudes toward parents, and the two attitudes continue to be related. The adolescent's attempt to break free of the parents is therefore probably accompanied by some antagonism toward authority figures in general (p. 214).

Baumeister's research has also proved fruitful by its recognition that the "deficit" identity crises of adolescence share several commonalties with the widely reported "mid-life" crises. Levinson's investigations, for example, suggested that mid-life crises are characterized by "emotional turmoil, despair, the sense of not knowing where to turn or of being stagnant and unable to move at all" (Baumeister, p. 215). And, even though some important differences separate adolescent and mid-life identity crises, Baumeister concludes that: "The tension between fear of unfulfilled potential and desire for stable commitments is thus common to the identity deficits of mid-life as well as adolescence." (p. 215). Hence, the critical issue may not be age but, rather, the struggle between desire and fear: the desire to actualize one's potential and the fear of making the necessary commitments to do so.

Identity conflict

In the type of crisis Baumeister calls "identity conflict" the adolescent is in an intolerable situation where it is "impossible to act without betraying oneself and one's loyalty to some other person, to an ideology, or to an institution" (p. 215). When action is taken under these conditions young people feel that they are traitors, that they have betrayed themselves, their friends or their ideals. A typical example of such a conflict occurs when the adolescent girl feels strongly that she loves her boyfriend, that he holds a special splendor which she desires, but simultaneous to this she recognizes that attachment to him will severely curtail her own goals as a person, will prevent her from going to university, or, from being able to sample the special splendor of other boys. Such conflicts are painful because *no matter which choice is made a desired option must fall by the wayside.*

In identity conflict it is difficult to maintain integrity because important components within one's identity are simultaneously threatened. As a result, feelings of imminent disaster loom in the margins of consciousness. Adolescents with identity conflict develop resentment of their life situation, and, even worse, a resentment of themselves for not being able to rise above it. Like the identity deficit, identity conflict leads to a paralysis of action, to an indecisiveness, and to the sinking feeling of living in a quicksand world.

Experiences associated with identity conflict

1. being torn and conflicted between desired opposites;
2. feelings of living in a world which poses unsolvable problems; a sense of being unable to solve basic life issues;
3. paralysis of action; fear of taking sides; feeling that one is always over-powered by circumstances;
4. feelings of betrayal, self-condemnation, of being a traitor either to oneself or to one's beliefs; free-floating guilt;

5. loss of a sense of coherence and consistency which, in turn, leads to a loss of integrity; alternating feelings of being worthwhile and worthless;

6. a sense of doom or imminent disaster;

7. hostile resentment to people or conditions which force decision-making in conflicted areas;

8. resentment, or envy, of peers who are not conflicted, who possess a clear identity and a clear mission in life.

The identity conflict stands in contrast to the identity deficit because there is no vacuum to fill; there is no need for exploration or experimentation. At bottom, the crisis is one of having to choose between conflicting needs and desires, all of which the adolescent is attracted to in one form or another.

Values and identity crises

Adolescence is the first developmental stage where values, beliefs and the pursuit of meaning are dominant impulses and the first where failure to achieve meaningful values may result not only in anxiety, but even in emotional disturbance and psychopathology. Part of the "youth predicament" in our culture is based squarely on the fact that we shun adolescents away from the activities and devotions their need structure impels them toward.

We accept outright the adolescent needs for popularity, for achievement and for esteem. Rightfully so, as they are fundamental to the psychology of youth. But these needs live in the psychological domain; they do not contribute to moral maturity nor do they speak to one's value needs. When we understand adolescent identity exclusively in terms of psychological needs, and thereby overlook their moral needs and value needs, we deny a spectrum of human experience which contributes in great measure to mature identity.

We seem all too willing to accept the idea that adolescents are children, and that their habits, their inclinations, even their troubles and anxieties are more like those of a child than of an adult. Few things are further from the truth. Adolescent intelligence is closer to the adult than the child; the adolescent body is adultlike in all respects except for wear and tear; adolescent inclinations, though showing occasional streaks of childishness, are essentially adult in focus. Finally, and of much greater importance than most adults care to note, the adolescent is impelled by moral energy just as is the adult, perhaps moreso since blunting encounters with social pragmatism have not as yet dulled their idealism.

Adolescent moral energy most typically strives to express itself in three vital areas: (1) the need to believe in something greater than oneself; (2) the need to relate to others in such a way that love, belonging and esteem are satisfied; and (3) the need to make meaningful contributions to family and society. Unfortunately, our society blunts all three: we provide little to pursue except material goods; we impede genuine relatedness by herding adolescents into age-segregated schools; and, finally, we prevent participation in virtually all socially valued, worthwhile work.

Adolescents don't take drugs, drop out of school or commit suicide because their needs for popularity, esteem or acceptance are thwarted. They succumb to pathology because, in human terms, their lifestyle is a charade —a fake existence of narcissistic immersion where nothing of genuine importance takes place. Young people cannot render worthwhile work or produce worthwhile goods; they are expected to redirect their needs for community relatedness into superficial peer gatherings or trivial social events. All this culminates in a personality lacking in self-esteem because nothing meritorious is undertaken; when action lacks substance so also does ambition.

Nearly unanimous agreement exists among investigators of psychological health that firm values are a prerequisite for healthy identity. Gordon Allport, in his pioneer research on this topic, concluded that six general categories are common to virtually all definitions of healthy personality. These include:

1. extension of self;
2. warm relating of self to others;
3. emotional security of self-acceptance;
4. realistic perception of the external world;
5. self-understanding, personal insight and a sense of humor;
6. a unifying philosophy of life (Allport, 1969, p. 307).

In the mature personality values play a critical role in the total health picture. Values which increase the ability to cope with stress, to handle tension, and to outlast anxiety increase ego-strength and make adolescents less vulnerable to the stress inherent to their lives. Values which allow one to extract meaning when meaning is not evident, which allow purpose to flower when all seems bleak, which encourage perseverance when defeat seems imminent, all contribute to a coherent sense of oneself, and in doing so, diminish the likelihood of an identity crisis.

On the other hand, values (or the absence of values) which incline the person to cope less ably with tension weakens positive self-esteem. Values which incline the person to believe that meaning is only myth, that life is chaos, that giving up one's freedom is not a significant loss, not only magnify life stress, they subtract from the coherence of identity, and thereby increase identity crises.

Identity crisis as serious but not disastrous.

The word "crisis" holds different meanings to different scholars. For Erikson, and those who follow his lead, it means a turning point, a juncture, or a critical life intersection where important decisions are made or important actions taken. These crises may meet with either a positive resolution, in which a strengthening of the ego occurs, or a negative resolution, in which the ego is weakened and adaptation is lessened. To others, however, the word "crisis" simply refers to a critical situation which may, or may not, produce consequences of significance, but which, nevertheless is profoundly experienced by the individual undergoing it. In a statistical sense, the latter viewpoint probably most corresponds to the majority experience during adolescence. In a theoretical sense, the former viewpoint is probably the most widely accepted.

In order to lessen the problems created by word entanglements, I would like to draw, once again, upon the insights of the originator of the concept of identity crisis, Erik Erikson. As always, his ideas are challenging and insightful even though they need not be considered the final word on the matter:

> Every adolescent is apt to go through some serious struggles at one time or another. The crises of earlier stages may return in some form as he seeks to free himself from the alignments of childhood because of both his own eagerness for adulthood and the pressures of society. For a while he may distrust what he once trusted implicitly; may be ashamed of his body, and doubtful of his future. He experiments, looking for affirmation and recognition from his friends and from the adults who mean most to him . . . He goes in for extremes — total commitments and total repudiations. His struggle is to make sense out of what has gone before in relation to what he now perceives the world to be, in an effort to find a persistent sameness in himself and a persistent sharing of some kind of essential character with others.

> *Far from considering this process to be a kind of maturational malaise, a morbid egocentricity of which adolescents must be "cured," we must recognize in it the search for new values, the willingness to serve loyalties which prove to be "true" . . . and thus a prime force in cultural rejuvenation* (my italic; 1960, p. 45).

Identity diffusion: The collapse of identity

> *Many a late-adolescent, if faced with continuing diffusion, would rather be nobody or somebody bad, or indeed, dead . . . than be not-quite somebody.*
>
> Erik Erikson

A solid identity requires a sense of direction and a healthy dose of certainty; when these are not attained the result is confusion — confusion about identity, confusion within identity, and confusion as to whether identity can ever be achieved. This final confusion, the *fear that a solid identity can never be achieved, is one of the most profound psychiatric outcomes of the adolescent identity project.*

Identity diffusion   never achieve

Some adolescents seem incapable of attaining a systematic self-definition or of maintaining themselves with any consistent style. As a result, their personality is a diffuse mixture of depression, acting out and bewilderment — a syndrome Erikson calls "identity diffusion." Identity diffusion is far more serious than identity crisis because *it involves a deterioration of the entire personality*. It represents a serious malfunction within identity formation.

As adulthood approaches and youngsters move away from the parental home, they find that they cannot handle new responsibilities with an impoverished identity. As a result, normal growth demands trigger an emotional breakdown, or a depressive withdrawal. Usually, all important life decisions are avoided, hence, the adolescent remains undecided about an occupation and is somewhat indifferent to all ideological issues.

In identity diffusion the youngster typically rejects any person or any experience which threatens the self. Such universal repudiation is not necessary for ordinary youngsters because they can handle threat without the ego fearing its own destruction. In identity diffusion, the strength of a positive self-definition is completely lacking; therefore, every threat is perceived as a total threat, and the person mobilizes all emotional resources for a fight to the bitter end.

It is worthy of special mention that some adolescents "normal" in their personality development may experience temporary, short-term episodes of identity diffusion. This most typically occurs during periods of exhaustion or fatigue, or after long periods of peer rejection or emotional discouragement. Among young people of adequate personality strength these reactions are abandoned after a few days or sometimes even after a few hours. This tendency to "backslide," that is, to show a temporary deterioration in ego strength, occurs with sufficient frequency during the adolescent period that it is thought of by experts as "normal," which is not the same as healthy. Normal simply means that it occurs with considerable frequency. "Healthy" means that it is beneficial to one's general well-being.

The subjective experiences which most frequently accompany identity diffusion are *shame, worthlessness* and *self-hatred*. The specific, immediate sensations include: the intrusion of sudden unwelcome thoughts into consciousness that have nothing to do with the task at hand; preoccupation, brooding and endless rumination about stressful events that return uncontrollably into the young person's stream of consciousness. These feelings not only debilitate one emotionally, they nurture attitudes, mannerisms and behaviors which distance the young person even further from friends (by now usually former friends) and family.

Because identity-diffused youth do not believe in their own worth, they desperately require the approval of others to obtain a sense of significance. Ironically, the approval they so desperately crave is usually repudiated because they are so convinced of their own unworthiness they think that anyone who likes them can only be an empty fool. (This is one reason they reject unconditional love, or unconditional trust, on first exposure to it).

Identity diffusion produces time confusion, hence the loss of time typical to normal youngsters exaggerates into chronic time disassociation; consequently, identity-diffused youth experience bizarre "time flights" and unexplainable (to them) time lapses.

How do we differentiate pathological from non-pathological identity diffusion? In general, when three or more of the following symptoms appear, identity diffusion has gone beyond "normal disturbance" and assumes the features of a serious emotional disturbance.

- Incapacity for personal intimacy, with resulting isolation, stereotyped interpersonal relationships, and a frenzied quest for intimacy with improbable partners.

- Diffusion of time perspective, with disbelief in the possibility that time may bring important change in one's life.

- Diffusion of industry, with inability to concentrate; a self-destructive preoccupation with narrow activities, and an abhorrence of competitiveness.

- The choice of a negative identity, expressed through utter disdain for community standards of desirability and propriety.

Some concluding comments on identity diffusion

The essential feature of all identity diffusion is the experience of piercing anxiety about an acceptable sense of self. Its symptoms may last weeks or months and result in significant impairment of social, academic, and occupational functioning. Uncertainty regarding long-term goals is expressed as an inability to choose a life pattern, a career or even friends. Bursts of impulsive experimentation are typical. Family relationships deteriorate and friendships virtually disappear. Relationships with other identity-distressed youth may increase, although, these are rarely rewarding friendships. Drug abuse may increase, and it usually is accompanied by episodes of despondency, apathy or depression.

Identity diffusion is not part of the normal growth process — it is a pathological exaggeration of an identity crisis, and it usually indicates a personality which remains troubled through the adult years.

Identity diffusion is a profound malfunction and, as such, it is beyond the scope of a book dedicated to investigating "normal" adolescence. As a rule, though not an unfailing one, identity diffusion follows a seriously troubled childhood and a history of interpersonal failures. Despite its serious nature, we sometimes observe "normal" adolescents going through episodes which resemble identity diffusion, but which are not as long lasting or as emotionally devastating as the real thing. This tendency to acquire short-term behaviors which resemble serious malfunctions make it extremely difficult to diagnose accurately the severity of adolescent identity problems.

Hey, Mr. Tambourine Man play a song for me,
I ain't sleepy and there is no place I'm goin' to,
Hey Mr. Tambourine Man play a song for me,
In the jingle-jangle morning I'll come followin' you . . .

Bob Dylan

chapter eleven

Negativism and Negative Identity

When one's negativism and anger is so powerful that every
statement is perceived as being unsympathetic or distant then
one's entire style and demeanor becomes contradictory.
Friedrick Nietzsche

The identity project is complicated by many, many factors, none of which is more perplexing to the student of adolescent behavior than the negativism which consumes so many young people. There is no easy way to account for negativism as part of the human condition, and, most assuredly, no easy way to explain its widespread presence in the adolescent community.

For some young people negativism shows itself in harmless eccentricities, in creative bursts of defiance or insubordination; for others, however, it lives as a hostile, seething hatred which may erupt into violence at any instant. For some youth, negativism and negation express themselves in stereotypic style, lighting up the sky like an exploding star then consuming itself in spent energy. For other youth, however, the habits of hostility and the patterns of negativism acquired during adolescence set the stage for a life-long warfare between self and others. In this chapter, we will delve into the dynamics of negativism in the hopes of better understanding the adolescent's struggle with society, and, as well, society's struggle with the adolescent.

Negative identity

As we have already indicated, for some youth the messages of socialization simply do not take hold. Among these young people, according to Erik Erikson, our century's most profound and productive theorist of adolescent behavior, resides a scornful hostility toward the roles offered as proper in one's family or immediate community. For these hostile youth, what is expected of them is met with refusal and rejection. These negational youth are consumed with a contemptuous disgust for the values of their families, their schools and of society itself.

Negative identity is more than merely rejecting what parents or teachers or society expect; it is actively and energetically doing the *opposite* of what is expected. Negative identity is a coping style adopted by youth who have had ideals paraded before them which seem unattainable, or equally important, by youth who believe that others have already attained these ideals with such a high level of superiority that they could never equal them.

Rollo May draws an interesting parallel which pertains to these angry, negative youth. "No human being can exist for long without some sense of his own significance. Whether he gets it by shooting a haphazard victim on the street, . . . or by rebellion, or by psychotic demands in a hospital, or by Walter Mitty fantasies, he must be able to feel this I-count-for-something and be able to live out that felt significance" (1972, p. 37). Among youth admitted for psychiatric care we commonly observe a negativism which is little more than a cry for significance, and their behavior, defiant though it may be, is really a plea for recognition and importance. They are engaged in a desperate fight for relevance. And, as Erickson comments, for some young people it is easier to "derive a sense of identity out of total identification with that which one is least supposed to be, than to struggle for a feeling of reality in acceptable roles which are unattainable . . . "

Unclear, and perhaps unknown, is why some adolescents are more attracted to "that which one is least supposed to be" than that which is hoped for or encouraged by parents and society. Once again, we draw upon Erikson:

> Such vindictive choices of a negative identity represent, of course, a desper-
> ate attempt at regaining some mastery in a situation in which the available
> positive identity elements cancel each other out. The history of such a choice
> reveals a set of conditions in which it is easier for the patient to derive a sense
> of identity out of total identification with that which he is least supposed to
> be than to struggle for a feeling of reality in acceptable roles which are
> attainable with his inner means (1968, p. 176).

For some teens the struggle to integrate the residue of their childhood self with their adolescent self, that is, their struggle to sustain a coherent continuity of self over time, just doesn't work. For them the total rejection of their "childish" past, choosing a lifestyle totally at odds with the juvenile past, is easier than to blend past with present. Hence, by choosing a negative identity, by standing in opposition to the childhood self, the adolescent creates a new "me" which exists beyond, and in opposition to, the childhood "me."

> For some troubled adolescents, it is better to be somebody totally other than
> what existed during childhood rather than struggle to reintegrate the past into
> a present and future having some continuity with one's previous existence.

There is often much relief following the choice of a negative identity, however destructive that solution may ultimately be (Kroger, p. 16).

Youth who feel that they are expected to blindly follow the paths established by their parents without their own feelings considered are prime candidates for negative identity. Their parents want them to do well, to achieve, to make the family proud; yet they may not care much about how their kids feel or what kind of people they really are. For many adolescents negative identity, when all is said and done, is primarily an attempt to strike out against their parents. As one adolescent put it when describing her angry, hostile friends: "They are all shooting themselves in the foot trying to make their parents dance."

The concept of negative identity has received wide audience in recent years and, as a consequence, the term has acquired a broader usage than Erikson intended. Some psychologists now use the term merely to refer to the adolescent tendency to defy convention or authority. This less technical usage helps us to focus on widespread correlates of negative identity which Erikson's psychodynamic interpretation does not deal with. For example, some youngsters who appear to be quite solid in their ego identity, who have been raised in a household which shows no noticeable symptoms of psychopathology, sometimes reject, or run away from, expected roles. Their rejection does not seem to be motivated by psychodynamic conflicts, or by difficulty in establishing continuity with their childhood selves, or even by a basic hostility toward their parents. Rather, it appears that these youngsters simply have no desire to act out the roles their parents want them to fill, no matter how richly they are rewarded for doing so, or how severely they are punished for not doing so. Social learning theorists like to think that these adolescents were simply "inadequately" socialized, and that if they had a more "effective" upbringing they would have learned to incorporate the expectations of their parents. Such explanations usually do not stand up well under close inspection. (I know several psychologists who were completely loyal to social learning theory before their own children became teenagers and began to reject expected roles and identities. None of these psychologists now believe that "inadequate socialization" adequately explains adolescent negativism — except when it is applied to other people's children!)

The contradiction arises when negation is manifested by healthy youngsters living in emotionally stable families. For these youth, negative identity does not seem to betray a disturbance within their personality, nor a disturbance within the family constellation, yet they show the same symptoms as disturbed kids from disturbed families. Our present understanding of negative identity falls well short of explaining this phenomenon.

Two points should be kept in mind when we try to understand the negativism of youth. The first is that any force that threatens the adolescent, whether real or merely perceived as real, will generate a negative, hostile reaction against that force from the adolescent. Second, the adolescent always tries to leave a stamp on the environment, and, any stamp at all is better than no stamp at all. In North American society, where youth are isolated from important events, segregated into schools, sometimes the only way they see to leave their stamp is through defiance or negation.

Parent hatred

> *I understand a fury in your words, but not the words.*
> Shakespeare, *Othello*

One of the most dramatic manifestations of adolescent negativism and anger is the way it is directed, rightfully or wrongfully, toward parents. Many households are brought, quite literally, to the point of collapse because of the defiant negativism of the adolescent who lives within it.

Few issues are more emotion-laden than parent-hatred; remarkably, at least to me, few scholars in the field of adolescent psychology even acknowledge the existence of this topic. Of the 20, or so, adolescent psychology textbooks published in North America between 1990 and 1992 (the time when I was writing this book) not one dealt in any systematic fashion with adolescent hatred of parents. Yet, during this same time, every city in North America held workshops by the hundreds for parents concerning topics such as "how to deal with youth who hate," and "how to protect yourself from your teenager." "Toughlove," the national organization created to protect parents from their own angry, hostile children, was founded because some kids are so hateful of everyone, including their parents, that they cannot be controlled by ordinary measures (York, 1982, 1984). Hatred is not the prevailing adolescent emotion, and should not be so perceived; it is, however, more prevalent than mainstream psychology seems willing to acknowledge.

On the other hand, some adolescents (especially early-adolescents) claim to hate their parents when it is doubtful whether "hate" really is the emotion they are experiencing. Not infrequently, older adolescents report having hated their parents, but they also report that this "hate" gradually disappeared during the course of adolescence.

Much can be learned by listening to what young people themselves have to say; like the experts, their words are not the final words, but they have a vivid awareness which demands our attention.

The following statements were written by young adults between the ages of 20-24, as part of my program of research on parent-teen relationships at the University of Alberta. The first three comments, provided by three different individuals, effectively demonstrate that adolescent "hate," though a painful and terrible experience, is not always as hateful, nor as permanent, as the young person thinks it is.

> Yes, I'm sure like most teens, I felt like I hated my parents. I felt like they wanted to totally control my life and not let me live my own. Now, I realize that they were doing the best they could and that they were just as scared as I was. I have vowed to myself, though, that I will not be quite as strict as they were. I guess a better way to summarize my feelings is to say that I hated their strictness but not them. I don't think I knew this at the time, though.

❖ ❖ ❖

> Yes, I especially hated my dad, but as I matured and gained more knowledge and understanding of him and his background, I realized that much of what he did was because of his upbringing, and problems in his life, not because he didn't love me, which is how I felt when I was younger.

❖ ❖ ❖

> I felt I was deprived normal, affectionate parents during my adolescence. I realized, not too long ago, that compared to others I am very lucky to have the parents I have. Also, I know that they did their very best in raising their children — the best that they knew how considering they came from a small town in Italy . . . My parents have made changes in their attitudes and discipline. I have come to realize that when I am a parent I will have to learn also.

The experiences which inspire "hatred" among early adolescents may inspire no such reaction among late-adolescents. Some early-adolescent hatreds are, quite obviously, brought into existence by abuse and violence; others, however, can be described as exaggerated emotional reactions of an immature ego quick to hurt and slow to mend. This latter phenomenon is spelled out rather directly by a university student recalling her adolescent attitudes toward her parents.

> I can remember hating my parents because of the things they wouldn't let me do. I hated them when they wouldn't let me go skiing in B.C. with my friends when I was fifteen, and again when I was sixteen and wanted to date a 22-year-old. I thought they just wanted to ruin my life and that they didn't want me to have any fun, but now I realize that they had their reasons for all of the things that they did and they just wanted what was best for me.

The following statement, written by a young woman in her second year of university, recalls the hatred she held toward her parents as an early adolescent and how it changed over the course of time.

> Between the ages of thirteen and fifteen, I hated my parents on and off. Now, however, I rarely hate them. I never hate my parents directly, just what they do. My feelings now are never as strong as they were as an adolescent. When I was an adolescent I hated them because of the limitations they put on my life. Now when I hate them it is usually because of some action. Hate is actually a pretty strong word, but I do still experience it; it just doesn't last so long.

Some parent-hatred appears to come about from a mixture of perceived and actual punishment for normal adolescent behavior.

> There were times when I especially hated my mom because my parents had marital problems and she was always the cause of it. I hated her because she was also very strict with me in terms of not letting me sleep over at my friend's place and not letting me go to certain events or places with my friends . . . I still resent what she did and still does do, but nevertheless, I will still love her. She will always be my mom.

From our investigations of early-adolescents' attitudes, we know unequivocally that some kids develop hostility toward their parents for nothing more than the legitimate demands of decent parenting. The causes of this hostility seem to be located within the youngster more than in the actual people to whom the hatred is directed. Their emotional reactions are, in effect, completely out of proportion to the situation. A surprising number of young adults who I have interviewed over the years admit to having owned such "unfair" hatreds.

Equally true, and far more tragic, is the fact that many young people live with parents who are disrespectful, abusive and punitive. Parents whose own pathology is more than any adolescent can be expected to handle on a day-to-day basis without experiencing some episodes of hatred. Here, in the words of one 21-year-old, is an all-too-familiar (in its general contours) response to the question "Was there ever a time in your adolescence when you hated your parents?"

> I resented my parents and truly did hate my father. My father represented everything that was going wrong in my life at the time. He was the cause for most of my grief, my distrust, and my humiliation. The hate was so intense that I wished he would die. I wished that he would not come home from work. I actually planned his demise on several occasions in my childish way . . . If you are asking if I am less hateful now, yes, I am. I realized somewhere along the way that there was no use in it all. I guess that I realized he was human and flawed, therefore allowed mistakes . . . I still hate what my father does but I don't hate him as a person. I separate the action from the person . . . I found that as you get older the events seem to fade so that they hurt less . . .

I don't wish him death anymore, but I often wonder if I would really care if he was gone. That is not hatred, it's indifference . . . When he hurts me now I feel it, but only momentarily.

Negativism and survival in the adolescent's world

Far from being an aberration, then, negativism can be seen to play and essential and constructive role in normal psychological development . . .

M.J. Apter

It can be argued, and has been done so rather persuasively by M.J. Apter (1983), that negativism plays a vital role in adolescent behavior. He claims that "the human propensity for negativism . . . is nevertheless essential for healthy psychological development and maturity." For Apter, the ability to stand in opposition is merely a variant of the ability to defend oneself, and both of these abilities are necessary if one is to attain any kind of durable identity capable of dealing with threats to one's integrity. "The development of a sense of personal identity, and its maintenance in the face of threat, *is fundamentally dependent on the capacity to feel, think and act in a negativistic way*" (p. 79).

Although negativism, as a theoretical concept, is held in low favor by investigators of adolescent behavior, Apter views it as a necessary force in the young person's struggle for uniqueness and distinctiveness.

By negativism will be meant the state of mind which one is in when one feels a desire, or a compulsion, to act against the requirements or pressures from some external source. This may mean refusing to do what others wish or even doing the opposite of what is required or expected in a given situation. It is a state of mind with which everyone must be reasonably familiar (p. 79).

Two of the most important challenges in the adolescent's identity quest are attaining distinctiveness and maintaining autonomy; negativism holds critical connections to both.

The aim of negativism now is to help the individual *to feel distinctive* in terms of "where he or she stands" in relation to a variety of issues . . . *in terms of autonomy* negativism lets the adolescent know . . . that it is possible to make up one's own mind about things rather than conforming to external pressures (p. 83, my italic).

The adolescent does not attain distinctiveness only by the pursuit of excellence, or by demonstrating unusual talent. Equally important to establishing uniqueness are the clear messages about what one is not; and, if one thinks about it objectively, it is far easier for teenagers to clearly define what they oppose, or resist, than what they defend or represent. Before the identity process can go anywhere, adolescents must be able to say (or act out) what they are not. "One's sense of distinctiveness, therefore can be gained and sustained by doing everything possible to demonstrate to oneself what one is not" (Apter, p. 80).

As far as behavior is concerned, in a moratorium culture it is far easier to make a statement about one's distinctiveness via negations than via affirmations. This fact is not lost on adolescents any more than it is on toddlers.

> After all, it can hardly be by chance that the two most obviously transitional periods of development — that from babyhood to childhood, and that from childhood to adulthood — are both characterized by negativistic behavior: in both cases the search for a new identity appears to be mediated by defiance of adult authority (Apter, p. 75).

In a thoughtful critique of the evolution of the self, Harwood makes reference to the kind of identity anchored in negativism or, in her terminology, "opposition." The relevance to adolescent theory is direct, especially her emphasis on the notion that negativism most typically occurs in a self which is not complete: "The self that defines itself in opposition has differentiated itself enough to know that it exists, but cannot trust or implement its own creative gestures." And, further, the self energized by negativism "obtains a sense of aliveness or power from opposing others; otherwise, it feels empty and restless, while always dissatisfied" (Harwood, p. 71).

And, of course, the negativism of youth cannot be addressed without taking into account their justified resentment of living on the margins of society, of being left out of the important social machinery, of being viewed as irrelevant or unworthy. In many ways, the rules which regulate adolescent life blunt their sensitivity to real human reactions. Thus insulated from consequences, many youth simply cannot read the reactions their behavior causes. They fail to comprehend how their behavior is, or is not, affecting the people around them, and as a result, the full impact of their negativism is rarely perceived with much clarity.

Confrontational politics and negativism

To understand why adolescents have so much negative energy, and possess such a strong propensity for confrontation, it helps to envision *the benefits which accrue from these traits*. Yet, it is by no means a straightforward matter. Sometimes it appears to outside observers (especially parents) that adolescent negation and negativism yield only unwanted outcomes. However, if one takes into account the narcissistic properties within the adolescent personality, negativism clearly offers some attractive benefits. I would like to suggest, more as hypotheses than anything else, the following as representing some of the benefits which accrue to the adolescent as a result of all kinds of confrontational politics, including defiance and negativism.

1. Confrontational behavior creates social scenarios in which the adolescent's egocentricity is given expression and becomes the focus of social attention. Since any expression of one's egocentricity is better than no expression, the emotional advantages of confronting parents, police, teachers, etc., in their immediate psychological totality, outweigh their disadvantages.

2. Negativism excites primitive emotional states, especially feelings of grandiosity and power, and these emotional states unto themselves, manufacture an invigorating, narcissistic pleasure.

3. Negativism elicits reactions of greater magnitude than virtually any other adolescent behavior; this carries tremendous reward value to a teenager since the failure to generate social response, in the teen community, is to be nobody, and to a fledgling identity to be anybody at all is better than to be nobody.

4. Confrontational argumentativeness is an effective way to obtain what one wants, especially when one's opponents possess only weak confrontational skills. It is common sense to do what works, especially when one has no empathy or respect for the person being confronted.

5. The act of taking an oppositional posture confirms to insecure adolescents that they have sufficiently differentiated themselves from their past, from their upbringing, or from their family that they now no longer merely learn about social conventions, but that they now judge them, evaluate them, even reject them. With a logic completely comprehensible to every oppressed person, they believe that the act of opposition confirms their equality to that which is opposed.

6. Through opposition adolescents create the opportunity to hate in others those things they despise in themselves. The shame, humiliation and self-diminishment so common to the adolescent experience inspires a self-contempt which a young person in the midst of identity formation simply cannot tolerate. To keep their world within manageable limits this hatred must be projected outward even when the recipients of this projection are parents or loved ones.

Anger and negativism

There are very few instances in human growth and development where the gap between one's capacity to think objectively and one's tendency to behave irrationally is greater than when adolescents are angry. Anger, unto itself, diminishes the ability to think clearly. However, when it exists as a perpetual feature of the personality, as is often the case in negative identity, its dampening effects on rationality are profound.

No one really knows why anger exists in such quantities in the adolescent community. Several theories attempt to account for it, but it is rare to find a practitioner in the field who believes any of them with conviction. Angry adolescents themselves rarely have much of an idea as to the origins of their hostility; often they cannot even predict what will trigger it. One "street kid" (a seventeen-year-old boy) told me: "I don't know why I hate so much. But I'll tell you this, around here it's a lot smarter to hate everyone than to hate no one."

Those of us who are not consumed by anger tend to think of it as a strong feeling of displeasure caused by a wrong; to us anger usually is aroused by an injury or an injustice. However, among many youth, anger is bound to no such specified conditions; rather, their anger exists as free-floating energy with a life and force of its own, ebbing and flowing with seeming unpredictability.

Angry youth perceive the objects of their anger as existing in a universe totally alien to the one in which they live. As a result, their world is divided into two camps: the "good others," and the "bad others." The practical outcome of this practice, as far as adolescent identity is concerned, is that it encourages one to think of oneself as completely different from the hated others. Through this separation one becomes not only more worthy and more special, one also becomes unanswerable to demands made upon the less worthy ones. (As one youngster put it: "The everybodies who are everywhere").

Part of the adolescent's sense of specialness is the belief that "I" am not like anyone else. This belief is sometimes distorted beyond recognition by the personal fable and the imaginary audience, eventually resulting in the belief that I exist in a class by myself and expecting me to be like everyone else insults my singular splendor. Even holding such expectations justifies my anger; no one has the right to treat me the same way that they treat everyone else. To hostile youth, equal treatment is an insult because it strips them of their "unique" qualities, it cancels their special entitlements, and, it lowers them to the hellish, contemptible level of their peers.

As the result of such entangled beliefs, some adolescents come to hold an open resentment of adults (especially parents and teachers) because of the very "virtues" which the adult has worked so hard to attain: fairness, impartiality, even-handedness.

Anger is a fairly efficient mechanism for young people because almost no one can retaliate either against it, or them. Teachers cannot retaliate unless academic achievement is valued; parents cannot retaliate if the adolescent is already alienated from their affections; passers-by in the impersonal adult world don't have a prayer. In a moratorium culture, hostile adolescents are remarkably immune from corrective measures. As Bob Dylan once penned: "When you ain't got nothing, you got nothing to lose."

Anger is a warfare emotion. Not by chance are angry kids described as "waging war against society" — or school, or parents. Without the external focus of "war," anger turns inward in self-destruction; with war it turns outward in self-preservation. Therefore, "anger-war" is initiated against anyone toward whom the adolescent is chronically anxious, jealous or fearful; the primary targets being parents, teachers, peers and society. Since one of the primary purposes of these wars is merely to sustain one's own anger, they do not require a very advanced justification; however, when a justification is found (or invented) it reinforces the rightness of the war being waged, and the courage of the warrior waging it.

This is one reason why angry, defiant youth are magnetized to those who praise their defiance, who perceive it as heroic, and, perhaps most importantly, who, through their ideology can lend moral or intellectual justification to it.

One of the many connective links between anger and negativism works something like this: The adolescent is emotionally agitated by feelings of free-floating anger, and these feelings eventually trigger negative behavior. The reactions this negative behavior incites from parents, teachers or peers forces the youngster to defend his or her actions by creating an identity of opposition to the hated, criticizing others. Once such an identity is forged the youngster defines his or her self within these very negations. Such self-definition firms their opposition to anyone who is not a total ally. Eventually their entrenchment within their negative self-definition becomes so powerful that to drop their negative behavior is to abandon the basis of their self-esteem. Hence, in a perverse irony, the best within their nature is defended by the worst in their behavior.

The adolescent belief system and its relationship to negativism

Adolescents need to believe that life is worth living and that goals are worth pursuing if they are to survive, with any dignity, the pain inherent to normal adolescence. In the absence of worthy beliefs, youth are susceptible to a loss in direction, and vulnerable to a wide range of psychological disturbances which are easily observed in their daily behavior if we know where to look. Adolescents want to believe in their worth as well as the worth of their society.

Failure on these counts sets the stage for a stunning range of youth problems which ultimately translate into societal problems.

Here I shall briefly describe three variations of belief bewilderment, each of which impacts upon young lives in different ways. The first is *transitory disbelief* which is a temporary belief network brought into existence primarily by normal intellectual and moral growth. The second is *reflective disbelief*, which is essentially metaphysical in concerns and rational in tack, and is commonly observed among reflective, intellectual youth. The third, and certainly the most serious as far as the mental health of the adolescent is concerned, is *chronic disbelief*, a disorder which may nurture more profound psychiatric ailments such as depression, and, as well, may precipitate self-destructive behavior such as drug dependency or suicide.

Doubt, skepticism and disbelief are abetted by the adolescent's developing intellect. As the adolescent grows through the series of intellectual transformations we know as formal thought, attitudes and beliefs are re-examined. Many youth question the authenticity of their moral convictions and religious beliefs — an act of self-inquiry they could not effectively transact in childhood. They begin to recognize social pretense and to discover realities beyond the imaginings of a more innocent mind. Self-examination, in the form of pensive introspection or analytic dialogue, becomes part of adolescent routine.

Adolescence is the first time in the life cycle when values, beliefs, moral viewpoints and philosophical issues are given vigorous intellectual inspection. The inspector is new to such ventures, and often does not know how to handle the disillusionment which accompanies such inspections. Intelligence outraces security, leaving a gap which adolescents experience as anxiety. It is a fitful state of affairs. The intelligence which unlocks mysteries of the outside universe simultaneously unleashes a host of internal riddles, many of which seem unfathomable to the perplexed adolescent.

The adolescent may be afraid to be himself or herself and, at the same time, afraid to be anyone else; afraid of losing oneself but, in a very real sense, not as yet in control of the self whose loss is feared. The disconnectedness brought about by this confusion is "projected" to the outer world, which, to the adolescent, further verifies the chaotic nature of life in general.

All of this culminates in a period of belief bewilderment which I call **transitory disbelief.** This is the young mind's reaction to intellectual perplexity, but is not, in a psychiatric sense, a patholological disorder. It is an adaptation to puzzlements beyond one's intellectual range.

Reflective disbelief differs from transitory disbelief in its greater preoccupation with philosophical models and lessened preoccupation with inner feelings. Transitory disbelief is the adolescent's reaction to what appears to be a shipwrecked personality; reflective disbelief is a more measured attempt to determine whether, in fact, the personality really is shipwrecked.

Reflective disbelievers are rarely filled with self-pity since the motivation behind their disbelief is intellectual investigation rather than psychological protectionism. Reflective disbelief is not at all rare among university students, and occurs to thoughtful youngsters in general. It is disbelief borne of intellectualization, therefore, it is a brand of youthful skepticism not cynicism.

Chronic disbelief, the disbelieving of everything, leads the adolescent to conclude that he or she is pointless or meaningless and so also are friends, parents, teachers. Everyone and everything is equally nothing. Chronic disbelief pervades the adolescent's entire scheme of things, and drains the sense of meaning and purpose. Accepting the insignificance which comes with chronic disbelief requires emotional insulation, and a good measure of it. The price youth pay for this insulation, however, is substantial. Their loss of relatedness uproots their social grounding, their loss of belief defeats their spiritual cravings, and their loss of ambition leads to an obsessive anchoring onto the present.

Chronic disbelief does not refer merely to periodic recurrence of common experiences such as apathy, doubt, listlessness or uncertainty. Rather, it represents a significant deficit which may culminate in the formation of classic neuroses such as obsessive-compulsive reactions, depression or chronic phobias. Pathological disbelief is a psychological crisis born of a value crisis, both of which derive from the absence of dignified goals.

One final discouraging point. Disbelief generates a sense of helplessness, which is perhaps the ultimate invisible boundary since it creates a paralysis of purpose that prevents the adolescent from taking hold, or worse, from desiring to take hold.

In summary, chronic disbelief among adolescents produces the following psychological profiles, all of which feed negativism, anger and defiance.

1. Cynicism, pessimism and fatalism all of which encourage adolescents to think of themselves and the people near them as meaningless.

2. Boredom and non-selectivity which prevent the adolescent from becoming engaged in relationships (or activities) which celebrate worthwhile personhood.

3. Absence of social interest, minimal desire to work with or help others. The belief that cooperative and charitable acts are stupid or self-defeating.

4. The inability or refusal to engage in productive work.

5. An absence of genuine intimacy relationships, "helper" relationships, and love relationships.

6. Social narcissism, minimal concern for the rights or feelings of others.

7. Spiritual emptiness.

Skepticism and cynicism. Skepticism and cynicism are qualitatively different phenomena which call into existence qualitatively different consequences. Skepticism is the attitude of questioning and doubting which is based upon uncertainty and the finiteness of human knowledge. As a philosophical doctrine skepticism claims that truth must always be questioned; intellectual inquiry, to the skeptic, is a process of ongoing doubt and examination. (Among the ancient Greeks skeptics believed that humans are incapable of attaining ultimate knowledge.) Skepticism treats doubt and uncertainty as legitimate facts, and, as far as adolescents are concerned, this means that one need not fear the unknown, and even more critical to the themes of this chapter, it means one need not be contemptuous of, or hostile toward, things and people which are not understood. For these reasons we see precious little genuine skepticism among negative youth. Their forte is cynicism.

Cynicism is bankrupt skepticism. Cynics disbelieve the sincerity of human actions and doubt that motivations can be altruistic or idealistic; they even question the value of living. A cynic believes people are motivated only by selfishness, and that the values we aspire to are no better than the ones we discard. Cynicism is the dominant attitude among nihilistic youth, yet it is far more than merely a "negative" outlook; it is a form of emotional protectionism which manipulates reality in order to soothe a frightened identity.

The cynic plays it safe by not believing in anything with an ethical or moral structure. If he follows a pattern of total disbelief, he is then disappointed in nothing. *Because he believes in nothing, he avoids the heartaches that come from having believed in something that ends in failure.* The device he uses is to deprecate any value which seems to hold forth hope (Bischof, 1970, p. 225).

Hence we see one fundamental difference between skepticism and cynicism: intelligence generates skepticism; fear generates cynicism. Another point separates skepticism from cynicism which is frequently overlooked by students of adolescent behavior: anger and hostility require an attitude of cynicism to sustain themselves. Cynicism is the fuel which keeps negativism burning within the adolescent personality. In return, the anger fueled by cynicism ignites negative behavior which causes others to behave scornfully toward the hostile adolescent and this scorn, in turn, creates further cynicism in an egocentric mind that cannot comprehend it. Hence, the relationship between cynicism and negativism is both circular and self-perpetuating — each increasing the power of the other.

The ability to formulate a philosophy of life, to construct life aims, to establish a solid sense of oneself — basic demands of the adolescent identity quest — are all impeded by cynicism. Perhaps the steepest price youngsters pay for their cynicism is that it cuts away the trust and love necessary to understand oneself. As Norman Cousins put it:

> Nothing is easier than to turn cynical; nothing is more essential than to avoid it. For the ultimate penalty of cynicism is not that the individual will come to distrust others but that he will come to distrust himself (1981, p. 48).

The attitude of cynicism becomes for many young people, in the course of time, a permanent mindset; a fixed perceptual filter which darkens the meaning of all human events. This attitude of darkness is even further encouraged by what clinical psychologists refer to as *defensive devaluation.*

Friederick Nietzsche once claimed: "Not a few, perhaps the majority of men, find it necessary, in order to be able to retain their self-esteem and a certain uprightness in conduct, *to mentally disparage all the people they know.*" This sentence, in addition to describing effectively the actions of some adolescents, summarizes perfectly the concept of defensive devaluation.

Defensive devaluation is expressed in constant griping about the ineffectiveness of teachers, in the incessant belittling of peers, in the repudiation of parents. Its purpose, pure and simple, is to lessen the pain of one's own insecurities and inferiorities by spotlighting real or imagined defects in others. Early adolescents (eleven- to fourteen-year-olds) are perhaps the world's premiere users of defensive devaluation. Having never held positions of responsibility, they possess virtually no first-hand knowledge of that which they so persistently devalue: teaching, coaching, parenting. With increased maturity their relentless detraction of others tends to become less blatant.

Belief and hope. Belief is the acceptance of something as true; it can be based on reason, prejudice or even fantasy. The power of belief is determined by the confidence held by the person that it is true. As we have already discussed, beliefs can inspire one to growth or they can encourage resignation and defeat. A young person can believe that the world is foul and ugly or fair and beautiful. Beliefs can be positive or negative, healthy or unhealthy, identity-enhancing or identity-stunting.

Hope, on the other hand, elicits the feeling that what is wanted, or believed, will happen; it is the exuberant anticipation or expectation that what is true will be. Hope is the soul of the future and it is, perhaps as fully as any reality in the domain of adolescent psychology, essential to mature identity.

> What gives hope its power is not the demonstrable accumulation of facts, but the release of human energies generated by the longing for something better. *The capacity for hope is the most significant fact in life. It provides human beings with a sense of destination and the energy to get started.* It enlarges sensitivities. It gives value to feelings as well as to facts (Cousins, 1981, p. 57).

Hope is what negative youth have in such complete scarcity. They have no belief in themselves, yet their needs for affirmation and recognition, impel them to trumpet themselves. The failure of hope causes the self to turn back into itself, a gesture of refuge-seeking which magnifies obsessive egocentrism. The adolescent self can escape its own protectionism only when it sees hope for itself outside itself; only when it views the outside world as just and legitimate, and as a place where even a brittle self can love and be loved.

Summary observations on negativism and negative identity

> *If you must hate . . . then hate that which should be hated:*
> *falsehood, violence and selfishness.*
>
> Ludwig Boerne

It appears to me, that negation, negativism, and their elaborated manifestation of negative identity, are, at bottom, not actions but reactions. And though adolescent negativism usually parades itself as an affirmation of this belief or a defense of that ideology, it usually reduces to fear, and to the unwillingness, sometimes the incapacity, to extend oneself to others in a way that encourages them to give love in return.

Many young people perceive their world through "negative morality," as a result, they believe that the goodness within themselves exists only in relation to the evil within others. Such a morality contributes to their need to see evil where it does not exist, and, as well, to their desire to believe that the intentions of others are hateful and malicious when they are not. These perceptions, in turn, perpetuate their hostile paranoia toward parents, teachers, police and the community at large.

Attributing "evil" to others may actually enhance one's emotional survival. When one thinks of oneself as morally superior to others (even when superiority is self-ordained) it provides the strength, the courage and, most importantly, the *justification* to oppose whatever or whoever is perceived as morally inferior. Hence, negational youth have a relentless fascination with ideologies which denigrate the objects of their hate — especially school, authority and parents. To them the act of degrading others confirms their own honor and worth.

These summary comments, quite obviously, leave many important questions unanswered. A few which immediately present themselves include the following:

- Why do adolescents perceive so many people, events and circumstances as threatening when they really are not threatening at all?

- What is it that is threatened when a youngster feels threatened?

- Why are adolescents so easily threatened in some areas, but so sturdy and resilient in others? For example, how is it that some kids fear their peers yet hold no apparent fear of police officers? Fear parental scolding but do not fear the risk of pregnancy?

- Why is the adolescent's perception of threat so influenced by style? That is, by the mode of interaction employed by the person with whom the adolescent interacts?

- Why are some youngsters obsessed with entitlements, rights and privileges but, seemingly, so completely unaware of their duties or responsibilities?

chapter twelve

Conformity and Identity

At the heart of the problem lies a deeper conformity . . .
conformity to the unquestioned assumptions of one's culture.

S. Putney

In the previous chapter, I tried to demonstrate that for some young people the messages of socialization simply do not take hold, and that parental teachings and societal expectations are rejected outright. This chapter deals with the other side of the coin: with youth who willingly, even eagerly, accept the teachings of their parents and follow enthusiastically the expectations of their society. These are the youngsters of conformism; their psychology is anchored in compliance, not rejection, and their identity emphasizes shared commonalties with family and community, not the differences which separate them.

The psychologists who have investigated the adolescent experience in North America have traditionally over-emphasized the tension between the parent culture and its adolescent children, and under-emphasized the harmony which exists between them. In the 50s and 60s, in great measure, because of the innovative and persuasive writings of Paul Goodman (*Growing Up Absurd*), Edgar Friedenberg, (*The Vanishing Adolescent*), and Kenneth Keniston (*The Uncommitted*), it was widely accepted that youthful conformity came at a frightful cost to integrity and individuality. In some circles, adolescent conformity was viewed as the youthful noble savage kneeling before the raised sword of a persecuting majority; an indignity that no healthy adolescent would succumb to without putting up a fight, symbolic or real.

Like many images born of speculative theory, the concept of youth as hot-blooded individualists heroically resisting their parent society is supported far more by myth than by data. Virtually all research conducted during the 70s, 80s & 90s indicates that the majority of youth in North America *willingly* accommodate to the general demands and expectations of their family, their school and their society. Equally clear is that, for most youngsters, conformism is chosen rather than forced, desired rather than resisted, and fits their emotional dispositions rather than opposes them.

One problem which impedes understanding is that "conformity" is an emotion-laden term, striking a blow as it does against the treasured values of autonomy and rugged individualism. The words which typically precede it, "herd," "mindless" and "bland," tell us a good deal about how the concept is thought of.

Conformity, as generally defined in the social sciences, is simply agreement on some trait, attitude or behavior, based on common group membership. Quite obviously, every group is necessarily characterized by some degree of uniformity, otherwise it would not be a group. And, equally obvious, every group is necessarily characterized by some insistence that its members behave so that their behavior is not harmful to the group.

As the term is used in ordinary language, "conformity" is too broad, at least for our purposes. We gain a bit more insight into the phenomenon of conformity when we consider three concepts which hold special relevance to adolescent behavior.

The first is **contagion**: the imitation of behavior without any pressure to do so from the group. Simply doing the same thing that others are doing. Imitation.

The second is **compliance**: when an individual yields to behavioral precepts more from obedience than from desire. Following orders. Doing what is expected.

The third is **internalization**: when conformity persists in the absence of group pressure or group reward, that is, when it is so much part of the person that it is freely and eagerly chosen. Over the course of time the behavior of the group becomes one's own behavior.

Youth watchers are in agreement that some youngsters conform simply from momentum, following in the jet stream of those who have gone before them. Theirs' is a conformity born of custom rather than thought, from inertia rather than initiative. In terms of what we described a moment ago, it can be thought of as a *combination of compliance and contagion.* Unflattering as it may be, many youth conform without much concern for what it is they are conforming to, and without much awareness of the alternatives available to them (a widespread trend among twelve-, thirteen-, and fourteen-year-olds). This type of follow-the-crowd behavior is social imitation in its most juvenile, least dignified form; fortunately for the adolescent identity project, all youthful conformity is not of this passive, convictionless type.

Some youngsters conscientiously choose their paths even though these paths are the same ones travelled by their parents or peers. Many youth believe fervently in the religion, the government and the ideology which defends their conformist choices; they have strong convictions, even intense passions, for their conformist posture. These are the youth Moriarty and Toussieng (1976) call "Ideological Conservatives," and we shall give them special recognition in this chapter.

Two themes focus every discussion of adolescent conformity. The first concerns conformity imposed from above by the weight and force of larger powers; conformity which is accepted because of an anxious fearfulness within the person who conforms. The second concerns conformity which is chosen more freely, which suits the needs and ambitions of the conformer; conformity to something or someone perceived by the person who conforms as worthy of allegiance. *The second brand of conformity is the focus of this chapter.*

Conventional conformity, anxious conformity

Conventional conformity is the term I have chosen to describe the type of adolescent conformity that comes into existence from a combination of *contagion*, (the imitation of behavior without any pressure to do so from the group); of *compliance* (when the youngster yields to behavioral expectations more from obedience than from desire); and, from *internalization* (when conformity persists without group pressure or group reward, in other words, it is so much a part of the person that it is freely and eagerly chosen). Conventional conformity, as used here, is not caused by underlying fears, anxieties or deficiencies; or, at least that is how it appears to those of us who observe this type of conformity. Conventional conformity is freely chosen, although it is only fair to report that a wide range of differences exist among youth as to how much thought actually goes into choices.

In conventional conformity the adolescent has difficulty even imagining himself or herself being too different from family, from peers, or from community standards. And even though their conformity unquestionably limits their life options and narrows the components which make up their self-concept, it does not seem to be motivated by a fear of rejection nor by a sense of social inferiority. Conventional conformity seems to be motivated by the desire to blend with one's peers, to adjust to social demands and expectations, and to comply with rules and regulations which, on face value, seem fair. And even though such malleability completely befuddles individualists, these are authentic choices which many, many adolescent choose. Conventional conformity is a very influential force in the adolescent identity project.

A different matter altogether is the "anxious" conformism of young people who really do not know themselves with any certainty or clarity, and who, therefore, *need the acceptance and approval of others in order to attain a sense of themselves*. Their conformity operates from a completely different dynamic: they perceive themselves as being different from, and less than, the people they are trying to be like, and, to them, conforming proves that they have bettered themselves. Their conformity is designed to win approval and recognition; conformity is an important competition with acceptance awarded to winners. Such conformity has a nervous, frenzied quality because conformity is not motivated by the merits of that to which one conforms, rather, it is motivated by fear and self-doubt.

Consequently, the behavior of anxious conformers is determined by the people they are imitating, and their values are determined by what is rewarded by the desired group. These anxiously conforming youth work hard to earn the goodwill of the group whose acceptance they seek; their identity project becomes consumed with making favorable impressions on desired others. In much popular literature, all conformism is portrayed as anxious conformity. As we shall see, this is not the case — at least not with adolescents.

Identity foreclosure and conformism

> *My beliefs give me my identity.*
> (J., a sixteen-year-old Hutterite
> boy living in southern Alberta.)

Foreclosure is the attainment of identity without experimentation; that is, deciding upon an occupation, a role, a marital status or a definition of oneself without examining or experimenting with any alternatives. In Erikson's understanding of the identity process, foreclosure occurs when the adolescent settles upon a set of identifications as forever characterizing his or her identity. It is the premature fixing of one's self image in such a way that one's development, one's potential, and, of course, one's self definition, are narrowed. Foreclosure is the curtailment of identity in exchange for certainty; and even though it derives from personal choices, these choices foreclose on life's options before they are ever experienced.

Foreclosure is the norm in traditional cultures where roles tend to be obediently accepted, and where (this is vital to our discussion) few other genuine options are available. Equally germane to our discussion, however, is the fact that foreclosure is a widespread phenomenon in technological cultures, such as our own, and it is an avenue of identity resolution selected, for whatever reasons, by many, many young people in the 90s.

At first glance foreclosure seems completely contrary to the demands of identity, especially since it eliminates the exploration and experimentation generally deemed essential to the identity project. And even though it holds many perils, foreclosure offers some attractive "solutions" to identity demands. First, it helps adolescents to focus their energy and to narrow their anxiously expanding range of options. It also reduces their uncertainty about whether *they are able even to follow a specific path.* Second, foreclosure gives the individual something to hang on to and to identify with. For many youth, *the very act of making a commitment* solidifies their sense of themselves, and proves to them that they can make significant, "adult" decisions. Foreclosure involves, for many young people, an interesting twist on how identity is usually achieved: rather than making commitments based upon their identity, they simply reverse the process and base their identity upon made commitments. Finally, foreclosure is one means by which young people can eliminate virtually all life options, and by so doing, they attach great significance, even exalt, the niche their foreclosure has created for them. In other words, they glorify their narrowness because they are their narrowness; and, in the logic of egocentrism, this makes their narrowness grand and glorious.

The popular wisdom of our era proclaims that identity foreclosure yields more negative than positive results. In fairness, however, it is difficult to verify this. Many youngsters, quite obviously, do regret their early choices and commitments, especially those who end up unemployed, on government "roles," in dead-end circumstances. On the other side of the coin, we know virtually nothing about those young people whose identity is forged early and who show no ill effects from it. Our culture places such a heavy premium on "freedom" and "choice" that we find it hard to accept foreclosure as a realistic way to cope with identity formation. But remember that some cultures in which identity foreclosure is universally adhered to have existed for hundreds of generations. Current research suggests that some religious communities, such as the Hutterites, which pressure their young into identity foreclosure *have far less social pathology than society in general.* But, of course, the Hutterite community constrains personal freedom far more than our government, or most of our citizens, find acceptable.

For many youngsters foreclosure is motivated by their fear of breaking away from an expected path, or from their fear of failure. Some youth have never been encouraged to diversify, or to branch out; in fact, they are pressured to behave exactly as their brothers and sisters behave, and to desire exactly what their elders desire. As well, some youngsters are so conventional in their own disposition, so ingrained in their allegiance to learned cultural habits, rituals and outlooks that *it does not even occur to them to be anything other than what they are expected to be.*

One unhappy consequence of foreclosure occurs when the identity chosen proves totally inappropriate to one's emotional, spiritual or economic needs. Or, when the identity chosen requires skills and abilities the young person thinks he or she possesses, but does not. In these instances, foreclosure, rather than enhancing identity, fails it. Rather than preparing adolescents to meet the demands of adulthood, it paints them into a corner. Foreclosure is especially damaging when it necessitates commitments from which it is extremely difficult to extricate oneself: early marriage, early parenting, and early withdrawal from school are foreclosures which, in our culture, usually backfire. These are the kinds of foreclosure that our society is beginning to recognize as being extremely costly not only to the emotional welfare of the young people involved, but also to the state in unemployment payments, in rent subsidies, in medical care for infants.

We may surmise that while adolescence is acknowledged by our society as a special time for role experimentation and the sampling of diverse identities, it is not so for all adolescents. Youth who foreclose upon their identity, in essence cancelling their moratorium, do not follow a universal path into adulthood. Some regret their foreclosure; others do not. For some the decision is conscious and premeditated; for others it is defensive, impulsive and reckless.

Youth who foreclose on their identities are the living opposites to the individualist Herman Melville, who once claimed: "It is better to fail in originality than to succeed in imitation." Foreclosed youth believe, in very important ways, that it is better to succeed in imitation than to fail in originality.

Our knowledge of the impact of foreclosure on adolescent identity has been advanced considerably by the able investigations of Jane Kroger. In her review of the empirical research concerning foreclosed youth (1989), she uncovered some interesting findings. For example, foreclosed youngsters tend to be happy within themselves, almost "smugly self-satisfied"; they are "authoritarian and unbending," conventional in moral reasoning and are "particularly drawn to the values of a parent or a strong leader who can show them the right way." Marcia's research supports the notion that the strength of foreclosed youngsters "is a rigid and brittle strength, rather like glass; if you push it one way, it is very strong; if you push it in a different way, it shatters" (1989, p. 37).

Kroger reports that foreclosures tend to be approval-seeking and that their actions are greatly influenced by the opinions of others. They are typified by less complex cognitive styles and tend toward conventional levels of moral reasoning. They report close relationships with their parents, whom they greatly resemble because their parents encourage adherence to family values and traditions. From Kroger's findings it appears that youth who foreclose are inclined toward both conformity and authoritarianism.

Foreclosure and authoritarianism. "The authoritarian character" is difficult to comprehend in a time of life, such as adolescence, when so many individuals are characterized by opposition, negation and hostility toward authority. Yet there can be no doubt that many youngsters prefer situations in which they are expected to obey unquestioningly. These youngsters tend to be markedly conventional, and, at least on the surface, appear to be clones of some ideal citizen conjured by an arch-conservative politician.

By now it should be evident that all youngsters are not defiant toward their parents, society or the school system. They are comfortable with society, admire it, and want to be a part of it. Among the college students I have interviewed who are, by their own description, "identity foreclosures," I have noticed a consistent tendency to prefer situations where one person sets the tasks, prescribes procedures, and judges results without having others share in the process. And, as well, to believe in the importance of strong authority in social relations; and, to recognize authority as a source of religious and political truth. All of these features typify authoritarianism.

A parallel feature which shows up among many foreclosed, authoritarian youth is a keen sense of self-discipline, by which I simply mean a well developed regulation of their personal conduct, a solid control of their impulses, and a genuine sense of their own values and ideals. Furthermore, they possess the ability to control their present behavior for the sake of later satisfactions. All in all, their features are virtually the opposite of youth typified by negative identity, by identity crises, or by identity diffusion. They are, in the literal sense of the word, conformists.

Conformity and traditionalism

Perhaps the most comprehensive study of adolescent coping styles ever conducted in North America was undertaken by Alice Moriarty and Povl Toussieng. In their classic book, *Adolescent Coping*, (1976) they provided insightful descriptions of the different styles by which adolescents reconcile their personal needs and desires with the demands and expectations of family, school and community.

In this chapter, I would like to focus on an aspect of Moriarty and Toussieng's study which has not received wide recognition, but which is, nevertheless, I believe, worthy of close investigation. Specifically, their findings which demonstrate that many adolescents cope with the demands inherent to their developmental stage *by adopting a style of traditional conformity in which they fervently (though not blindly) follow the paths established by their parents, their school and their community.*

Moriarty and Toussieng investigated how adolescents cope with the demands of established family while at the same time experimenting with new values. In the next several pages, I shall discuss the two groups of young people who fit the mold of "traditional conformism." *These youngsters were divided into two groups, "The Obedient Traditionalists" and "The Ideological Conservatives."* Both groups tell us a great deal about adolescent conformity and how it can direct and shape personal identity.

The obedient traditionalists

The young people who embraced this coping style were easily the most other-directed, the most authoritarian, the least defiant, and the least questioning of all the subjects in this research project. As with any concept which categorizes individuals, a certain amount of definitional spillage must occur. However, in terms of their behavior, their attitudes and their beliefs, the obedient traditionalists were the most similar to one another of all the groups of adolescents in this study.

The defining feature of the conformism of the Obedient Traditionalists is *narrowness.* Their emotional tone is one of constraint, and their trademark is adapting to the expected and the conventional. In most regards, their style of coping, and their techniques of interaction, are highly authoritarian. They earnestly prefer social settings in which one valued person sets the tasks, prescribes the procedures, and judges the results without excessive participation of others in the decision process. In their religious beliefs and in their political ideology, they believe in authority as a primary source of truth, and as well, they tend to perceive the rejectors of authority as heretics who, in one way or another, will pay a price for their heresy.

These youngsters showed a strong bond to their family and to their community, and they strongly believed in the rightful authority of both. Their adherence did not seem to come from mere imitation; they *genuinely* identified with their community and its customs, and their respect for parents and tradition extended with remarkable consistency to their inner life.

The emotional life of obedient traditionalists is calmer than adolescents who are at odds with society — especially youngsters undergoing identity crises or negative identity. In the interviews which provided much of the data for this research, the obedient traditionalists described events they participated in, such as family vacation trips, with a remarkable "lack of detail and color, even though many of these young people are highly intelligent" (p. 11). They are consistently characterized by a low level of affectivity; they do not react easily, or naturally with feelings or emotions, and they do not, as a rule, carry with them the diffuse, free-floating feel of emotionality and exuberance typical of more passionate youngsters. Adolescents who adopted this coping strategy do not appear to be emotionally conflicted about their future. In fact, they do not appear to experience major conflict about anything, and in this regard they are quite different from many of their peers. (Most research conducted since the pioneer work of Moriarty and Tousseing, confirms the widespread existence of these conformist youth in the adolescent community).

In school, in the arena of peers, and in their relationship with teachers, these youngsters are solid, effective and well organized. They do not oppose school because their value system accords so well with it. They enjoy competition and accept matter-of-factly the basic capitalist tenet that competition produces both human and material excellence. As Moriatry and Tousseing observed: "Quite clearly, too, these youth welcome competition and savor their own excellence. At the same time, they are unpretentiously modest about their own accomplishments and particularly strive to avoid bragging." They avoid trouble at school because they tend to be conscientious, responsible, and to know the value of hard work.

The obedient traditionalists express their religiosity by attending church. The social aspects of church attendance impact them more than any other group of adolescents. The powerful, soul-shaping religious experiences reported by more passionate teens ("the religious moment") are rarely reported by these youngsters.

Their shallowness of religious emotion does not imply a lack of religious conviction, or a weak belief in the moral righteousness of their church. These young people are solid believers, but emotion does not invigorate their beliefs. It appears that they follow parental and religious standards because:

> They feel they are right, comfortable, and an asset in establishing a reputation for moral decency. They see no reason to question any of these standards or to move outside of tradition to experience solely for the sake of experiencing (p. 14).

Experience for the sake of experience is not a moving force in the lives of most Obedient Traditionalists, and this is but one of many features which sets them apart from more experience-centred peers. A wide range of insulators protects them not only from the storm and stress of adolescence, but from the anguish inherent to life in general. They are well armored, and even more to the point, their armor fits their personality and their life goals extremely well.

Although Obedient Traditionalists are as intelligent as any adolescent group, they tend not to be intellectual or introspective; they are not overly intrigued by intellectual concepts, by radical ideas, or even simply "things of the mind." Rather, "On topical issues requiring more reasoning and independent judgment, obedient traditionalists . . . often find it difficult to make more than vague, tentative, verbal formulations" (p. 15). (Part of this characteristic, however, is definitional since conventional adolescents who are more intellectual in their style are classified as "ideological conservatives." They are described shortly).

The avoidance of intellectual depths is paralleled by their avoidance of passionate emotional relationships. "They are less likely to seek, or to feel comfortable with special closeness or depth of feeling . . . they protect themselves from intense feelings of enthusiasm or ecstasy, as well as from disappointment or sadness in the event of loss" (p. 17). Many of the young people known as "obedient traditionalists," because of their emotional tightness and their behavioral narrowness, eventually evolve lifestyles that resemble what Anna Freud called "asceticism," and what Karen Horney called "excessive self-control."

In general, it is safe to say that these young people hold a solid pride in themselves and their community, showing high esteem for their own ability and positive regard for their community. They possess a firm, though narrowly entrenched sense of self worth, so much so that they tend to condemn notions of worth different from their own. Quite obviously, their self-image is positive, and, especially in their community of allegiance this positive sense of self is encouraged and rewarded by most of the adults they interact with.

Ideological conservatives

These youngsters share many features with obedient traditionalists, especially their tendency toward narrowness, emotional protectionism and adherence to the social order. The major differences between these conventional youth is that the ideological conservatives are *more intellectually able to formulate an ideology which explains and defends their attitudes.* "They differ from obedient traditionalists in the extent to which they vigorously develop and defend their chosen stance. They define their points of view more rigorously, pursue their goals with more determination, and are more often openly critical of views different from their own" (p. 37).

In "bull sessions," or in intellectual discussions, it is these youngsters who provide the intellectual justification for conformism to their less intellectual peers; and, it is they who defend intellectual conservatism before their more individualistic, anti-establishment peers. "Having forged definite credos out of their own logical thinking and personal convictions, they are able to offer more refined justifications for their beliefs, which are vitally and internally a part of their being" (p. 37).

These youngsters hold a firm and well developed sense of moral righteousness because, in their own minds, the justification for their narrow, traditional behavior is both richly and honestly defended.

> . . . they hold their opinions to be uncontroversial, absolute, and unquestionably right. Therefore, they often appear to be dogmatic, unspontaneous, and highly judgmental of persons who have less determination or self-control in personal behavior, or who are less clear about their own values (p. 37).

Their behavior is quite resistant to peer pressure, at least in areas where their ideology prevails, and they tend not to torment themselves over the appropriateness of their actions — which are endorsed by the authoritarian adults they interact with at home, at school and at church.

Among this group of conventional youth the real function of ideology is to defend the status quo, and, by implication, "me" who has so completely identified with it. Theirs is not a comprehensive ideology, although, in fairness, neither is that of most other adolescent groups. Ideology is the complex system of ideas, beliefs and attitudes that constitute an extensive philosophy or world view. In this usage of the word, "ideology" overstates the thinking of these youngsters. Their thought more closely resembles "intellectualization"; that is, the analysis of a problem in purely intellectual terms to the neglect of its emotional considerations. The real purpose of intellectualization is to formulate a conceptual fortress which defends one against the complexities of the larger world — not to build an ideology by which to better understand the larger world.

Ideology demands a certain degree of intellectual consistency, and perhaps more so than in any other group of teens, this consistency is maintained by selective perception, by seeing what one wants to see.

> In order to maintain such an uncompromising stance, the ideological conservatives have to curb and make special use of their often keen senses. If they allow themselves to observe all the facts, they may have difficulty in being as sure of what they believe as they regularly are, and wish to be (p. 3).

As we have previously observed in our analysis of foreclosed youth, of youth struggling to keep their world within manageable limits, and of youth whose thinking processes are monopolized by egocentrism, *stability is maintained by blinding oneself to unwanted or undesired perceptions while highlighting approved and sanctioned perceptions.*

> They have to use their perception . . . in a highly selective fashion, so that nothing will disturb their inner serenity. Thus, large areas of perception are blocked out completely, even when overwhelming evidence foists itself upon them (p. 38).

The intellect of "ideological conservatives" is subordinated to their ideological needs, consequently, their intellect is used as much to justify their beliefs as to honestly and openly investigate them. They are remarkably vulnerable to propaganda which supports their beliefs, and virtually immune to propaganda which contradicts it. Ideological Conservatives represent one very important subset of youth destined to become the "Idealistic Reformers" described in the Chapter Three.

In the social sphere these youngsters are more self-assured than many of their peers, partly because they possess an intellectual competence which renders clarity to their social world, and partly because their beliefs so thoroughly match those of the school and family power structure. As well, they manifest a commendable self-discipline as exemplified by their effective management of their daily conduct, the control of their impulses, and their habit of controlling present behavior for future satisfactions.

They believe in their community and they aspire to be leaders in it; they accept the prestige that comes from adult approval and they actively pursue it. They tend to delay onset of dating, to keep emotional investments low key, and to prefer friends who are wholesome and morally strict. As well, they are likely to disapprove of smoking, drinking, and use of drugs for reasons which usually include: damage to the body, interference with their personal ambitions, needless expense, or conflict with parental or religious injunctions.

Their ability to extend (through philosophy and theology) the concepts of God and Worship which they learned as children make them less reliant upon ritualized church attendance, and in this regard, they differ from the obedient traditionalists for whom religious belief without church attendance seems blasphemous. As a result, they "are less constant in attending church and performing religious ritual and are less likely to use their religion habitually for social outlets or for parental approval than the latter" (p.43).

In conclusion, research conducted during the past three decades supports the observation that many young people are conformists in both the narrow and the broad sense of that term.

In this chapter, I have attempted to describe some of the defining characteristics of two groups of conformist youth: the obedient traditionalists and the ideological conservatives. These youth demonstrate to us, in a very literal way, that the identity project of all young people is not confused by identity crises, by negative identity, by hostile confrontations with society, or even by fundamental differences with parents. For many adolescents, conformity is the heart and soul of the identity project.

chapter thirteen

Turning Points in Identity

Truthful moments in unfolding selfhood

The ideas and attitudes that young people hold about themselves exist in the fluid world between permanence and change, and as such, they possess alternating and not always predictable qualities. Precious little is etched in stone, and even that is etched tentatively rather than boldly. If during adolescence, change and tentativeness are the reality, permanence and firmness are the goals. Thus, whether we speak of self-concept, personal identity or gender definition, during adolescence, each of these exist as transformative concepts. For most teens, these changes occur not in random forays, but in a dialectic of progression-consolidation-progression with occasional episodes of regression.

Experiences which hold the power to change the course of a young person's life are what Anselm Strauss calls "turning points." These truthful moments, whether subtle or brutal, precipitate vital changes in how young people think about themselves, and as such, they are experiences from which youth emerge a "person different." And, as far as identity is concerned, nothing is more important than an event which causes a person to become someone different. The differentness may be for the better, or for the worse; it may bring pride or shame. It does, however, always bring change. And change is what adolescent identity is all about.

A turning point need not be a crisis, but all crises are turning points. As used in this chapter, a turning point is more subtle than a crisis. Buying an automobile may be a turning point, crashing it may be a crisis; joining a gang which does drugs may be a turning point, injecting heroin may cause a crisis. Turning points have life-changing consequences, but they come from ordinary human realities easily observed in the day to day life of young people everywhere.

Some turning points occur as the result of reaching important milestones (what David Elkind calls "markers"). As when a teenager graduates from high school, or is named to the official roster of the hockey team, or experiences first sexual intercourse. A young women, described for me one of her adolescent turning points:

> One day I will certainly never forget is the day I got my first menstrual period. I told my mother and as her eyes filled with tears she said I was all grown up — I was a woman now! Wow! That very experience changed the way I thought about myself and throughout adolescence I struggled with trying to be a new me!

Other turning points occur with an unexpected change in legal or social status, as when a sixteen-year-old is informed by the health clinic that she is pregnant, or when a government letter informs a nineteen-year-old he is now a soldier. Turning points force us to take stock of a new status, and to reassess things in general, but even more importantly, they require us to re-assess and reinterpret ourselves, our goals, our identities.

Many of the "turning points" which cause us to change the path of our identity are not public events, rather they are private experiences which initiate a new way of looking at the world, and even more importantly, how "I" fit in this new world. I refer to these as "psychological" turning points.

Psychological turning points in adolescent identity

Meeting a challenge. Whether self-imposed or imposed by others, meeting important challenges may signal to the person that he or she is now slightly more, slightly better than before. Making it through "death week" in football season, passing an audition for a role in the school play, or being accepted into a formerly inaccessible gang, are all challenges met; and upon being met the person, in some measure, is greater for it. It is the element of being "greater" that nurtures not only one's identity, but also one's sense of rightness about oneself. Identity is measured by living up to certain standards; meeting challenges is one way teens confirm to themselves that they are able to meet family, societal and personal standards.

Meeting a temptation may also promote a new or more expanded image of oneself. Strauss summarizes the significance of such an achievement: "One potent form of self test is the deliberate courting of temptation. Failure to resist it is usually followed by new tests or by yielding altogether" (p. 96). When one masters a formerly irresistible temptation, growth is signalled. The person now exists in a different relationship to the object of temptation, and in a different relationship to the self. An enticement that cannot be resisted proves that the individual is "lesser" than the temptation; mastery proves the opposite.

A hallmark of mature identity is the belief that one can handle temptation. (Talk to any social worker about this. The consistent feature of street youth, of virtually all adolescent alcoholics and drug abusers, is their inability to handle temptation, and their conviction *that they do not possess the ability to resist temptation,* whatever, the temptation may be.)

Accepting personal inconsistencies. When a boy thinks of himself as fair and reasoned yet knows that he is a wide-eyed fanatic in the sports arena, he experiences conflicting images of himself. This conflict does not derive from a neurotic split in his personality, but rather from different responses to different demands from different circumstances. This matter is of special importance to younger adolescents because to them it is confusing to recognize what appear to be irreconcilable opposites within themselves. That they hate their mother on Monday and bake her a birthday cake on Tuesday; design a professional career on Wednesday and decide to drop out of school on Thursday. This makes Friday a fearful proposition.

Recognizing the conflicting aspects within one's own personality creates a perplexing realization, namely, that one aspect of identity prevents another from being actualized.

> When a child begins to look at himself or herself as having stable character-
> istics and no longer as a series of actions, the realization becomes possible
> that some of these stable tendencies are an obstacle to the realization of other
> traits he or she may desire to have. In this case, there is self-inconsistency:
> when a trait is a part of a person's self-definition or of his or her ideal self,
> when a second trait interferes with the actualization of the first, and when
> the person could eliminate the conflict but prefers to do nothing (Blasi &
> Oresik, p. 73).

Self-inconsistencies do not cause identity crises. They do, however, make clear the extent to which the self is out of sync with itself, and they also generate anxiety and frustration which younger adolescents perceive as a serious malady when, as a rule, it is not.

Role excellence. When a young person performs a new but important role with unexpected excellence, and thereby confronts the potential in a completely new form, a turning point in development is underway. Such achievements cause the young person to think "I am greater than I thought." A parallel example occurs when the adolescent surpasses someone held in high esteem, such as an older brother or sister, or, even more importantly, mother or father. Or, as frequently occurs in adolescent romance, when one discovers an emotional maturity or depth that he or she knows the partner can neither equal nor nourish. When the adolescent's loyalty to the parent, or the lover, is powerful, surpassing them may actually encourage retreat from the adolescent's own excellence. Since self-assessment is greatly influenced by *comparative* skills, *comparative* intelligence, *comparative* beauty, special dilemmas are posed when we actually go beyond not only what we were, but beyond the very standards of comparison upon which our identity is based. Such advances, and there are many of them during adolescence, effect not only how we evaluate ourselves, but also how we evaluate those who evaluate us. Few things are more relevant to identity. Worthy of special mention here are those youth who, for essentially unknown reasons, walk away from, deny, refuse to take ownership of their own excellence. It is as if their own excellence threatens their identity by creating possibilities or options beyond the brittle boundaries of their narrow self-definition. This phenomenon is not based on the fear of failure, quite the contrary. It is the fear of excellence, and the fear of having to change one's self-concept in order to accommodate to this very excellence.

Role reversals. Another turning point occurs when one looks forward to, even relishes, roles or activities that were formerly viewed with suspicion or disdain. Here again the turning point may be pleasurable or painful. The adolescent girl who fantasizes erotically about her new boyfriend, who con-trives ways to meet with him alone, who skips school in the afternoon to be with him, may not know how to identify the creature she has become. Only a few months ago she despised girls who engaged in sex, scolded girlfriends who skipped school to be with boys, and was altogether disbelieving that sexual desires could wield such force. Here again we observe that the shock of unexpected change does not throw the teenager into disrepair, but it does demand recuperation time *and a new way of looking at oneself.* Perhaps it will require her to revise how she views her morality, her behavior, her attitudes toward sex and sexuality. Then again, she may simply put these contradictions on the back burner and let them simmer. Living with the edgy nervousness of self-contradiction is, in an experiment-oriented youth culture such as ours, simply a fact of life. Nevertheless, these moments of looking at oneself in a new way, these instances of self-contradiction each play their role in the accumulation of self-knowledge and in the eventual formation of one's per-sonal identity.

Developmental friendships. Developmental friendships are bondings in which one friend has special qualities needed for the wholesome development of the other. Not only do developmental friendships satisfy the need for togetherness and loyalty, but they also nurture growth in a way ordinary friendships cannot. They are perfectly suited for adolescent friendships where each partner has immaturities which need the strength and guidance of a friend not equally limited. For many young people developmental friendships usher in a higher level of personal integration — a significant turning point in their maturing process. Here Peter Madison describes such a friendship taken from the case studies he has made of this topic:

> Fred had certain qualities particularly lacking in Bob and required by him for his own development. Two of these qualities are prominent: Fred's interest in and evaluation of ideas and all that we mean by the "liberal arts" in education and his freedom to oppose and criticize authority. Bob was badly in need of being opened up to intellectual, cultural and human values and freed from the overly technical and materialistic outlook he had on education when he came to college. Bob needed to break out of the constraints of parental obligation and to oppose such authority. Fred was an expert at rebellion (p. 117-118).

Most 40-year-olds remember well their best adolescent friends. (Many, in fact, remain as best friends.) At no time in life are friends more vital to emotional well-being than during adolescence. To have an intimate comrade on your side of the struggle, to share exhilarations, is important for all of us, but especially for (as one adolescent girl described herself) "a lonely, struggling soul, scratching on alien terrain."

Developmental friendships have special herbal powers, fortifying emotional strength in a way ordinary friendships cannot. This strength nourishes and encourages the solid identity every adolescent strives for.

Betrayal. The opposite of the helpful enhancement embraced within a developmental friendship is the bitter reversal of betrayal. Betrayal hits young people with such crunching force that it shakes their faith in friends and friendships, especially when it comes from a parent, a hero or a loved one. Betrayal may come from abandonment, as when a friend deserts you or simply forgets you exist; or in the form of rejection, as when excluded (symbolically or physically) by peers, parents or teachers.

Betrayal hits the adolescent with greater emotional devastation than most other "turning points" for several reasons. First, betrayal opens the spillgates of an anxiety dammed since infancy — the fear of separation, "separation anxiety." Many psychoanalysts, especially John Bowlby and his followers, believe that separation anxiety is the deepest and the darkest of all our deep, dark fears. To be betrayed is to be cut off, separated, in a way that resurrects the painful childhood fears of losing mother or father. Second, betrayal casts into doubt one's desirability, for, by definition, one is desired less than that for which one is betrayed. But even more importantly, it confirms (at least for the moment) that one is not loveable, and as, Polansky has stated "the issue of being lovable is of tremendous importance to the human psyche" (p. 53).

In her study of adolescent runaways who end up as street kids (becoming a runaway is one of the gravest behavioral turning points in our culture) Webber discovered several common threads which connect the backgrounds, attitudes and desires of street kids. Significantly, "Betrayal is the most common experience among them . . . many street youths feel profoundly betrayed by significant adults, usually one or both parents, or surrogate parents assigned by the state . . . " (1990, p. 28).

Betrayal is insult on a grand scale. How its pain is negotiated may represent a turning point in the way a young person protects, discloses and shares himself or herself. Betrayal clouds over all future relationships, especially when formed by the storms of adolescence. Paradoxically, it is often the pain of betrayal which entrenches respect for loyalty and allegiance in the adolescent's value system.

BEHAVIORAL TURNING POINTS IN ADOLESCENT IDENTITY

The turning points discussed thus far can be thought of as "psychological" experiences which influence identity formation. They carry considerable force, yet, they are most assuredly not the only turning points to change the direction of a young life.

I would like to shift the focus from psychological turning points to "behavioral" turning points, even though while doing so I recognize that behavior is never completely separate from its psychological correlates. This shift is necessary because, in our culture, certain behavioral options, when exercised, exact a profound toll on the adolescent's entire life. When these turning points occur the adolescent takes a turn which, in many instances, paralyzes identity. That is to say, these turning points actually shape and mold the person, an absolutely devastating blow to the identity process. Two of the most critical behavioral turning points in our culture are: becoming pregnant, and dropping out of school.

Teenage Pregnancy

There are no illegitimate children — only illegitimate parents.
L.R. Yankwich, U.S. District Judge (1928)

Pregnancy, quite obviously, is a behavioral turning point of profound significance; for some youngsters it becomes the single most important event in their entire adolescent identity project.

The perplexity surrounding our current understanding of teen pregnancy is given candid summary by Ginzberg (1988), who after an exhaustive investigation into prevention and intervention strategies concerning teen pregnancy, surmised: "The search for effective interventions is *seriously compromised by the scarcity of knowledge about the determinants* of individual adolescent behavior." And, even though we know the incidence of teen sexuality at virtually every developmental level, we have no clear understanding why teens engage in sexual intercourse in the first place, or why they often make no attempt to prevent pregnancy. Nor do we understand why teens invent, then cling to, irrational or absurd beliefs concerning pregnancy; especially the near-universal fable "It can never happen to me."

(As I have attempted to demonstrate throughout this book, the adolescent thought process is prone toward self-serving, egocentric conclusions whenever vital "self" issues such as sexual intercourse, pregnancy or child-rearing are concerned.)

In our culture it is rare to think of a fifteen-year-old female as a woman unless she is pregnant or a mother. In all other phases of her existence, in her schooling, and in virtually all of her interpersonal interactions, she is thought of either as a teen, or as a girl. Pregnancy provides instant womanhood, and some theorists believe this, unto itself, is an incentive for pregnancy.

Among women aged fifteen to nineteen, pregnancy is increasingly prevalent. From a base of 95 per 1,000 in 1972, the rate increased to 111 per 1,000 in 1981, and the evidence suggests that the climb is continuing. About 45 percent of teen pregnancies terminate in medical abortion, and some 5 to 6 percent in miscarriages (Ginsberg, p. 72).

Mothers under age fifteen experience a rate of maternal deaths two and one half times that of mothers aged 20-24. Teen mothers also have a higher rate of nonfatal complications than non-teen mothers; the younger the mother the higher the risk for such complications of pregnancy as toxemia, anemia, prolonged labor, and premature labor; teen mothers are 92 percent more likely to have anemia, 23 percent more likely to experience premature birth than mothers in their 20s.

The babies of teen age mothers also face severe risks beginning before birth. Teenage pregnancies more frequently end in miscarriage and stillbirths than pregnancies of older women. Babies born to teenagers are more likely to be premature, to have low birth weights, to have low Apgar scores, and to die within the first month and within the first year. Low birth weight contributes to cerebral palsy, mental retardation, epilepsy and is a major cause of infant mortality. The Carnegie Council on Adolescent Development (1989) reports that total medical costs for low-birthweight infants average $400,000. (By the time you read these figures they will be much higher).

The behavior patterns of teens contribute to their own poor health, and to the poor health of their babies. In the words of a mid-wife who works with teens, "They do not eat nutritional foods . . . junk foods, lots of Coca Cola and soda." And while it is widely observed that pregnant teens who do take advantage of the prenatal care available to them do produce healthier babies than those who do not, many teens simply will not, without great prompting and reassurance, look after their own prenatal needs, or the needs of their fetus (Moore, p. 19-20).

It is, of course, not really necessary to document the fact that many youngsters are psychologically and morally immature; it is virtually impossible for them to be otherwise in a society where all important work and responsibility is reserved for adults. But this immaturity is never more painfully evident than when it is confronted with raising a child. As one thirteen-year-old mother said, describing her reactions to her newborn child:

> You know, sometimes I look at him and he don't seem like he's mine. I guess I'm not used to him yet. Even in the hospital, right after he was born he didn't seem like he was mine. It's hard to think he's what I had in me for nine months. After he came out of me, the doctor put him on my stomach. 'Get that messy thing off me!' I yelled at that doctor. Maybe he don't seem like he's mine 'cause he can't talk yet. Now, my little cousin, he's different. He's three years old and he seems like he's mine, but he ain't. It's funny, I know he ain't a baby doll, but he don't yet seem like he's a real baby, like my cousin. He's sorta in between (Frank, 1983, p. 54).

The adult years following teen pregnancy

The impact of teen motherhood is dramatically summarized by Arthur Campbell:

> The girl who has an illegitimate child at the age of sixteen suddenly has 90 percent of her life script written for her. She will probably drop out of school; even if someone else in her family helps to take care of the baby, she will probably not be able to find a steady job that pays enough to provide for herself and her child; she may feel impelled to marry someone she might not otherwise have chosen. Her life choices are few, and most of them are bad.

By age 29 about 50 percent of women who had their first child as a teen had obtained a high school diploma, while over 95 percent of those who did not have their first child until after age twenty had obtained a high school diploma. Mothers without a high school diploma are twice as likely to live in households receiving Aid to Families with Dependent Children. Women whose first child was born in their adolescence produce more children in their lifetime than women whose first child was born after adolescence.

Teenage mothers pose a substantial cost to the state in welfare payments alone. "A major source of new applications/acceptance on welfare rolls is the young teenage mother who, in the absence of a wage-earning male, frequently has no other source of income to cover living expenses for her child and herself" (Ginsberg, p. 30). A significant factor for teen mothers is longevity: "Although many adults who go onto the rolls leave within a relatively brief time (less than two years), many teenage mothers remain for a decade if not longer" (Ginzberg, p. 30). The Carnegie Council (1989) reports that the United States spent more than $19 billion in 1987 in payments for income maintenance, health care and nutrition to support families begun by teenagers.

Dropouts

In a single purpose moratorium such as the one we presently have in place in North America, the fulcrum upon which successs pivots is the school system. Success within the school system does not guarantee success, but failure in school virtually guarantees failure outside school.

By abandoning access to certified (credentialed) work, dropouts drastically reduce their ability to support themselves or contribute to society at large. Our society simply does not have any effective ways whatsoever (as of 1992) to channel the dropout into economic self-sufficiency. Opportunities are for "stay-ins" not drop-outs.

Reasons for dropping out of high school, quite obviously, vary from person to person. However, one of the leading investigators of this topics concluded that the primary reasons for dropping out of school prior to graduation include the following:

1. boredom with what goes on in the classroom;
2. lack of understanding of the value of a diploma for later job prospects;
3. absence of family encouragement to complete high school;
4. the lure of the street and one's peers; (Ginsberg, p. 28).

Counting dropouts in North America is not an easy matter. No uniform method for counting, or even determining what a dropout is, exists in Canada or the United States. Administrators claim to follow specified procedures when they calculate the annual number of dropouts, but their statistics are not always accurate, and their methods of calculating the dropout rate vary from year to year and from school to school. In Chicago, students who leave school before graduating are classified into 19 separate "leave codes," only one of which is called "drop out." Other leave codes include "lost—not coming to school," "needed at home," "married" and "cannot adjust."

Numbers, of course, cannot lie, but their "crunchers" can. School funding is based on average daily attendance, thus dropouts deny the school needed revenue; however, a ghost student on the class roster, but not in the classroom, brings in vital school dollars. Dropout rates in most cities are tabulated annually. "Thus, if fifteen percent of a high school freshman class drops out in a given year, the official dropout rate is put at fifteen percent. Yet, four years later when the students gather in the school auditorium to receive their diplomas, only half of the original class may still be in school"(Hahn, 1987, p. 261).

A practical course is to ask the dropouts themselves. This, too yields blurred data. Many reasons are given by dropouts for dropping out, including: poor grades, dislike for school, distance from peers, marriage, jobs. *The most common reasons for dropping out of school are poor academic performance and pregnancy.* Over forty percent of dropouts reported grades of mostly Ds in school. Only about thirteen percent of the males and about eight percent of the females claimed they dropped out to help support their family. (Some studies report the incidence as low as three percent in this category).

Just as high achieving kids have a wide range of reasons for school success, dropouts have a wide range of reasons for failing. In one study of New York City youth, about one-third blamed themselves, another third their home life, and another third the schools. What is more clear:

> Young people at risk of dropping out resist the social control, competition, and order that characterize classrooms. In the High School and Beyond survey, one in five male dropouts indicated they couldn't get along with their teachers; more than one in 10 had been expelled or suspended (Hahn, 1987).

Fuhrmann (1990, p. 168) suggests that school dropouts, as a group, have the following distinguishing features: poor family relationships, a history of truancy, trouble with authority, friends who are dropouts, parents with low educational achievement. As well, dropouts are more impulsive, complain of a greater number of bodily ailments, have low occupational aspirations and have trouble keeping jobs once obtained.

From the available research it is virtually impossible to isolate "most important" variables. Some educators give greatest weight to data showing that dropouts are behind grade in reading, that they are likely to have already failed one grade, and that they dropout in direct ratio to their low scholastic ranks (Conger, 1984, p. 423). Others are more impressed with data indicating that dropouts are characterized by low self-esteem and poorly structured goals. Or that these youth are more influenced by frustrations from which they are trying to escape than by longer-term goals toward which they are striving.

These adolescents tend to live more for the moment, responding impulsively, planning little, showing little sustained, goal-directed activity and seeking immediate gratification.

Turning points versus Breaking points

The turning points of pregnancy and dropout hold profound significance for adolescent identity because the freezing of life options paralyzes the quest for mature identity. When self-definition fixates inwards, losing its social and communal components, it, in effect, is stunted. An identity turned inward upon itself becomes increasingly narcissistic and self-serving, and decreasingly allocentric and other-serving. Identity really amounts to little more than "survivalism."

The "character development" our society is so urgently trying to cultivate in youth involves many things, but inherent to it is the sharing of oneself, one's abilities and one's resources. Mature identity cannot take hold in the fledgling adolescent until giving, as well as receiving, has been ingrained into the character. The significant feature of identities molded by "breaking points" such as pregnancy or dropping out of school, is that identity becomes channeled into a frightened and protective self, resulting in the relentless pursuit of consumer goods, and a narcissistic obsession with self-indulgence rather than social participation. The end result: stunted personal identity and fragmented social identity.

chapter fourteen

Further Issues in Adolescent Identity

In the preceding chapters, I have described several critical components to the adolescent identity project, starting with the basic ingredients to a healthy identity. As we subsequently discovered, there are many variations to the basic identity themes: hostile negative identity; crises within the identity process; conformity and conformism; and, psychological and behavioral turning points in the journey toward identity formation.

In this final chapter, I would like discuss three final concepts which, in my opinion, do not receive sufficient attention in contemporary discussions of adolescent identity. The first concerns the *relationship between worth and identity*, especially the relationship which binds worthwhile actions with healthy identity and worthless actions with diminished identity. The second concerns the extent to which young people in our culture spend so much time *trying to prove themselves in games and gamesmanship*. The third concerns the extent to which young people, especially those whose lives are invested in worthless activities and excessive gamesmanship, *experience alienation —the subversion of identity*.

WORTH AND THE ADOLESCENT IDENTITY QUEST

Adolescence is not a good time of life for feeling worthwhile about oneself. In North American culture, this is primarily due to three general circumstances interlaced with the youth paradox. First, little opportunity exists for youth to engage in worthwhile work or to participate in inherently meaningful activity. Second, the youth culture itself is based on a shallow superficiality which is often riddled with hypocrisy and high egocentrism. Third, the public school, in which youth spend their daylight hours, like most institutional settings, rewards conformity and uniformity.

It is important to recognize that when young people do not possess a solid sense of their own worth they tend to think poorly (not neutrally) of themselves. Youngsters low in self-worth tend to resent themselves with the same matter-of-factness with which they resent other unworthy people. This lived sense of worthlessness is most prevalent among those who make no important differences in their interpersonal world. As far as adolescence is concerned, dignified self-worth is inseparable from real actions.

> In this children cannot be fooled by empty praises and condescending encouragement. They may have to accept artificial bolstering of their self-esteem in lieu of something better, but what I call their accruing ego identity gains real strength only from wholehearted and consistent recognition of real accomplishment, *that is, achievement that has meaning in their culture* (Erikson, 1959, p. 88, my italic).

And yet, if what Erikson suggests is true, that adolescence is the period during which the individual must acquire certain skills and insights in order to negotiate the demands of parenthood, occupation, and selfhood, it is equally true that the entire preparation process is contingent upon two key factors: the parent society's willingness to provide opportunities for growth, and the youth's desire to attain adult status. The transformation from child to adult is sabotaged when young people believe that society is simply unworthy of their efforts.

When any minority group is denied access to legitimate accomplishment or genuine achievement the public attitude toward that group deteriorates. As the ability to involve oneself in important work lessens so also does the ability to earn social esteem. Two inevitable outcomes flow from this: the oppressed group disaffiliates from the larger group; the oppressed group invents its own standards of worth.

We are confused about the nature of worth and its relationship to youth partly because our entire culture has trouble distinguishing the worthwhile from the worthless, but even more so, because we have infantilized adolescents so much we have lost sight of how they differ from children. We think that if we provide them with affection and love, their sense of worth will flourish. This is not so. (When love and affection are given to children it does enhances their sense of worth because, for children, worth is based upon received love. Adolescents require much more). For adolescents, giving and receiving love or affection satisfies only their needs for love and affection. Worth during adolescence (and, in this regard, it differs significantly from childhood) is *based upon doing not upon receiving*. In more elementary form: youth must do things of worth to possess feelings of worth. Genuine actions produce genuine worth; counterfeit actions produce counterfeit worth.

Worthwhile Work

Worthwhile work contributes to the important events of one's life. When completed it leaves the worker with a feeling of having done something important. It draws upon legitimate talents. Worthwhile work can also be understood in terms of what it is not. It is not work where one worker replaces another without noticeable loss; it is not work where the worker does not know to what end or purpose labor is directed; it is not work where pay is the singular motive.

Young people are intrigued with worthwhile work because they want to think of themselves as worthwhile and they do not, except of necessity, coldly detach themselves from the outcome of work. They are inherently geared to invest themselves in their work; this is but one of many benefits inherent to their egoism and narcissism. Since the work available is rarely worthwhile, adolescents cultivate cynicism to buffer the resentment which inevitably accompanies meaningless work. There is no pride in undignified work — there never has been. It simply does not enlist worthwhile capacities, it is not interesting, it isn't useful.

Once young people become convinced that "work" really means worthless work (bear in mind that the vast majority of young people have never held a worthwhile job) they quickly learn substitutes for achieving their sense of worthwhileness. For most youth, self-worth eventually becomes entrenched in these substitutions, and the quality of these substitutions goes a long way toward defining the quality of their personal identity.

Several things should be made clear. Youth are not entitled to the "best" jobs in our society; neither should they be exempt from jobs requiring tedious labor; neither should they be paid more than they deserve for their work. To insist otherwise is nonsense.

Youth are not the only ones who suffer from the lack of worthwhile work. As psychiatric literature attests, job-related problems are at the heart of most adult pathology. Our intent is not to slight adult variations of work pathology. Our concern here is with young people in modern North American society and the problems they encounter in attaining a decent sense of self-worth. And, perhaps even more importantly, the consequences which accrue to society and to young people themselves when they are unable to develop a sense of their own worth. These consequences include: an emotional tone of neutralism and a moral tone of ethical indifference; early-resignation, and paralytic cynicism; an obsession with instantness, especially instant gratification; a minimal sense of history or time connectedness; and, the robotic pursuit of material goods. And finally, perhaps of greatest economic consequence to society-at-large are youngsters who sense of unworth contributes to the likelihood that they will become school dropouts or that they will become pregnant. In a society which has become increasingly aware of the fiscal price paid for the disaffection of our youth, this represents a "worth" predicament of immense proportions.

All youth problems, quite obviously, do not derive from lack of worthwhile work. However, all youth problems are aggravated by it and all solutions to youth troubles are impeded by it. It is easy to devise worthwhile work which youth would naturally gravitate toward and which, at the same time, would prove greatly beneficial to society. The great farms of this continent, the ancient forests, and the million streams, rivers, and lakes are natural productive laboratories for working people of all ages. Government and private industry could gainfully utilize millions of workers in urgently needed ecological projects.

The strategies for making honest work available to eager youth are beyond the scope of this book. The task here is to demonstrate the legitimacy of designing strategies for coping with this problem and to point out some of the consequences of failing to do so.

What then can we conclude?

First, that a lack of purpose results in an impaired ability to prepare for the future, an unwillingness to commit oneself to action or belief, and, perhaps most critical to youth, a lessened capacity to cope with the day to day pressures of normal existence. Without a passable sense of purpose adolescents are far more likely to surrender to the depersonalization of school or to the manipulations of peer puppeteers, and to the obsessive craving for material goods.

Second, the absence of a worthy identity fosters boredom, which unto itself, nourishes a wide range of emotional disturbances since it contributes to both moral disenchantment and behavioral disengagement.

Third, the ways youth come to identify their own sense of worth is contaminated by the artificial measuring sticks we provide for them. For many young people worth is based on what they wear, what they display. (As one commentator put it: "I buy, therefore, I am"). The painful outcome is a demeaning cycle in which young people pursue meaningless work so that they may purchase essentially worthless goods in order to bolster an artificial sense of worth.

GAMES, GAMESMANSHIP AND PROVING ONESELF

Most humans beings today waste some twenty-five to
thirty years of their lives before they break through the
actual and conventional lies which surround them.

Isadora Duncan

Games represent one of the few means by which adolescents can transform their routine of insignificance into events of importance. When youth cannot find important, meaningful activity they invent games of *reduced* expressions. These expressions I call "game proof" because their real purpose is to prove worth.

Honest work and dignified involvement are extremely difficult for adolescents to attain, even for those who persistently pursue them. Youth in our culture don't have too much opportunity to say of anything important: "I am responsible for that." They live in a world where recognition, acceptance, or acknowledgment derives, in very large measure, from participation in games, or game-like activities, or interpersonal relationships consumed more by gamesmanship than honest relatedness. As Musgrove (1964) stated in his landmark essay on youth in modern society, the young in our in our society are:

playing furiously at adult games but resolutely confined to a society of their own peers and excluded from serious and responsible participation in the world of their elders.

Many youth simply lose sight of the fact (some of the younger ones never see it in the first place) that they are involved in games. Not only are they lured by the hope of obtaining a certain amount of recognition but, after playing the game long enough, they actually come to evaluate their own worth in terms of their game performance. Once their identity is defined, or even greatly influenced by, games, they lose contact with that inner resource which impels a more dignified self assertion. The entire sequence holds significant consequences for the formation of healthy identity, and the seeming lack of it among so many young adults.

Games are not inherently wrong; but when they sidetrack normal growth, or replace it with artificial goals and ambitions, they are in essence, socially sanctioned forms of self-diminution.

In the course of time, if challenges are stern enough, social praise powerful enough, and the game complex enough, the adolescent comes to define himself or herself in terms of the very games which were originally invented simply to fill a void. When this lock occurs, defining oneself in terms of a game less substantive and less worthwhile than oneself, young people come to think of themselves, and encourage others to think likewise, in terms of rituals and performances. The self, hungry for proof of itself, settles for this exchange, not recognizing the stage is set for one game replacing another, each of which encourages self-definition via game competency.

Games, obviously, are not the true issue. They are clutched to lessen the pain of living in a community where adolescents are not taken seriously, are not accorded much respect, and are given little chance to act with impact. Embroiled in a social arena governed by game proof rather than person proof, young people quickly discover that they must play or get out. When they opt to play they are proclaiming, whether consciously or not, that they are willing to exchange their natural impulse for genuine assertion for the learned desire to pursue gamesmanship.

For adolescents to admit that some of their games are not really tests of skill, endurance or courage, and, rather, that they often are nothing more than juvenile contrivances, only robs them of what they most desperately crave: self-affirmation, self-validation, and self-worth. Hence, they rarely admit to themselves or to others that their games are merely games.

In teen society, peers are the only game in town. Youth are the players, the school is the playing field and adults the referees. It is a predicament of growing up found in every moratorium culture.

> As schools get larger, as they come to embrace more and more of the students' lives, as the power of their elders to dictate to them is weakened, and as their interactions with adults become fewer and more attenuated, young people are thrown more and more upon their age-mates for stimulation, for status, for satisfying social relationships, and for companionship in whatever activities, serious or trivial, they choose to pursue (Musgrove, p. 29).

The weaker one registers upon the real world, the greater the need to prove oneself in the contrived world, hence, marginal adolescents who make no impact on the real world are prime candidates for game proof. Conversely, adolescents who are taken seriously by adults, who hold important responsibilities, however defined, are less inclined to exchange genuine proof for game proof.

Adults, of course, hold a vested interest in the petty games of the adolescent community. They perpetuate smallness and reward the adolescent for not trying to become involved in the exclusivity of adult significance. Being seduced into games confirms for adults that teenagers are not yet ready for responsible roles. Adults fully understand, whether they speak it aloud or not, that when permitted to do important work adolescents, for all intents and purposes, cease to be adolescents.

A brief comment to the reader: Over the years some of my students have pointed out that the word "game" holds a specific meaning to many individuals, especially those conversant with Berne's school of Transactional Analysis. And, as well, to those people who use the term "game" in a colloquial sense to convey the idea of "playing the game," that is, to act according to unwritten rules, or to behave as required by custom.

In Transactional Analysis, a game may be viewed as an "ongoing series of complementary ulterior transactions progressing to a well defined end"—even when that end is not in the best interests of the player. The outcome to such games is rather predictable, and is called the game's *payoff*. A payoff consists of bad feelings for each of the players from having been downgraded or discounted. "Examples of such bad feelings might include the sadness of the Victim, the malice and triumph of the Persecutor, the concern of the Rescuer." And, finally, as far as the games of transactional analysis are concerned, "Even though it may have started smoothly, the games ends with a payoff unpleasant for all involved. The true aims of the game are masked" (Polansky, p. 194).

Several of these ideas are pertinent to adolescent games, but the emphasis in transactional analysis on the psychological origins of games is too strong for our immediate purposes. Many adolescent games, to be sure, are characterized by styles which resemble the Victim, the Persecutor and the Rescuer. In my understanding of adolescent games, however, the focus is more upon *the social conditions which necessitates the invention of the games in order for young people to validate themselves.*

An important parallel with transactional analysis, however, is our shared belief that one of the primary motivations for adolescent games is the need to be "stroked." That is, to be recognized, praised or admired by the peer group. As here discussed, however, "games" are not intended as a parallel concept to the concept of script, so effectively popularized by transactional analysis. A script is "the life plan that someone wishes to carry out, or believes he is fated to carry out; it is likely to be largely unconscious" (Polansky, p. 195). Adolescent games are less psychologically determined than scripts, and their purpose is more of an attempt to address the satisfaction of an unsatisfied need, than the acting out of an unconscious impulse.

In essence, game proof, is the means by which the adolescent attempts to prove himself or herself to an outside world which is unconcerned with this very adolescent.

ALIENATION: THE SUBVERSION OF IDENTITY

There are certain times and occasions in this strange mixed affair we call life
when a man can take his whole universe for a vast practical joke.

Herman Melville

For the most part, when writers, teachers or parents use the term "alienation" in relation to adolescence, they are referring to a rather specific form of
"self-alienation." That is, to the condition in which the young person is out of
touch with his or her own emotional needs, in which thoughts, inclinations and
yearnings are blocked from awareness, and, in which important capacities are
never actualized. This form of self-alienation is what Branden (1983) has
labeled "the disowned self," a form of self-separation in which we "cease to
recognize our body, our emotions, our thoughts, our attitudes, our aspirations,
our abilities as ours. We thus radically restrict and impoverish our sense of
self" (p. 141).

Self-alienation distances the self from itself.

We have less access to our inner signals, and consequently we become more
dependent on signals from others. We need others to tell us what to think,
how to live, when to express which emotion, what is appropriate and what
is inappropriate, and so forth. By ourselves, we barely exist; our sense of self
is often reduced to little more than a sense of anxiety. In such a state of
self-alienation, we are prone to becoming approval addicts, love addicts,
group-membership addicts, system and structure addicts, belief-system addicts, guru and leader addicts, escape from pain/inner emptiness/anxiety
addicts (Branden, 1983, p. 141).

Of the psychodynamic psychologists, Karen Horney drew the most explicit
parallels between alienation and psychological disturbance. To Horney "self-
alienation" described the state in which the person feels that his or her self is
illusory and unreal. In essence, alienation signals a shift in consciousness away
from one's "real" self with a resultant loss of cohesion and togetherness. It is
not as profound as "self-extinction" which Horney saw as a form of neurotic
behavior in which the person retains no sense of their personality as a
self-experiencing, self-directive entity. In self-extinction one endeavors to live
through the lives of others, seeing oneself only as a reflection of others.

Alienation is not described uniformly by psychologists because it contains
moral, psychological and social ingredients, the relative strength of which are
disputed. Harry Stack Sullivan, the eminent psychoanalyst, described alienation as the estrangement from "significant others." Kenneth Keniston (whose
greatest insights were directed toward young adults rather than adolescents)
claimed that youthful alienation is characterized by the rejection of cultural

values, a distrust of society, and a profoundly pessimistic world view. Keniston, also describe a "developmental estrangement" in the adolescent identity process which is triggered by the emotional void created when the adolescent must abandon childhood ties and roles and replace them with adolescent behaviors and relationships. Such developmental estrangement is a mild form of alienation widely observed in the growing up process in moratorium cultures, and it is instrumental in the adolescent coming to grips with fundamental "Who am I?" and "Where am I going?" questions. Which are, of course, integral to the adolescent identity project.

Walliman (1981) concludes that the term "alienation" has lost much of its utility because of overuse and lack of precision in its deployment. He observes that even though alienation is frequently used in popular and scientific circles, "its precise meaning remains so unclear that many have questioned its value." Because the term has been imprecisely used it has also been recommended that the term be either abandoned or more rigorously defined. Hence, Walliman further claims that alienation "is at best a sophisticated term denoting a variety of conditions that could, without loss of clarity, be just as well apprehended with numerous other words" (p. 1).

Despite these limitations, the term has a rich history in literature, widespread recognition among non-professionals, and hence, a practical utility to youth watchers which exceeds considerably Walliman's rather negative assessment of this concept.

How is alienation experienced?

A recurring theme among alienated youth is that the contempt they hold for their own society is counterbalanced by an elevated image of other cultures they have never experienced first hand — a trait also observed among youth undergoing identity crises. Though alienated youth may themselves belong to a recognizable subculture, they are likely to think of themselves as post-culture, anti-culture or, beyond culture. Indifference to the strengths and virtues of the larger community with an accompanying obsession for its defects is symptomatic of virtually all alienated youth in Western culture.

Perhaps the most effective way to describe alienation is in *the ways it is experienced*. That is, the moods, sentiments or attitudes it creates within the subjective world of the adolescent who is, in fact, alienated. Although this represents only one avenue of exploration, it merits investigation.

The core experiences of alienation can be classified into three general categories:

1. alienation experienced as meaninglessness;

2. alienation experienced as powerlessness, and;

3. alienation experienced as estrangement or isolation.

Youth whose alienation is *experienced as meaninglessness* tend to perceive their future as empty or pointless, and their personal actions as having no significance or relevance. Generally, they believe that their own life, perhaps even all life, is without any grand purpose or design. This tends to cancel the relevance of values, hence what we call a "value crisis" typically accompanies alienation experienced as meaninglessness. The condition of valuelessness engenders a spiritual emptiness which we can loosely think of as "moral alienation."

Youth whose alienation is *experienced as powerlessness* (which character-ized the 80s much as meaninglessness characterized the 70s) inclines youth to live as though they have no control over their social world, that they are pawns on a chessboard they did not create. These youngsters could never fit our cultural image of "rugged individualists" because, in their hearts, they do not believe in their own actions or talents. They rarely are surprised by their own failures or those of individuals who struggle against institutional bureaucracy or impersonal bigness. Their style is one of accommodation and adjustment because they do not believe they can make a difference to anything they oppose. Much of what outside observers (including teachers and parents) perceive as acceptance of institutional rules and regulations is really a form of alienation which parades as compliance. In most high schools, it is surprisingly difficult to tell the difference between those students who genuinely believe in the school and what it stands for, and those students who simply follow orders because they lack the self-confidence, the self-direction or a belief network to oppose anything.

Powerlessness is perhaps the most easily observed modern embodiment of angst — the dread inherent to the realization that our existence flows toward an undetermined future which must be filled by choices and actions. This realization produces an anxiety which panics in the face of personal decisions, and even more so, at honoring the consequences of these decisions. Among youth in the 90s powerlessness shows itself as the inability to effect change, and worse, the loss of any desire for change. When a sense of powerlessness combines with narcissism it produces an identity in which the primary features are social apathy, psychological indifference and a permanent preoccupation with self-indulgence.

Youth whose alienation is *experienced as isolation* manifest an estrange-ment from society-at-large (the classic definition of social alienation) or as estrangement from one's self (psychological alienation). Alienated youth are disconnected from significant others, and frequently lack the skills or social attractiveness to draw others to them. Their isolation makes worthwhile interaction with others virtually impossible; they protect their isolated selves with emotional insulation, or, as we increasingly observe in the 90s, with asceticism or excessive self-control. Although isolation from self and others helps alienated youth to maintain their emotional equilibrium, it magnifies their estrangement and their alienation by keeping others at such a distance that they cannot benefit from their love or kindness.

Our understanding of adolescent alienation

The experience of alienation is understood differently from different theoretical perspectives. Here I shall briefly overview four separate attitudes toward alienation:

1. alienation as illness;
2. alienation as a normal phase of adolescent development;
3. alienation as a normal phase of development which holds pathological potential; and,
4. alienation as a legitimate style of identity.

The first describes alienation as a significant emotional disturbance whether it occurs among adolescents or adults. (None of the prevailing theories deal with childhood alienation). This viewpoint asserts that alienation derives from weaknesses and defects within the personality, the family structure or the socialization process.

The second viewpoint asserts that alienation is normal in the statistical sense owing to its frequency of occurrence among youth in a moratorium culture. Adherents to this viewpoint believe that most forms of alienation derive from a combination of intellectual perplexities, emotional dislocations, and the inability to meaningfully read the future. The developmental features of adolescence (especially rapid intellectual growth and increased emotional richness) contribute to feelings of meaninglessness, powerlessness and isolation, but these feelings are not pathological. Alienation, from this framework, is essentially a by-product of adolescent intellectual transformations and psychological metamorphoses.

The third viewpoint claims that adolescent alienation is a "normal" developmental phenomenon which may assume pathological proportions. This viewpoint receives wide audience among psychotherapists, psychiatrists, social workers and other professionals coping with the surge of young people who manifest traditional school phobias, sexual obsessions, parent-hatred or self-hatred *in addition to* their classic symptoms of alienation. Among these youngsters, emotional disorders actually magnify their alienation because they keep them from satisfying their needs for love, belonging and esteem. The defects of one strata magnify those of another.

Finally, alienation is understood by some experts as a unique, even legitimate form of identity. This viewpoint emphasizes that estrangement from society can be a choice, an active manifestation of self-definition. Individuals showing this type of alienation incorporate into their personal identity that which most youth dread: emotional distance and social separateness. The young person for whom an alienated status becomes integral to identity is not emotionally paralyzed or even excessively anxious about "estrangement." Quite the contrary, this identity promotes an heroic individualism, a scornful defiance which encourages the feeling of *being elevated beyond society's masses rather than merely separate from them*. The blatant expression of their individuality, even when it contradicts the expectations of society, is the central factor in their identity.

Alienation-as-identity is observed most frequently among older adolescents, early adults and university students. As well, a wide range of youngsters with allegiance to fringe cultures which overlap with, but are neither submerged within nor completely separate from, the prevailing culture. Alienation-as-identity, as described in the affirmative, non-pathological manner of these pages, rarely embraces middle or early adolescent youth.

Bibliography

Adams, G.R. & Adams, C.M. (1985) Developmental issues. In *Recent Developments in Adolescent Psychiatry*, edited by Hsu, L.K. & Herson, M. New York: John Wiley & Sons (p. 14-30).

Adams, Gina, Adams-Taylor, Sharon & Pittman, Karen. (1989) "Adolescent pregnancy and parenthood: A review of the problem, solutions and resources." *Family Relations, 38*, 223-229.

Alford, F.C. (1988) *Narcissism*. New Haven: Yale University Press.

Apter, M.J. (1983) Negativism and the Sense of Identity. In *Threatened Identities*, edited by G. Breakwell. New York: John Wiley & Sons.

Atwater, E. (1988) *Adolescence* (2nd ed.). Englewood Cliffs, N.J.: Prentice-Hall, Inc.

Baker, M. (1985) *"What will tomorrow bring?"* . . . *A study of the aspirations of adolescent women*. Ottawa, Ont.: Canadian Advisory Council on the Status of Women.

Baumeister, R.F. (1986) *Identity: Cultural Change and the Struggle for Self*. New York: Oxford University Press.

Benditt, T.M. (1982) *Rights*. Totowa, N.J.: Rowan & Littlefield.

Bishop, J.H. (1989) "Why the apathy in American high schools?" *Educational Researcher, 18* (1), 6-10.

Blasi, A. (1988) Identity and the development of the self. In *Self, Ego and Identity: Integrative Approaches*, edited by Lapsley, D.K. & Power. New York: F.C. Springer-Verlag.

Blasi, A. & R.J. Oresick (1987) Self-Inconsistency and the Development of the Self. In *The Book of the Self*, edited by P. Young-Eisendrath & J.A. Hall. New York: New York University Press.

Blos, P. (1962) *On Adolescence*. New York: Free Press.

Boyer, E.L. (1983) *High school: A report on secondary education in America*. New York: Harper & Row.

Branden, N. (1983) *Honoring the Self*. Los Angeles, Ca.: J.P. Tarcher, Inc.

Bronfenbrenner, U. (1986) "Alienation and the four worlds of childhood." *Phi Delta Kappa, 67*, 430-436.

Brooks-Gunn, J. & Furstenberg, Frank F. Jr. (1986) "The children of adolescent mothers: physical, academic and psychological outcomes." *Dev. Review, 6*, 224-251.

Burns, D.D. (1986) The perfectionist's script for self-defeat. In *The Pleasure of Psychology*, edited by D. Goleman & D. Heller. New York: New American Library.

Bursten, B. (1977) The Narcissistic Course. In *The Narcissistic Condition*, edited by M.C. Nelson. New York: Human Science Press.

Bursten, B. (1986) Some Narcissistic Personality Types. In *Essential Papers on Narcissism*, edited by A.P. Morrison. New York: New York University Press.

Carnegie Council on Adolescent Development. (1989) *Turning Points. Preparing American Youth for the 21st Century*. Washington, D.C.

Catterall, J.S. (1987) "On the social costs of dropping out of school." *The High School Journal, 71*(1), 19-30.

Centre for Educational Research and Innovation. (1983) *Education and work: The views of the young*. France: Organization for Economic Co-operation and Development.

Chandler, M. & Ball, L. (1990) Continuity and Commitment: A Developmental Analysis of the Identity Formation Process. In *Coping and Self-Concept in Adolescence*, edited by H. Bosma. Berlin: Springer-Verlag.

Coleman, J.S. (1975) *Youth: Transition to Adulthood*. Chicago, Il.: University of Chicago Press.

Conger, J. Janeway. & Peterson, A.C. (1984) *Adolescence and Youth* (3rd ed.). New York: Harper & Row.

Conrad, D. & Hedin, D. (1987) *Youth service: A guide for student reflection in youth participation programs*. Washington, D.C.: Independent Sector.

Cooper, A.M. (1986) Narcissism. In *Essential Papers on Narcissism*, edited by A.P. Morrison. New York: New York University Press.

Corson, D., ed. (1988) *Education for work: Background to policy and curriculum*. New Zealand: The Dunmore Press.

Cousins, N. (1981) *Human Options*. New York: Berkley Books.

Csikszentmihalyi, Mihaly & Larson, Reed (1984) *Being Adolescent*. New York: Basic Books, Inc.

Danzig, Richard & Szanton, Peter. (1987) *National Service: What Would It Mean?* New York: D.C. Heath & Co.

Davis, Richard A. (1989) "Teenage pregnancy: A theoretical analysis of a social problem." *Adolescence, 24*, 19-27.

Dept. of International Economic and Social Affairs. (1986) *The Situation of Youth in the 1980s and Prospects and Challenges for the Year 2000*. United Nations.

Dyfoos, J.G. (1990) *Adolescents at Risk*. New York: Oxford University Press.

Elkind, D. (1967) "Egocentrism in adolescence." *Child Development, 38*, 1025-1034.

Elkind, D. (1974) *Children and adolescents*. New York: Oxford University Press.

Elkind, D. (1978) "Understanding the young adolescent." *Adolescence, vol. XIII*, no. 49, p. 127-141.

Elkind, D. (1987) "The child yesterday, today and tomorrow." *Young Children, 42*(4), 6-11.

Enright, R.D., Lapsley, D.K. & Shulka, D.G. "Adolescent egocentrism in early and late adolescence." *Adolescence, 14*(56) 687-696.

Enright, R.D., Levy Jr., V.M., Harris, D. & Lapsley, D.K. (1987) "Do economic conditions influence how theorists view adolescents?" *Journal of Youth and Adolescence, 16*(6), 541-559.

Erikson, E.H. (1946) Ego development and historical change. In *The psychoanalytic study of the child, vol. 2*, edited by R. Eissler, pp. 359-395. New York: International Universities Press.

Erikson, E.H. (1956) "The problem of ego identity," *Journal of American Psychiatric Association, 4*, pp. 56-121.

Erikson, E.H. (1959) *Identity and the life cycle: Selected Papers.* New York: International Universities Press.

Erikson, E.H. (1960) "Youth and the life cycle," *Children.* March-April 7, p. 43-49.

Erikson, E.H. (1968) *Identity, Youth and Crisis.* New York: W.W. Norton & Co. Inc.

Evans, R.I. (1967) *Dialogues with Erik Erikson.* New York: Harper & Row.

Flaste, R. (1988) "The myth about teenagers." *The New York Times Magazine,* Oct. 9.

Flavell, J.H. (1963) *The developmental psychology of Jean Piaget.* New York: Van Nostrand.

Frank, D. (1983) *Deep Blue Funk and Other Stories: Portraits of Teenage Parents.* New York: Ounce of Prevention Fund.

Freud, A. (1966) *The Ego and the Mechanisms of Defense.* (Rev. ed.) *The writings of Anna Freud. vol. 2.* New York: International Universities Press.

Friedenberg, E. (1959) *The Vanishing Adolescent.* New York: Dell.

Friedman, M.I. & Willis, J.L. (1981) *Human Nature and Predictability.* Lexington Books.

Fromm, E. (1964) *The Heart of Man.* New York: Harper & Row

Fromm, E. (1973) *The Anatomy of Human Destructiveness.* New York: Holt, Rinehart & Winston.

Fuhrmann, B.S. (1990) *Adolescence, Adolescents* (2nd ed.). Glenview, Il.: Scott, Foresman/Little Brown Higher Education.

Gendlin, E.T. (1987) A Philosophical Critique of Narcissism. In, *Pathologies of the Modern Self,* edited by D.M. Levin. New York: New York University Press.

Ginsburg, G. & Opper, S. (1969) *Piaget's Theory of Intellectual Development.* Englewood Cliffs, N.J.: Prentice-Hall, Inc.

Ginzberg, E., Berliner, H.S., and Ostow, M. (1988) *Young People at Risk: Is Prevention Possible?* London: Westview Press.

Glass, D. (1968) Theories of consistency and the study of personality. In *Handbook of Personality Theory and Research.* edited by E.F. Borgatta and W.W. Lambert. Chicago, Il.: Rand McNally.

Goleman, D. (1985) *Vital Lies, Simple Truths.* New York: Simon & Schuster.

Greenberger, Ellen & Steinberg, Laurence. (1986) *When Teenagers Work: The Psychological and Social Costs of Adolescent Employment.* New York: Basic Books, Inc.

Gurwitsch, A. (1985) *Marginal Consciousness*. Athens, Oh.: Ohio University Press.

Habermas, J. (1973) *Legitimation crisis*. Boston, Ma.: Beacon Press.

Hagenhoff, C.; Lowe, A.; Melbourne, H. F. & Rugg, D. (1987) "Prevention of the teenage pregnancy epidemic: A social learning theory approach." *Education and Treatment of Children, 10*(1), 67-83.

Hahn, A. (1987) "Reaching Out to America's Dropouts: What to Do?" *Phi Delta Kappa. 69*, 256-263.

Hamburg, D.A. & Takanishi, R. (1989) "Preparing for life. The critical transition of adolescence." *American Psychologist, 44*(5), 825-827.

Hamilton, V. (1982) *Narcissus and Oedipus: The children of psychoanalysis*. London: Routledge & Kegan Paul.

Heath, D.H. (1977) *Maturity and competence*. New York: Gardner Press.

Henninger, M.G. (1989) "The adolescent's making of meaning: The pedagogy of Augustine's confessions." *Journal of Moral Education, 18*(1), 32-44.

Hewitt, J.P. (1989) *Dilemmas of the American self*. Philadelphia, Pa: Temple University Press.

Hoffer, E. (1951) *The True Believer*. New York: Harper & Brothers.

Hoffman, E. (1987) "What confronts today's youth." *Junior League Review*, p. 8-13.

Horney. K. (1939) *New Ways in Psychoanalysis*. New York: W.W. Norton.

Horney, K. (1945) *Our Inner Conflicts*. New York: W.W. Norton.

Horney, K. (1950) *Neurosis and Human Growth*. New York: W.W. Norton.

Ingersoll, Gary M. (1989) *Adolescents* (2nd ed.). Englewood Cliffs. N.J.: Prentice-Hall, Inc.

Inhelder, B. & Piaget, J. (1958) *The Growth of Logical Thinking*. New York: Basic Books.

Jackson, A.W. & Hornbeck, D.W. (1989) "Educating young adolescents. Why we must restructure middle grade schools." *American Psychologist, 44*(5), 831-836.

Johnson, S.M. (1985) *Characterological Transformation*. New York: W.W. Norton.

Kean, T.H. (1989) "The life you save may be your own. New Jersey addresses prevention of adolescent problems." *American Psychologist, 44*(5), 828-830.

Kiell, N. (1967) *The Universal Experience of Adolescence*. Boston, Ma.: Beacon Press.

Kimmel, D.C. & Weiner, I.B. (1985) *Adolescence. A Developmental Transition*. Lawrence Erlbaum Associates.

Knight, M.B. (1988) "Children teaching culture." *Equity and choice*, 1r, #2, 5-8.

Kohut, H. (1971) *The Analysis of the Self*. New York: International Universities Press.

Kohut, H. (1977) *The Restoration of the Self*. New York: International Universities Press.

Kroger, Jane (1989) *Identity in Adolescence*. London: Routledge and Kegan Paul.

Kubey, R., & Csikszentmihalyi, M. (1990) *Television and the Quality of Life*. Hillsdale, N.J.: LEA Publishers.

Lapsley, D.K. & Rice, K. (1988) "History, puberty and the textbook consensus on adolescent development." *Contemporary Psychology, 33*(3), 210-213.

Lapsley, D.K., Enright, R.D. & Serlin, R.C. (1985) "Toward a theoretical perspective on the legislation of adolescence." *Journal of Adolescence, 5*(4), 441-466.

Lapsley, D.K. & Power, F.C. (1988) *Self, Ego and Identity: Integrative Approaches.* New York: F.C. Springer-Verlag.

Lasch, C. (1978) *The Culture of Narcissism.* New York: W.W. Norton.

Lasch, C. (1984) *The Minimal Self.* New York: W.W. Norton.

Lewis, H.B. (1987) Shame and the Narcissistic Personality. In *The Many Faces of Shame*, edited by D.L. Nathanson. New York: The Guilford Press.

Lipsitz, J. (1984) *Successful schools for young adolescents.* New Brunswick, N.J.: Transaction Books.

Lloyd, M.A. (1985) *Adolescence.* New York: Harper & Row.

Looft, W.R. (1972) "Egocentrism and social interaction across the lifespan." *Psychological Bulletin. 78*, p.73-92.

Lowen, A. (1983) *Narcissism: Denial of the True Self.* New York: Macmillan Publishing Co.

Maddi, S. (1989) *Personality Theories: A Comparative Analysis.* Chicago, Il.: Dorsey Press.

Madison, P. (1969) *Personality and Development in College.* Reading, Ma.: Addison-Wesley.

Manaster, G.J. (1989) *Adolescent Development.* Itasca, Il.: F.E. Peacock Publishers, Inc.

Marcia, J. (1987) The identity status approach to the study of ego identity development. In, *Self & Identity*, edited by T. Honess & K. Yardley. London: Routledge and Kegan Paul.

Martin, M.W. (1985) *Self-deception and self-understanding.* Lawrence: University Press of Kansas.

May, R. (1975) *The courage to create.* Toronto, ON: Bantam Books.

McGuire, P. (1983) *It Won't Happen To Me: Teenagers Talk About Pregnancy.* New York: Delacorte.

Mead, L.M. (1986) *Beyond entitlement.* New York: The Free Press.

Millstein, S. (1988) *The Potential of School-Linked Centers to Promote Adolescent Health and Development.* Carnegie Council on Adolescent Development.

Millstein, Susan G. (1989) "Adolescent health. Challenges for behavioral scientists." *American Psychologist, 44*(5), 837-842.

Mitchell, John J. (1971) *Adolescence: Some Critical Issues.* Toronto, Ont.: Holt, Rinehart, & Winston.

Mitchell, John J. (1972) *Human Nature: Theories, Conjectures and Descriptions.* Metuchen, N.J.: Scarecrow Press.

Mitchell, John J. (1973) *Human Life: The First Ten Years*. Toronto,On.: Holt, Rinehart, & Winston.

Mitchell, John J. (1974) *Human Life: The Early Adolescent Years*. Toronto, Ont.: Holt, Rinehart, & Winston.

Mitchell, John J. (1975) *The Adolescent Predicament*. Toronto, Ont.: Holt, Rinehart, & Winston.

Mitchell, John J. (1978) *Adolescent Psychology*. Toronto, Ont.: Holt, Rinehart, & Winston.

Mitchell, John J. (1980) *Child Development*. Toronto, Ont.: Holt, Rinehart, & Winston.

Mitchell, John J. (1985) *The Nature of Adolescence*. Calgary, Alta.: Detselig Enterprises.

Mitchell, John J. (1989) *Human Growth & Development: The Childhood Years*. Calgary, Alta.: Detselig Enterprises.

Moore, K.A. (1982) *Private Crisis, Public Cost: policy perspectives on teenage childbearing*. Washington, D.C.: Urban Institute Press.

Moriarty, A.E. & Toussieng, P.W. (1976) *Adolescent Coping*. New York: Grune & Stratton.

Moschis, G.P. (1978) *Acquisition of the Consumer Role by Adolescents*. Atlanta, Ga.: University of Georgia.

Musgrove, F. (1964) *Youth and the Social Order*. Bloomington, Il.: Indiana University Press.

Muuss, R.E. (1982) "Social cognition: David Elkind's theory of adolescent egocentrism." *Adolescence, vol. XVII*, No. 66.

Muuss, R.E. (1988) *Theories of Adolescence* (5th ed.). New York: Random House, Inc.

Muuss, R.E., ed. (1990) *Adolescent Behavior and Society* (4th ed.). New York: McGraw Hill, Inc.

Neitzsche, F. (1968) *The Will to Power*, edited by W. Kaufmann. New York: Vintage.

Nelson, M.C., ed. (1977) *The Narcissistic Condition*. New York: Human Sciences Press.

Newcomb, Michael D. & Bentler, P.M. (1988) "Impact of adolescent drug use and social support on problems of young adults: A longitudinal study." *Journal of Abnormal Psychology*, 97(1), 64-75.

Newman, P.R. & Newman, B.M. (1988) "Differences between childhood and adulthood: The identity watershed." *Adolescence*, 23(91), 551-557.

Nightingale, E.O. & Wolverton, L. (1988) *Adolescent Rolelessness in Modern Society*. Carnegie Council on Adolescent Development.

Oakes, J. (1985) *Keeping track: How Schools Structure Inequality*. New Haven: Yale University Press.

Ortman, P.E. (1988) "Adolescents' perceptions of and feelings about control and responsibility in their lives." *Adolescence*, 23 (92), 913-924.

Orwell, G. (1983) *1984*. New York: New American Library.

Otto, L.B. (1988) "America's youth: A changing profile." *Family Relations, 37*, 385-391.

Paget, Kathleen D. (1988) "Adolescent pregnancy: Implications for prevention strategies in educational settings." *School Psychological Review, 17*(4), 570-580.

Peck, R.F. & Havighurst, R.J. (1960) *The Psychology of Character Development*. New York: John Wiley & Sons.

Piaget, J. (1967) The mental development of the child. In *Six Psychological Studies by Piaget*, edited by D. Elkind, New York: Random House.

Peterson, A.C. (1988) "Adolescent development." *Annual Review of Psychology, 39*, 583-607.

Polansky, N.A. (1991) *Integrated Ego Psychology*. New York: Aldine de Gruyter.

Posterski, D. & Bibby, R. (1988) *Canada's Youth Ready for Today*. Canadian Youth Foundation.

Pulver, S.E. (1986) Narcissism: The Term and the Concept. In *Essential Papers on Narcissism*, edited by, A.P. Morrison. New York: New York University Press.

Putney, S. & Putney, G. (1964) *Normal Neurosis*. New York: Harper & Row Publishers.

Rogers, D. (1985) *Adolescents and Youth* (5th ed.). Englewood Cliffs, N.J.: Prentice-Hall, Inc.

Rothstein, A. (1984) *The Narcissistic Pursuit of Perfection*. New York: International Universities Press.

Santrock, J.W. (1990) *Adolescence*. Dubuque, Ia.: Wm C. Brown Publisher.

Satinover, J. (1987) Science and the Fragile Self: The Rise of Narcissism, The Decline of God. In *Pathologies of the Modern Self*, edited by D.M. Levin. New York: New York University Press.

Schine, Joan G. (1989) "Adolescents help themselves by helping others." *Children Today, 18*(1), 10-15.

Sebald, H. (1984) *Adolescence: A Social Psychological Analysis* (3rd ed.). Englewood Cliffs, N.J.: Prentice-Hall, Inc.

Silbereisen, R.K., Eyferth, K., and Rudinger, G. (eds.) (1986) *Development as action in context: Problem behavior and normal youth development*. New York: F.C. Springer-Verlag.

Sowell, T. (1987) *A Conflict of Visions*. New York: William Morrow.

Steinberg, L. (1989) *Adolescence* (2nd ed.). New York: Alfred A. Knopf, Inc.

Stiffman, A.R., Earls, F., Robins, L.N., Jung, K.G. & Kulbok, P. (1987) "Adolescent sexual activity and pregnancy: Socioenvironmental problems, physical health and mental health." *Journal of Youth and Adolescence, 16*(5), 497-509.

Stolorow, R.D. (1986) Toward a Functional Definition of Narcissism. In *Essential Papers on Narcissism*, edited by A.P. Morrison. New York: New York University Press.

Strauss, A. (1959) *Mirrors and Masks*. Glencoe, Il.: Free Press of Glencoe.

Thornburg, H.D. (1982) *Development in Adolescence.* Monterey, Ca.: Brooks/Cole.

Tice, Carol H. (1989) "Youth opportunity: A private sector investment in prevention." *Children Today, 18*(2), 20-23.

Toulmin, S.E. (1977) Self-knowledge and knowledge of the self. In *The Self,* edited by T. Mischel. Oxford: Basil Blackwell.

United States General Accounting Office. (1986) *School dropouts: The extent and nature of the problem. Briefing report to Congressional Requesters.* Washington, D.C.: Author.

U.S. Department of Education. (1988) *Youth indicators 1988: Trends in the well-being of American youth.*

Wallach, M. & Wallach, L. (1985) "How psychology sanctions the cult of the self." *The Washington Monthly,* Feb., 46-54.

Walliman, I. (1981) *Estrangement.* London: Greenwood Press.

Webber, M. (1991) *Street Kids.* Toronto, Ont.: University of Toronto Press.

Wegner, D.M. & Vallacher, R.R. (1980) *The Self in Social Psychology.* New York: Oxford University Press.

Weiss, E. (1950) *Principles of Psychodynamics.* New York: Grune & Stratton.

Weiss, P. (1980) *You, I, and the Others.* Carbondale, Il.: Southern Illinois University Press.

William T. Grant Commission on Work, Family and Citizenship. (1988) *The Forgotten Half: Pathways to Success for America's Youth and Young Families.* Washington D.C.

William T. Grant Foundation, Commission on Work, Family and Citizenship. (1988) *The Forgotten Half: Non-College Youth in America.* Washington, D.C.

William T. Grant Foundation, Commission on Work, Family and Citizenship. (1987) *Dropout Prevention A Book of Sources. National Committee for Citizens in Education.* Washington D.C.

Wilson, W.J. (1987) *The Truly Disadvantaged: The Inner City, the Underclass and Public Policy.* Chicago, Il.: University of Chicago Press.

Wolf, E.S. (1977) "Irrationality in a psychoanlaytic psychology of the self." In *The Self: Psychological and Philosophical Issues.* Oxford: Basil Blackwell.

Wurmser, L (1987) Shame: The Veiled Companion of Narcissism. In *The Many Faces of Shame,* edited by D.L. Nathanson. New York: The Guilford Press.

Printed in Canada